The VC squad leader stood and looked into the forest. Except for the corpse, all he saw out of place were leaves ripped by the grenade, bark scarred by its shrapnel. He looked where the Americans had broken through the brush on the side of the trail and saw it was also a blind marker designed to fool a follower.

Now anger started to course through the squad leader. These Americans were nibbling at him, killing his men one at a time. Well, they had to be taught they couldn't do this; they must not be allowed to succeed; they must die; he must kill them. Or die himself in the attempt...

Also by David Sherman
Published by Ivy Books:

The Night Fighters

KNIVES IN THE NIGHT (#1)

MAIN FORCE ASSAULT (#2)

OUT OF THE FIRE (#3)

A ROCK AND A HARD PLACE (#4)

A NGHU NIGHT FALLS (#5)

CHARLIE DON'T LIVE HERE ANYMORE

The Night Fighters, Book 6

David Sherman

IVY BOOKS • NEW YORK

Library of Congress Catalog Card Number: 88-62389

ISBN 0-8041-0313-5

Manufactured in the United States of America

First Edition: April 1989

For Tam Cragg. Born in Vietnam of a Vietnamese mother and an American soldier father. Today he is a United States Marine. In one person, he is the embodiment and legacy of the Combined Action Program. Semper Fi, Tam.

AUTHOR'S NOTE

The U.S. Marine Corps' Combined Action Program was real. A few young Marines, usually commanded by a three-stripe sergeant, sometimes by a corporal, rarely by an officer, would be sent into a Vietnamese village. These Marines and a Navy corpsman lived in that village and worked with the people and trained and led the local Popular Forces (civilian militia) until they rotated back to The World or got killed in action or until the area of that village was considered so secure that American men-at-arms were no longer thought necessary to defend it from the Vietcong or the North Vietnamese Army. These eighteen-, nineteen-, and twenty-year-old Marines believed in what they were doing; they were dedicated to their jobs: helping and defending their friends and neighbors—the villagers. CAP was a generally ignored and neglected backwater of the war. The Marines and PFs often suffered from a lack of essential supplies, but they also had a degree of autonomy and freedom unknown to conventional military units. The events in this novel are fictional, and I doubt if any CAP did any such thing as is depicted here. But if one of my CAP veteran brothers told me his unit had done something like this, I'd be inclined to believe him. The CAP in this novel is loosely based on the one I served with in Ky Hoa village, Quang Tin Province, during the summer of 1966.

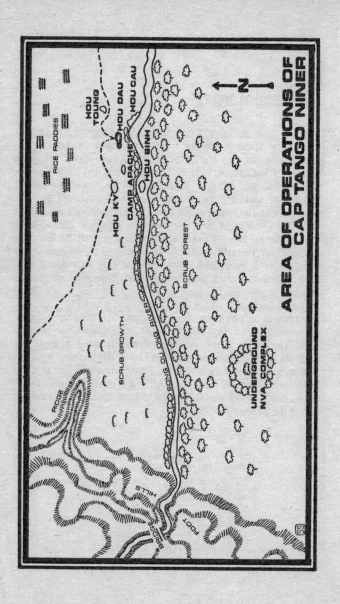

AREA OF OPERATIONS OF
CAP TANGO NINER

RICE PADDIES

HOU TOUNG
HOU DAU
HOU CAU
CAMP APACHE
HOU BINH
HOU KYO

SCRUB FOREST

SCRUB GROWTH

SONG DU SONG RIVER

RIDGE

HILLS

FOOT
BRIDG

UNDERGROUND
NVA COMPLEX

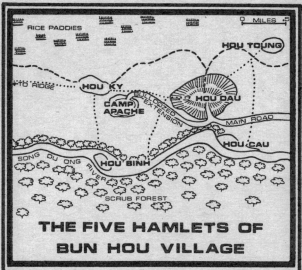

THE FIVE HAMLETS OF BUN HOU VILLAGE

RICE PADDIES

0 MILES 5

HOU TOUNG

TO RIDGE — HOU KY

HOU DAU

CAMP APACHE

BULLDOZED EXTENSION

MAIN ROAD

HOU CAU

SONG DU ONG RIVER

HOU BINH

SCRUB FOREST

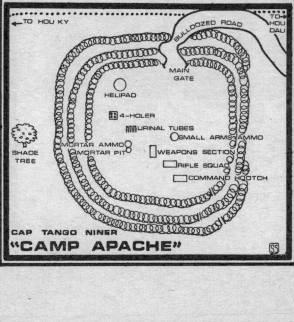

"CAMP APACHE"

TO HOU KY

TO HOU DAU

BULLDOZED ROAD

MAIN GATE

HELIPAD

4-HOLER

URINAL TUBES

SMALL ARMS AMMO

MORTAR AMMO

MORTAR PIT

WEAPONS SECTION

RIFLE SQUAD

COMMAND HOOTCH

SHADE TREE

CAP TANGO NINER

CHAPTER ONE

Before Dawn, March 5, 1967

Corporal "Tex" Randall sat slumped against a large-boled tree a few feet from the riverbank. His eyelids drooped, and his head nodded. He shook himself awake, arched the aches out of his back, and silently shuddered. He blinked a few times at the dull dots of orange glow bobbing on the Song Du Ong River: fishermen plying their trade at night—the lights served both to attract fish to the fishermen's nets and to notify anybody watching that these boats were innocent fishermen, not Vietcong. Randall worked his jaw to collect saliva and swallowed. He stared at the luminous dial of his watch: 0330. He seemed to stare at the watch for a long time before the minute hand moved past the half hour. He breathed deeply, an unsounded sigh.

He listened to the background sounds of chirring locusts. A night flying bird cawed its way through the dark, and a prowling "fukyoo" lizard gave its hunting cry. Somewhere a bored dog that didn't feel like going back to sleep just yet barked at the moon. No other dogs answered. The seven men near Randall in the ambush site made no noise of their own. Either they're all alert or they're all sleeping like babies, Randall thought. He grimaced and blinked a few more times. Then he shifted his back against the tree until he found a more comfortable position and waited, trying to stay alert. After a while his eyelids drooped again, his body sagged, and his head nodded until his chin settled on his chest.

An unexpected noise snapped him awake. He listened tensely for the noise to come again. The locusts chirred uninterrupted, the lizards *fukyooed* through the night, and the nocturnal birds cried. A wry smile twisted Randall's lips—he realized the noise that had awakened him was his own snore. Wasn't that long ago no way I would have done that, he thought. He glanced at his watch again: 0340. He stifled a groan. Isn't this night ever going to end? He decided to exercise the patrol leader's prerogative, do the one thing he could to stay awake that none of his men could do. He moved from his position, left his comfortable spot against the tree, and checked his men's positions.

Lance Corporal "Billy Boy" Lewis lay nearby, his head pillowed on his arms. Next to him the PF named Vien squatted, scratching under his shirt and yawning widely, soundlessly, to stay awake. Beyond them PFC "Dumbshit" Dodd lay prone, staring out over the river, while the PF the Marines called George curled tightly in slumber. In the other direction, PFC Rip Van Anderson, whose nickname was "Rip Van Winkle," lay napping lightly on his back. He woke when Randall knelt at Traun's side to exchange a few quiet words. Rip Van Winkle didn't have anything to say, though. He'd been sleeping, so if anything was happening, he didn't know about it. Randall returned to his tree. He checked the time again: 0355. In five minutes he'd radio in his hourly situation report, "Doghouse, Rover Two. Situation as before, over," then wake Tan to take the next two-hour watch and give the radio to Lewis. Then he could sleep without thinking he was derelict in his duties.

He sighed and found himself wishing for some of the action Combined Action Platoon Tango Niner had had in the good old days, the days when more often than not at least one of the three patrols the platoon put out every night had some kind of contact. He hadn't had any trouble staying awake on patrol then. One good thing about life being so boring, though: It had been two months since anybody in Tango Niner, Marine or PF, had been killed.

Eventually the sun got around to rising. It does on a very regular basis every morning; it's just that on some nights it seems to take a lot longer to get around to it than it does on other nights.

The eight men of the all-night patrol stood and stretched, twisting the night kinks out of their bodies. They emptied their bladders into the river and hitched out-of-kilter uniforms back into place. They sucked on the insides of their mouths to loosen the night gunk, hawked and spit and tried to make themselves feel human again. Randall pointed at Lewis. The wiry lance corporal cradled his rifle in his arms and balled his fists in front of his face. When he took his hands away, the right end of his mustache drooped Pancho Villa style and the left end flew away in a Guardsman swoop. He led the way toward the hill on which sat the barbed-wire compound the Marines called Camp Apache.

The night fishermen were gone from the river now; the last of them had headed home at false dawn. In all the hamlets of Bun Hou village, the farmers and woodsmen were rising, heading for riverbank or rice paddy or honey bucket to void themselves. Dogs barked joyfully here and there, happy that people were waking to pay attention to them. Young children clambered aboard the broad backs of thousand-pound water buffalos and tapped their heads with willow switches to guide them to the fields. The people were preparing themselves for another routine day in the peaceful floodplain of the Song Du Ong River.

The Marines and PFs of Tango Niner were through with their sixtieth consecutive night of excruciating inactivity.

A few hours later.

"Come on, Jay Cee. You shitting me, man."

Sergeant J. C. Bell bent his neck to look up at the very tall black man who had spoken. "Watch yourself, Stilts. You never know when someone will say something about his favorite turd."

"You wouldn't say that, Jay Cee," Corporal "Stilts" Zeitvogel said, and grinned down at the six-foot-one sergeant. When he grinned like that, his mouth looked like it held too many teeth. "I'm bigger than you are. Now, what's this shit about calisthenics?"

"Stilts, you long, skinny dip, I got too much weight on you for your height to scare me. And that's no shit. I want all hands on deck for calisthenics in five minutes."

"You been in the goddamn sun too fucking long, Jay Cee."

"And you've been hanging out with Swearin' Swarnes too long, Stilts. Round everybody up for jumping jacks and deep knee bends and the rest of that good kind of shit. Unless you want to wait until the full heat of the day to do it."

"You picking on my honcho again, Stilts?" another voice said.

The sergeant and the corporal turned and looked down at the speaker, who was standing arms folded across his chest next to Bell. It was Lance Corporal "Short Round" Hempen. Where Zeitvogel at six feet five inches was the tallest man in Tango Niner, Hempen's five feet four inches not only made him the shortest Marine in the unit, it was also the minimum height for a Marine.

"Pick on you, too, Short Round, I want to." Zeitvogel sneered.

"Go ahead and try it, you tall-ass fucking stringbean," Hempen said with a snort. "I'll take you off at the kneecap, sombitch, you try it. You won't never be able to field a roundball team that can beat a junior high girls' team."

Bell took advantage of the appearance of his third fire team leader—Zeitvogel was leader of the first fire team—to give his order to another of his NCOs. "Round up your people, Short Round. We're doing PT today."

"Say what?" Hempen yelped. "You dinky dau, Jay Cee? You want me to get Doc Rankin, check you out, take your temperature or something?"

"Don't get cute with me, dammit, just get your people, fall in over there." He pointed at the open area between the squad tents and the white painted circle that was Camp Apache's helipad.

Hempen abruptly stepped next to Zeitvogel, being very obvious about changing sides.

"*Now*, goddammit!" Bell shouted. "Things have been too slack around here; everybody's getting soft. We're going to do some good PT every day, starting today, and get everyone back in shape. Move."

Zeitvogel and Hempen stood staring at Bell. The sergeant opened his mouth to start chewing on them as only a Marine sergeant can. They were saved by the sudden appearance of another person.

"Chay Cee," said Lieutenant Phao Houng, commander of Tango Niner's Popular Forces. "You come me. We talk." He was very agitated about something and bounced up and down on the balls of his feet.

"What's happening?" Bell asked.

"You come me," Houng repeated, and pulled on the short sleeve of Bell's utility shirt. "Toot-sweet, we talk."

"Get everybody out there," Bell said again to the other two. "Now." He followed Houng to the southeast corner of the compound, where they could talk without interruption.

"My son," Houng said as soon as they were alone. "I know where he is. We go get him." His voice quivered, and his eyes were open wide.

Bell was stunned by Houng's statement, and it took him a few seconds before he could respond. "Your son? Where is he? Tell me everything you know. We'll get this passed up the line, and somebody will rescue him." His words came fast; they tumbled over each other.

Bell knew Houng had enlisted in the Army of the Republic of Vietnam, the ARVN, in 1960. He had fought valiantly against the Vietcong and the North Vietnamese for six years and had won several decorations for personal bravery. In the summer of 1966—he was a sergeant by then—his division commanding general transferred him to the Popular Forces as a lieutenant charged with raising a PF platoon in his home village of Bun Hou. In 1965 the Vietcong had attacked his home in retribution for his activities as an ARVN. They had raped his wife and left her and his daughter in his house, which they burned down—they expected the women to die in the flames, but they were saved by Phao Thien, Houng's brother, who was the hamlet chief of Hou Ky. When the Vietcong left, they kidnapped his seven-year-old son to serve as a laborer. For nearly two years Houng had had no information on where his son was being held or even if he was still alive. Now he came to Bell with the very startling news that he knew where his son was.

"We go get him, Chay Cee," Houng repeated, in Vietnamese this time.

Bell shook his head. "We can't," he said, also in Vietnamese. "Tell me everything you know. We'll get the people who do that sort of thing to go get him."

The PF lieutenant looked speculatively at the Marine sergeant. "Who does that sort of thing?" he asked.

"I don't know. Somebody must."

Houng considered his good friend for a moment, then seemed to make a decision. He pulled a folded and stained sheet of paper from his shirt pocket. "Here, this is where my son is," he said, and unfolded the paper. It was a hand-drawn map of the southern part of a valley. "A Shau," Houng said, identifying the valley. Trails were shown on the map, and a curlicued circle indicated a VC base camp. An annotation in the margin said the camp was the home of a VC regimental headquarters and was normally guarded by two companies of Main Force Vietcong, more than two hundred well-trained soldiers.

Bell whistled. "Three MAF might want to run a two-battalion operation in there, wipe that place out."

"What will happen to my son if two battalions go in there?"

Bell looked at his friend. He knew the boy's chances of survival weren't great if two battalions went in on a search and destroy operation, but he couldn't say that. "I think somebody can find a way to deal with this and get your boy out safely." But he didn't know who or how. "Are you sure they've got your son in there?"

Houng nodded and handed over a photograph. It wasn't much of a photo; it was grainy and had been taken in bad light, obviously from concealment. But the features of the large-eyed, sad-looking boy in the picture were clearly identifiable. The boy stood slightly stooped, as though standing up again after putting down the bucket next to his feet. Armed men in black pajamas with armbands Bell knew were red were in the background of the black and white photo.

Bell looked into the hurt, anxious father's eyes looking at him and asked, "You haven't seen your son in years. How sure are you this boy is your son?"

"I am sure." The PF lieutenant handed Bell another photograph. This one was older and was cracked in a couple of places. A large-eyed boy standing next to a shrine beamed at the camera. "This was taken two years ago, a few months before the Vee Cee came to kill my family, to punish me."

Bell examined the two photos closely. Despite the differences in age and surroundings, the two pictures were obviously of the same boy. "Let's take this to Scrappy, get someone working on it."

After Bell and Houng showed the map and photos to Lieutenant Burrison and told him the story, Burrison sent a radio message to Captain Hasford and the captain came out to visit Tango Niner. Then the daily hot meal bird came in. After they ate, it was time to give the night's patrol orders. It was too late for PT that day.

CHAPTER TWO

Phao Kha Ai

Phao Kha Ai was about what you think of when you think of a seven-year-old boy. He was energetic, he was curious, he was physical. He was eager to please, and he was the apple of his mother's eye. He started running and playing kick ball with the other children as soon as his mother let him out of the house in the morning and kept at it until time for bed—except for taking time out to herd the water buffalo to their grazing and back again and occasionally helping weed the kitchen garden. He also spent a few hours every day sitting in the hamlet square with the other young children of Hou Ky.

The children squatted together in concentric semicircles in front of their teacher, slates balanced on knees. They chanted their lessons in unison for the teacher and were praised when they got them right, yelled at or cajoled when they made mistakes. And the teacher had a switch he hit the children with whenever he thought they weren't quiet enough or were not paying attention or when they were too slow to learn his lessons. He often found reason to hit Ai with his switch.

The teacher was a dour-faced man from a village Phao Kha Ai didn't bother to remember the name of; geography wasn't a subject he had much interest in. Like most of the children of Hou Ky he didn't expect to ever wander far from his village. And why should he? Life was good in Hou Ky. There was enough to eat, there were thatch roofs to stay dry under when it rained, there was a forest to play hide and seek in, there were other children to play kick ball with, and riding the water buffalo when he took them to pasture was lots of fun. Hou Ky was the best place in the entire world.

His mother tried to interest him in geography. If he knew geography, she could tell him where his father was. His father wasn't there—that was all Ai needed to know about where his father was. [That and the fact that where his father was, was not the same place the teacher was from.] His mother always told him not to talk about his father to the teacher. That was fine with him. There were lots of children in the hamlet without a father, and none of them liked to talk about the missing parent; they were jealous of the children whose fathers were at home. He didn't understand when his mother told him his father was away fighting a war in which men from the north were trying to conquer men from the south so the north could rule the south and take away their good lives. Part of the reason he didn't understand was that some of the other children's fathers were away fighting in the same war—only it seemed some of them were fighting on the other side. Which didn't make much sense to him, because if they were fighting on the other side, how could the other side be from the north? His mother told him his father was a hero. Besides, the teacher hit him too much, and Ai didn't like him.

But the teacher kept insisting that the children understand geography. That was so they could understand the war that was taking place somewhere other than Hou Ky. Why the children should understand the war that was going on someplace else was a mystery to young Ai, except that his father was away fighting in it. He didn't tell the teacher that, though. What need did he have of geography more than to know where the rice paddies were, where the river was, the good places to hide in the forest, and how to get to Hou Cau and home again on market days? It was a mystery. But that was the adult world to a seven-year-old —full of mysteries.

The children laughed a lot at the teacher; he talked funny. The teacher didn't think he talked funny, though. He kept trying to make the children talk the same way he did. That was silly; the children talked right. Why didn't the teacher stop making all those harsh sounds when he talked and speak in softer tones as the people of Hou Ky did? That was another reason not to bother with geography; the people who were where the teacher was from talked funny. Ai didn't want to go where people talked funny.

At first the teacher was a novelty to the children—he didn't only talk funny, he dressed strangely as well. Instead of wearing the same kind of loose shirt and pants the men of Hou Ky wore, clothes that never bound and never stuck to the wearer so the men never got uncomfortable from their clothes, he wore tight clothes. Tight like the pastel tunics the women wore, though his clothes weren't pastel or white like the ones the women wore—more the color of skin that was protected too much from the sun. And he had to wear a strip of leather around his waist to keep his trousers up, a very strange thing for trousers that fit so tightly. Ai knew the teacher's clothes weren't comfortable;

he often had to pluck at the sides or bottom of his shirt because it was twisting on his body, and sometimes he had to pull the seat of his trousers out from between his cheeks. Sometimes the teacher wore a proper hat like everybody else wore, a flat cone straw hat. Most of the time the teacher wore a hat shaped like a bowl with a broad lip, but the hat wasn't any good as a bowl. When you turned it upside down so its opening was up, you couldn't set it down because its bottom was so sharply curved that it rolled over until it rested against its wide lip. The teacher wore an armband on his left sleeve and a triangle of cloth around his neck.

The children delighted in the decorations he wore and at first tried to decorate themselves the same way. It didn't make any sense to them when he told them that they couldn't wear the armbands, that only certain people could and they'd have to wait years before they were those certain people. Besides, why did the armbands have to be a particular color? After all, not everybody had red cloth to use. The children were somewhat mollified when the teacher told them he would give each of them a checkered triangle to wear around the neck. But only when they earned them. Okay, it was a game.

One other thing about the way the teacher dressed. The leather strap he used to hold up his trousers wasn't tied like one would tie a length of cord around one's waist to hold up too-loose pants or to carry things from. The strap was extravagantly fastened by a piece of metal. Not only was the fastener made of metal, it was designed for that purpose. Metal was expensive and was used only when it was far better than anything else that could be used for its purpose. Cooking pots had to be made of metal so they didn't burn in the fire. Knives for harvesting rice were metal but had to be well cared for or they would rust away. Needles for making and repairing clothes were metal. Ax heads had to be made of metal or they wouldn't chop much firewood. The best fishhooks were metal. Some expensive chests for storing ancestor offerings and other valuable things had metal hinges. There was a chest with metal hinges in Ai's home. Whenever his mother talked to him about his father, she took something remarkable from that chest and rubbed it lovingly between her fingers, then let him hold it. The remarkable thing was a medallion, a piece of metal that had no purpose other than hold a design and be held and rubbed. The fact that the teacher fastened his leather strap with a piece of metal that was designed for that purpose was more awe-inspiring to the children than was the red enameled star in its middle.

Ai envied that piece of metal the teacher called a buckle. He wanted to have one someday himself, though what use he had for a strap of leather to hold up his pants was beyond him. Maybe he had to learn about geography so he could go away. Maybe if he went to visit somewhere else, he could get one. He started paying attention to the geography lessons.

He learned many wondrous things in geography. He learned that there were two countries far across the ocean at the very edge of the world. The people of those two countries were giants, and they spoke a language even more different from Vietnamese than the teacher's strange talk was different from that of the people of Hou Ky. Ai thought that was very strange; how could people understand them when they spoke if they talked that differently? Those giants had many things made of metal, even machines that flew through the air and dropped bombs that shook the earth and made greater thunder than did a storm. Those people were very powerful, the teacher said, and wanted to rule the entire world. Each of them had come to

Vietnam to oppress the people and the people fought them off, and this fighting was what the war was. Ai wondered about that; it was not what his mother said—she never mentioned giants from across the ocean when she told him his father was fighting in the war. Ai had trouble understanding how the two countries of giants were different from each other and thought they might actually be the same place but with different names. Why not? He himself had three names. He wondered if the ocean was to the north; that was where his mother said the other people came from. But the teacher said one of the countries of giants was across the ocean to the east and the other was across the ocean to the west. Ai wondered: If the world was round like the teacher said it was, did the two oceans go all the way around? And if the countries were the same place, the only difference was which ocean you crossed to get to them. Actually, Ai wasn't too sure about this ocean business at all. To the east were rice paddies and cane fields and other villages, not oceans. To the west were the forest and mountains, not oceans. But he applied himself and tried to figure it all out.

Ai had a little sister. She was a dumb little girl, but that didn't seem remarkable. His two best friends both had little sisters, and they were both dumb little girls, too. He simply accepted that little sisters were dumb little girls. Except for one thing. Ai's dumb little sister had a better understanding of geography than he did. She also paid better attention than he did when their mother talked to them. One day when the teacher was helping harvest the rice she snuck into the teacher's house and stole his geography book. She didn't actually steal it; she returned it when she was through explaining geography to her brother. But it was stealing nonetheless because she had gone into the teacher's house when he wasn't there and taken it without permission. She sat down with Ai at the table in their home and showed him the maps in the geography book and how the two countries of giants were in different places and where the north was compared with where Hou Ky was. She even drew a map of Hou Ky and a map of Bun Hou so he'd get the idea of maps. After that the geography lessons started to mean more.

The teacher had friends who came to visit him now and again. Well, maybe they weren't friends. But they treated him with respect, and he was respectful to them. Those friends of the teacher dressed mostly like the people did, in loose black garments, but not completely. Sometimes they wore proper hats like the people of Hou Ky; sometimes they wore strange hats dull green in color, fitting close to the scalp and with a brim in the front only. Most of those friends had red armbands like the teacher did; a few of them had triangles of checked cloth around their necks. And they all carried rifles.

The visitors spent some time talking to Ai's uncle, Thien, who was the hamlet chief. They gathered everyone into the hamlet square whenever a special one of them came to visit; the special one dressed like the teacher did and carried a pistol in a leather pocket on his belt. He talked to the people for a long time, and he yelled and waved his arms a lot when he talked. He told stories of things happening far away; his stories used many words like "oppression" and "liberation" and "confession." When the special visitor stopped talking and yelling and waving his arms and went to rest in the teacher's house, the people of Hou Ky talked about him in hushed tones and said they didn't believe him. Every time the teacher's visitors left, they always took as much food as they could carry. They never paid for the food; they said it was for "the Revolution." Sometimes they took one or two or three young men with them, and those young men also carried as much food as they could. The young men who were taken didn't always act like they wanted to go away.

When the visitors first started coming, Ai was very excited about it. Hou Ky didn't often get visitors from farther away than Hou Dau or Hou Cau, two of the other hamlets in Bun Hou village. But the teacher's friends weren't very friendly. They ordered and demanded instead of talking and asking; they were harsh men. So Ai ignored them when he could.

Ai continued to take the buffalo to graze and weed the kitchen garden when necessary and run and play kick ball with the other children. And he applied himself to his lessons when the teacher taught. Especially geography.

Then one day it finally occurred to him where the teacher's village was. The teacher was from the north.

This was something Ai had to think about. The teacher said the Vietnamese people were fighting giant conquerors who came from across the ocean to the west and other giant conquerors who came from across a different ocean to the east. Ai still wasn't sure about those oceans, no matter what his little sister showed him on the maps. His mother told him his father was away fighting a war against invaders from the north. He knew his mother never lied to him. Did that mean the teacher was lying?

Ai had never seen a giant from across the ocean, conqueror or not. But he had seen the teacher's friends. There was the one who dressed like the teacher, whom the people thought wasn't telling the truth—and wasn't nice about the way he didn't tell it. And the others, who dressed more like the people did but carried rifles, also ordered and demanded. Given what his mother told him and the evidence of his own experience, Ai came to the only conclusion he could: The teacher was lying about the war. If he was lying about the war, what else was he lying about? Were those oceans real? Maybe the teacher made up the maps. Ai stopped applying himself so much to his lessons.

Then came a day the teacher's friends were visiting, including the one who dressed like the teacher did. Ai wasn't paying attention during the lessons. He was looking off over the rice paddies and thinking about a new game he and some of the other boys were talking about but hadn't yet played because they suspected their mothers would get very angry—racing their water buffalo—when a line of fire lanced across his back. Ai fell away from the pain and turned in time to see the switch descending again. He rolled away from the second blow. The teacher screamed at him for his inattentiveness and shook the switch vigorously. Wide-eyed and afraid, Ai mumbled something about paying better attention and retook his place in the concentric semicircle. The teacher had the children continue chanting their lessons from the point where they had been interrupted.

Ai looked attentive and mindlessly chanted the lessons with the others. But his back hurt from the blow, and inwardly he boiled with anger. He almost stopped chanting when, out of the corner of his eye, he saw the teacher's special friend smiling at him. It was a wicked smile.

After the evening meal the teacher's friends gathered everybody in the hamlet square in front of the teacher's special friend so he could tell them his stories that used many words like "foreign devils" and "liberation" and yell at them about "sacrifice" and "aid to the Heroes of the Revolution." Ai was still angry, and his back still stung from being hit. While he half listened, he looked at the teacher's other friends, the ones who wore red armbands and carried rifles. He thought that they were from the north and that his father was away fighting them because they wanted to take away his freedom. Not that he understood what freedom was; he suspected that if they took his freedom away, it meant he wouldn't be allowed to play kick ball and run in the forest and eat sugarcane anytime he wanted to. He thought about it, and the more he thought, the angrier he became. Until he finally jumped up and shouted.

"You are lying! There are no giants from across the ocean. You are from the north, and you want to take our freedom away. I know because my father is away fighting you. My father is a hero. I hate you and I want you to go away."

Absolute silence thudded down on the square, and all eyes turned to Ai, who stood there with his resolve dissolving. Then he felt arms wrapping themselves around him. His mother enveloped him and hushed him. He melted to her, suddenly terrified. He felt her fear through the trembling of her body, and it became magnified in him.

The special friend smiled his wicked smile and kept talking. Only this time he talked about "reactionaries" and "reeducation." No one said anything to Ai or his mother or even looked at them. Gradually she stopped trembling, and her quieting transmitted itself to him. By the time the special friend stopped talking and shouting and waving his arms, Ai thought maybe everything was all right. But he didn't look forward to being in the semicircles tomorrow; he was afraid the teacher would slip up behind him and hit him again with his switch—he'd have to be more than usually attentive to avoid being hit.

Oil lamps came on in the houses when the sun went down. People talked a little in the early night, and small groups of men squatted together over the day's final cigarette. In one house, then another, then another, and finally in all of them, the lamps were snuffed for the night and everybody lay down to sleep. Half the night passed quietly except for the occasional bark of a disturbed dog. Then Ai was awakened by his mother's scream.

Rough hands pinioned the boy but didn't stop him from thrashing about with every bit of undeveloped muscle his seven-year-old body had. He added his cries to his mother's and sister's screams until a wad of cloth was rammed into his mouth. He heard a thump of fist hitting flesh followed by the thump of a small body falling hard, then his sister stopped screaming. His mother's cries continued, though muffled and frequently cut off in midpitch. Ai heard the ripping of cloth, and guttural grunts, and wet noises from where his mother was. But the darkness inside his house was complete, so he couldn't see what the men were doing to her—and wouldn't have understood it if he had.

Eventually, after a second man took him from the first and that first man did something to his mother, silence came to the house, silence that matched the silence outside. Then someone spoke, and Ai tried to cry out again, but the cloth crammed his mouth too full and he couldn't. Why did the men want to burn down his house? What did they mean, leave the woman and girl here? It didn't occur to him to wonder what they had planned for him. Not yet, he didn't wonder. But he learned soon enough.

A match was struck and a lamp lit. In the light Ai saw his sister lying in a heap at the foot of the bed. His mother lay crumpled on it; her clothes were torn mostly off her, and her head lolled to the side, her eyes open. He saw blood between her legs and understood that the men had done something very bad to her. He kicked out and tried to wrench himself free, but the man holding him was too strong. The man laughed and shook him violently until he stopped kicking.

One man lit a torch from the lamp and touched the torch to the back wall and both side walls of the house. The men filed out, one carrying Ai. The man with the torch was the last through the door. He brushed the torch along the door frame as soon as he was out. Then he threw the torch onto the roof of the house. Laughing, the men turned away from the fire and headed west, toward the finger ridge that led down from the mountains.

Away from Hou Ky the man carrying Ai dropped him, then squatted down and bound his hands with a length of cord. The cord was long; the man drew its end up and looped it around the boy's neck and held on to it to lead him along. Ai had to almost trot to keep from being yanked off his feet and strangled. As it was he stumbled many times and was choked every time he did.

The next day he was bound in a less hazardous manner. His captors kept walking, mostly westward, for several days. They fed themselves morning and night. Each morning they untied his hands and gave him the sparse remnants of their meal—they didn't feed him at night. Some time after the boy thought he couldn't go any farther, they reached a broad, long valley and marched across it. There he was thrown into a cage and left, ignored, for several hours. Then his new life began.

Every day for two years Ai was fed a small bowl of plain rice morning and night. He carried honey buckets, tended garden, carried various objects he had no knowledge of, dug holes when they moved to a new location, and filled the holes when they left an old location. Two or three times a week he and the other laborers were treated to a lecture on the Revolution and how all must work at the direction of the Party for the good of the Liberation. He didn't understand any of that; all he knew was he didn't like the Revolution, the Party, or the Liberation. Not if they meant he had to work like this and never play. He was always hungry and tired. He didn't know he was undernourished and wasn't growing anymore. And he had no way of knowing how close he was kept to the edge of death.

CHAPTER THREE

That Afternoon

Second Lieutenant "Scrappy" Burrison stood a safe distance from the helipad and watched the helicopter swoop down, straight at Corporal "Big Louie" Slover. Bell stood to one side of Burrison; Lieutenant Houng, fidgeting nervously, stood on his other side. Other Marines and PFs lounged around the compound, more or less looking like they were perimeter security.

Slover was a humongous black man who never wore a shirt inside the compound; he preferred to let his ebony skin shine in the sun. He was the proud possessor of two orange Ping-Pong paddles, which he used to guide helicopters onto the white circle. He stood facing the circle with his back to the wind and held the paddles out to his sides to show the pilot the copter was level, then brought them down sharply when the helicopter was directly above the pad and everything was clear under it. His ebony skin never glistened after a helicopter came in; his chest, neck, and head always turned a dull gray from the dust and debris kicked up by the bird's rotor wash.

The helicopter came down fast, the way they always did when touching down in the boonies, and a man in pressed utilities leapt out and dashed from under the whirling rotors before the wheels of the UH-34 had settled onto the white circle. A .45 pistol was holstered on his web belt, captain's bars shined on his collars, and he carried a box tucked under one arm. The helicopter eased down on its wheels and squatted, its blades spinning slowly, looking like nothing so much as a Japanese science-fiction movie Grasshopper-That-Ate-Tokyo. It used to be that helicopters never sat on the ground when they came to Camp Apache; they dropped their passengers or cargo and took off immediately to orbit if they had to wait. But there hadn't been any enemy activity in Bun Hou village for two months, and now the pilots chose to take a break when they drove someone out to Camp Apache. Slover wiped ineffectively at the dust on his chest and joined Burrison, Bell, and Houng.

"What a coincidence," Captain Hasford said when he reached the CAP leaders. "I was coming out here today anyway when I got your message. I brought you a present." He held out the box. "Something new came down the pike, but I'm not sure what to make of it. Let's go sit down and you can tell me why you called—after you open that." He pointed at the box, which Burrison had taken.

The five men headed toward a cluster of beach chairs and folding hammocks set up near the southeast corner of the compound. They settled themselves comfortably, Hasford looking straight south toward the Song Du Ong River and the others arched around him so they could look over the southern vista or at their visitor. Burrison used his K-bar to slice the tape sealing the box. He stared at its contents for a long moment, then looked questioningly at the captain.

"One of each for every Marine and PF in Tango Niner," Hasford said. He reached into the box and pulled out two patches and two pins, which he handed to Bell and Houng. They were a long shield shape, red, with a rampant eagle like the one on the Marine Corps emblem in their middle. A scroll hovered above the eagle's head, and American and Vietnamese flags draped down from poles clutched in the eagle's talons. "The new emblem of the Combined Action Program," Hasford said.

Bell blinked at the patch and pin he held. He liked them. They were an attractive design, and the flags clearly symbolized the Americans and Vietnamese working together—and he liked the Marine eagle holding the flags. As soon as he could get some paint, he'd add the emblem to the sign next to the main gate. But what the hell, he wondered. "Marines don't wear unit patches," he finished his thought out loud.

"CAC Marines do now," Hasford said.

"CAC?" Bell repeated. He and Houng exchanged quick glances.

"Combined Action Companies," Hasford explained, a wry smile curving his lips. "There's been a total reorganization. All CAP units are being combined under Combined Action Groups as CAGs. You're an official unit now." He hesitated, then plowed on. "A lieutenant colonel from tanks has been made commander of CAP; his name's Corson. Don't sweat him not being a grunt," he added quickly when he saw concern flicker across the faces of Burrison and Bell. "He's been involved with the program since at least last September and really believes in it. Listen to me, Brute Krulak and Uncle Lew really want this." "Uncle Lew" was Lieutenant General Lewis Walt, commander of

III Marine Amphibious Force—the Marines in Vietnam.
"Brute" Krulak was Lieutenant General Victor Krulak,
commanding general Fleet Marine Force Pacific, Walt's
boss. "Uncle Lew thinks Colonel Corson is the man for the
job. I've met him; I think he is, too." He hesitated again,
then went on. "Because of my involvement with Tango
Niner and a few other CAPs—excuse me, CACs—I think
I'm going to be made CO of one of the CAGs."

"CAC?" Bell said again. "What's the matter, doesn't
anybody around here speak Vietnamese? Captain, I
thought you did."

Hasford shifted his shoulders in a slight shrug. "They
didn't ask me."

"We're going to have to get it changed, you know that,
don't you?"

"Probably," Hasford agreed. "But if I'm in a CAG
headquarters, I don't have to worry about it. Hell, Jay Cee,
sergeants are going to be running every CAC. Want to
know why? Because sergeants can handle anything, that's
why."

"Thanks, pal."

Burrison had sat puzzled through the exchange. "What
are you two talking about?" he finally asked.

The others broke out laughing. When they stopped, they
explained it to him. Between more laughs, they told him
that the pronunciation of the acronym CAC sounded exactly like a Vietnamese slang word for penis.

"Oh, shit," the young lieutenant murmured when he
heard the explanation.

"Khong," Houng said, "not shit, cac," and he laughed.

"So what did you want to see me about?" Hasford finally asked. Burrison and Bell turned it over to Houng.
The PF lieutenant handed the Marine captain a copy of the
map he had earlier shown Bell and Burrison—it was Bell's

idea to make the copy; he thought Hasford might want to take it and didn't feel quite comfortable being left without one. Houng talked rapidly in Vietnamese. Hasford had little trouble understanding him as he spoke very fluent Vietnamese, much better than Bell did. The captain examined the map carefully while he listened to Houng's tale of hearing on what the Americans called the "Jungle Telegraph" about where his son was being held by the Vietcong, a slave laborer in one of their base camps. Occasionally he asked a question, but mostly he let Houng talk. Finally he knew enough and sat back, his eyes unfocused somewhere in the distance as he thought about it.

"That's a tough one," he said when he broke his reverie. "The A Shau is in the Third Marine Division's area. As far as I know, they don't have anything scheduled for that area. But what do I know?" Until he was officially transferred to CAP, Hasford was in the G-2 staff, intelligence section, of the First Marine Division. "I'll talk to some people I know in Three MAF operations and intelligence shops, see what I can find out about anything that might be planned for that area, or if they can do anything with this information. If nothing else, they might want to send in a Force Recon team to check it out; a regimental HQ is something they should be interested in."

The three CAP leaders looked at each other when Hasford mentioned Force Recon. The captain saw their looks and interpreted them correctly.

"This is different from before," Hasford said. "That Vee Cee senior sergeant you captured blew it when he told G-2 about the greasy guy in the tight pants. Anyway, the aerial recon I arranged for didn't show any activity where he said they had that communications center." He paused, half hoping, half knowing it was a vain hope, that one of the three would tell him about it. What he suspected was that the Vietcong had established a communications center deep in the hills west of the Song Du Ong floodplain. When Tango Niner couldn't convince Marine authorities it existed, they went into the hills themselves and destroyed it. That was what he thought, but he didn't know for sure—and nobody in Tango Niner was going to tell him how right he was. What they had done was highly unauthorized and would get them in deep trouble if the wrong people found out about it. When nobody said anything he continued. "This time the information comes from a reliable source—" He nodded at Houng. "—so they might want to check it out. Maybe we can get your son back for you."

Houng said nothing and didn't let his face show that he knew Hasford knew he wasn't going to be able to accomplish anything.

A little while after that Hasford walked back to the helicopter that had brought him out to Camp Apache and left, leaving his promise he'd let them know anything he found out.

By then it was too late for the PT Bell had wanted; it was time to draw the night's patrol orders and chow down.

The big topic of conversation at evening chow was Houng's son.

"Where the fuck's the A Shau Valley?" Tex Randall asked.

"You know where Laos is?" Zeitvogel asked him back.

"Yah, it's where the Ho Chi Minh Trail is."

"The A Shau's near there."

Randall frowned. "Sounds like a bad place."

"So deep in Indian Country, it makes Camp Apache look like Central Park in New York," Hempen said.

Lewis snorted. He had grown up in the Bronx and knew Hempen was from Florida. "Man, I can sure tell you ain't

never been in New York. Gangs take over Central Park at
night; even cops don't go into Central Park at night." He
paused to concentrate on chewing a dry piece of overcooked pork chop. He swallowed and continued. "Central
Park at night is one badass mo-dicking place. Ask Big
Louie, he'll tell you."

"Shee-it, what's Big Louie know about New York? He's
from New Jersey."

"Paramus," Slover said. "It's right across the tunnel
from New York." He nodded. "Yah, Central Park's a bad
place at night. Bun Hou's a lot safer."

"No shit," Hempen said. "Bun Hou is safer than anyplace, anymore. Hell, you don't even run the risk of getting run over by a Mack truck here."

"Didn't used to be," Lewis said through a mouthful of
overspiced applesauce. "When it wasn't, it was still safer
than Central Park."

Slover stared thoughtfully at Lewis for a moment, then
said, "You know, Billy Boy, when I was back on the block
in Paramus, I thought I was some kind of tough shit, had
my own gang and everything." He shook his head. "How
bad I was then wasn't nothing. Today I could take on that
whole gang all by my lonesome, even if it had a leader as
badass as I was then, and kick ass something fierce on
them. You know what you and me should do when we get
back to The World and get out of the Crotch?" He didn't
wait for an answer. "We should go to the mayor of New
York and ask him how much he's willing to pay us to clean
house on that place. Have us a field day, maybe get rich."

Lewis bunched his fists in front of his face and twisted
—he did it to give himself time to think about Slover's
suggestion. By the time he pulled his hands away—the
right end of his mustache shooting straight out to the side
before it hooked forward like a longhorn steer's horn, the

left end curving sharply out and ahead like the horn of a fighting bull—Slover was talking again.

"You and me, Billy Boy, we go back to The World, go see the mayor. Two of us, that's all it'll take, kick ass on those gangs, make Central Park safe at night. Shit, dude, we do that, they'll make us mayor."

Lewis started talking about Slover's idea, agreeing that it was a good one and that they should certainly do exactly that when they got back to The World, but he was interrupted by Randall and Zeitvogel.

"Shitcan that," Zeitvogel said. "It don't have one goddamn thing to do with Houng's son."

"I bet the A Shau Valley's worse than Central Park," Randall said. Then he asked, "Anybody got a map of that place?"

Slover didn't wait for anyone to answer; he knew the only map of the A Shau anywhere near Camp Apache had to be the hand-drawn one Houng had. "I bet I can get one from my cousin Os," he said.

"I got a good look at Houng's map," Zeitvogel said. "It sort of looks like this." He started arranging empty C-ration cans, wadded condiment packages, peanut butter tins, and other effluvia of their meal into an impromptu sandbox map on the sheet-metal-on-sandbag table.

"How many men are guarding it?" someone asked.

"What's the terrain like?" someone else wanted to know.

"What kind of escape routes they got, in case someone runs a battalion operation in there to find their asses?"

"They got tunnels, or is it just bunkers?"

"How many laborers are held there?"

"Think they got any POWs?"

"What about a small team? What if Recon wants to send in a team to scope it out? Does that team—how big's a

recon team, four men, five men?—have a chance to grab
his ass and get out without getting caught?"

And so it went. The group of men around the table
steadily grew until nearly all the Marines of Tango Niner
were gathered around it, and so were many of the PFs. As
a matter of fact, all the Marines except Bell and Burrison
got in on it along with the twelve PFs who were patrolling
with the Marines that night. They discussed all the tactical
possibilities until it was time for the first patrol to go out.
They talked about almost everything connected with a rescue operation, but no one mentioned the one thing that was
on everybody's mind.

Houng spent that same time in the command hootch
visiting the Marine officer and sergeant. The three of them
didn't talk about what was on everybody's mind, either.

"Where's your patch, Short Round?" Bell asked the short
lance corporal who was leading the all-night patrol, which
was the first one to leave. He looked beyond Hempen to
where his six men—two Marines and four PFs—waited.
The PFs all proudly wore their new CAC patches on the
left sleeves of their shirts, but neither of the Marines did.
Bell wore the red patch on his own shoulder; the pin was
on the flap of his left shirt pocket.

"Patch? What patch?" Hempen looked up at the sergeant, looking as innocent as he could.

"Your CAC patch."

"It's in the hootch. I tied it onto the tent post by my
rack." Hempen tried to look eager, tried to sound as though
he was saying he had done exactly what he'd been told to.

"That's not where it's supposed to be, Short Round. It's
supposed to be on your sleeve."

Hempen beetled his brow and looked at Bell seriously,
as though trying very hard to understand the strange words

spoken to him. Then he looked at the Marine emblem stenciled on the left breast pocket of his shirt. He cocked his hip and looked up at Bell again. "Jay Cee," he said somberly, "the last time I looked I was a Marine, not a doggie. Marines don't wear unit patches on their uniforms."

Bell groaned. He resisted the impulse to close his eyes. He knew he was going to have trouble getting the Marines of Tango Niner to wear the CAC patches. He knew, as did the rest of them, that the only time Marines had ever worn unit patches on their uniforms had been during World War II, when the Corps had had six divisions.

"Short Round," he said, his voice filled with menace despite its softness, "if you don't have that patch on your shirtsleeve tomorrow, I'm going to give your fire team to Billy Boy."

Hempen's eyes widened, and he swallowed; it was a threat he could take seriously. "Aye-aye, Jay Cee," he said. "Will do. Tomorrow ole Short Round here is going to look like he's in the fucking Army." He spun around and headed toward his men before Bell could say anything else.

That was the only kind of excitement Tango Niner had all night, most of the Marines not wearing their new CAC patches and being ordered to sew them on the next day. It was another quiet night for the three patrols and the dozen or so men guarding the perimeter. It was the sixty-first consecutive night without any enemy activity in Bun Hou village. They managed to get through it.

CHAPTER FOUR

March 7, 1967

The night of 6 March was the sixty-second consecutive night on which the fighting men of CAP Tango Niner had to stay awake without any help from the Vietcong or the North Vietnamese. They were getting damn tired of having to do everything by themselves. At least one thing did happen to relieve the tedium.

When the helicopter brought in the evening hot meal it also dropped off two small cans of paint, one red, one yellow—substitutes for the Marine Corps colors of scarlet and gold—a paintbrush and two stencils. After he ate, J. C. Bell took the paint, brush, and stencils and walked across the bare, red dirt hilltop to the main gate. A crowd gathered to watch him paint a Marine Corps emblem in the upper left hand corner and the new Combined Action Company insignia in the upper right of the hand-painted sign that stood next to the gate. When he finished, he stepped back to admire his handiwork.

The sign read:

CAMP APACHE
USMC
HOME OF Combined Action Platoon T-9
IT TAKES TWO TO TANGO
CHARLIE GONNA DIE HERE
BARRY SADLER, EAT YOUR HEART OUT

"Sure looks good with the emblems on it," Bell said to nobody in particular.

"Fucking A," everybody agreed.

Stenciling the sign and getting the patches sewn onto sleeves occupied the Marines enough that Bell never got around to PT that day.

Then they had their sixty-second consecutive boring night. To relieve his boredom, Bell didn't even have the distraction of chewing on anybody for not wearing the new CAC patch. All the Marines had the patch on their sleeves and the pin on their pocket flaps—some of them had even ordered copies of the patch from a seamstress in Hou Dau so they could have one sewn on each of their shirts.

The seventh of March started out much the same. It changed in midafternoon, just as Bell was ready to go out to lead his Marines through what should have been their third day of calisthenics but was now scheduled to be the first.

PFC "Swearin'" Swarnes rogered the message that came over his radio and hung the headset back on the nail sticking out of the tent pole near his head, right where it belonged so he could hear incoming traffic without having to wear the headset all the time. He stared at the radio for a second, then said to it, "Fuck you very much, too. I bet your cock is just as big as the one on an asshole Ken doll."

"Ken dolls don't have cocks, Swearin' Swarnes," Bell said from his side of the canvas wall that separated the radio room from the commanders' quarters in the command hootch tent.

"No shit," Swarnes said back. "And I'll bet that cock-sucker could fuck a Barbie doll without having to drill a cunt hole in one." He paused a beat and added, "Barbie and Ken dolls don't have assholes, neither." Swarnes didn't get his nickname because of the onomatopoeic resonance of it, not by any means. He earned his nickname the old-fashioned way—he was the most foulmouthed man in Tango Niner.

"What's your problem?" Bell stepped into the radio room and stared hard at the radioman.

"Jerk-off railroad-tracker sent a message no one can goddam do a fucking thing about Houng's piss-ant son." He said it without looking at Bell.

"Watch your fucking mouth when you're talking about officers, Swarnes," Bell warned.

"Fuck him," Swarnes said. His jaw was clenched, and he still didn't look at the sergeant. "Fuck a whole bunch of ossifers."

"What was the exact message?"

Swarnes looked at the pad of paper lying in front of him on the narrow countertop on which the radios were mounted. "'Regret cannot comply at this time with your request of five March. Will confirm in person at first opportunity.' Dipshit."

"Swarnes, we've got a war going on, remember? It's important to us that someone try to get Houng's son out of there, but there might not be any units available to do the job."

Swarnes spun around in his folding chair to look defiantly at Bell. "Then why the fuck don't they send a god-damn Recon team to eye-fuck the goddamn situation, see if any-fucking-thing is really the hell there?"

"I don't know," was all Bell said, and he said it quietly. It was a sore point with the sergeant that Recon never seemed to be available to check out any information Tango Niner passed on and never was able to get any information to them when they needed it to save lives.

"You know what we got to do, don't you?" Swarnes concentrated so hard on making his voice firm, the kind of voice he hoped no one could argue against, that he forgot to swear.

"Do I?" Bell asked. "Do we have to do it?"

"You know good goddamn well we have to. No-fuck-ing-body else gonna do it. Who the fuck you think's left for shit duty like that?"

Bell stared hard at the radioman for a long moment, his face a stern sergeant's mask that effectively hid the emotions roiling through his mind. "Is that a fact," he said flatly, then left the tent in search of Lieutenant Burrison, the PT momentarily forgotten.

Bell didn't talk to anybody but the lieutenant, whom he found lounging in the collapsible hammocks in the southeast corner of the compound, and nobody saw Swarnes leave his radio room or anyone go in to visit him. But within fifteen minutes all the Marines in Tango Niner and about half of their PFs were gathered in small clumps around the compound talking about Captain Hasford's message and what they were going to do about it.

"Does everybody agree to it?" Bell asked the assembled Marines shortly before the helicopter arrived with the daily hot meal. He had earlier come up with some feeble excuse to get all the PFs off the hill so the Americans could talk alone. Nobody said so out loud, but they all knew that the PFs knew why Bell wanted them to leave. "We aren't going to do it if anybody objects." All the enlisted Marines—except Swarnes, who remained at his radios—were gathered around the sheet-metal-on-sandbag tables near the middle of the compound. Lieutenant Burrison stood, arms folded across his chest, off to one side; the meeting was properly run by the sergeant.

"Only objection anybody's going to make is when I take over your job after we shitcan you if we don't do it," Zeitvogel said.

"After *you* take over his job!" Slover said in a voice that rumbled from somewhere deep inside his massive body. "I'm senior to you. We shitcan Jay Cee, I take his job."

"See what I mean?" Zeitvogel said.

"What we do, Wall," Randall said to Corporal Dennis McEntire, the machine-gun team leader, "is after we shitcan Jay Cee if we don't do it is we let those two fight it out, then after they wipe each other out, you take Big Louie's job and I take Jay Cee's." McEntire, like Slover, was a massive man. He was called "Wall" because he was "not tall enough to be a tree and not fat enough to be a bear."

McEntire was four inches taller than Randall and outweighed him by some sixty pounds of solid muscle. He displayed his bulk to the smaller corporal and snarled. "I think you got that backward, Tex."

Billy Boy Lewis turned to Hempen and said sotto voce, "Short Round, when them dumbass corporals get through taking each other out, it's gonna be you and me running this show."

"You know it, Billy Boy."

"Shut up!" Bell roared. Everybody shut.

"I say again," Bell said in a parade-ground voice that

was heard a quarter mile away in Hou Ky hamlet, "does anybody have any objections?" Still, no one had said out loud what it was they were going to do.

When nobody spoke up, Randall looked around at the other Marines to see if any looked like they were considering speaking. None did, so he said, "It's like Stilts said, Jay Cee. The only objection is if we don't do it."

"All right, then," Bell said in a lower voice, but still loud enough for Swarnes, fifty meters away in the command hootch, to clearly hear him without straining. "This isn't going to be easy. It's going to take a lot of planning, and we have to pull it off without a hitch the first time, because we won't get a second chance." He paused for long enough to look each man in the eye. "Not everybody will be able to go on this one. If we all go, that's too many to be able to move that far without being detected and not enough to defend ourselves when we get spotted. A small team, no more than six men, has the best chance of being able to get in and out alive. The men who go have to be the best at evasive movement—and the toughest fighters. Now—" He hurried so no one had a chance to voice any objections to being left behind. "—to as great an extent as possible everybody will be involved somehow. Some of you who don't go will be involved in the operational planning, some will help with the logistics, and somebody has to arrange for transportation. Everybody gets in on it. Are there any questions?" Bell almost immediately wished he hadn't asked.

"Who's going?" It seemed like twenty men asked that question simultaneously.

"I haven't decided yet."

"Make sure I do," about twenty of them said back. Then somebody asked, "Who you gonna keep here with you and Scrappy?"

Bell glared at them, trying to decide which of them had said that.

Then the deluge of serious questions and suggestions began:

"We need maps, where we gonna get the maps?"

"The A Shau is what, thirty, forty miles away? We can walk there in a couple of days. What's the terrain like between here and there?"

"No, we can't walk it in a couple of days. There's heavy jungle between here and there."

"What do we know about bad guys along the way?"

"How long's this mission going to take?"

"Right, how long? How many days' rations we got to carry?"

"Is there any drinkable water along the way, or do we have to hump it?"

"Are there any friendly forces around there? Don't want to get shot up by the good guys, you know."

So it went for several minutes. Some things Bell had thought about already, some things he hadn't thought of yet. He had almost no answers for any of the questions— not yet, but they'd come. "That's it for now, people," the sergeant finally said, holding his hands up for silence. He had to shout it out a second time before everybody heard him and stopped talking. "I'll take everything you said into consideration," he said when the cacophony subsided. "Tonight Scrappy and I will start the preliminary planning. I'll keep you informed of what's happening. And I want every good idea every one of you has to offer. Now, you're all dismissed except the patrol leaders. It's time to give the orders for tonight's patrols."

"Say what?" the objections started.

"Patrols?"

"Tonight?"

"Cut us a hus, Jay Cee."

"We got more important shit to do, Jay Cee!"

"As you were, people," Bell bellowed. "We still have a job to do, and that job is providing security for Bun Hou. That means patrols tonight."

Shortly after that the daily hot meal arrived. Then the men of CAP Tango Niner suffered through their sixty-third consecutive boring night.

CHAPTER FIVE

March 8, 1967

Sergeant J. C. Bell was already awake when the sun rose above the horizon and flooded the Song Du Ong floodplain with light; he had taken the last shift on the night's radio watch rotation. He climbed out of the bunker where the radios were kept overnight and watched Tex Randall and his three Marines trudge in through the compound's back gate after their all-night patrol. Ten minutes earlier the four PFs who had patrolled with Randall had peeled off from his small column and gone home to Hou Ky, where their wives or mothers were rising and starting to fix the morning meal. Those PFs would eat lightly and then get a few hours' sleep before heading to the rice paddies to work the afternoon away.

Randall and his men walked to the side of the command hootch tent and stared at the C-ration boxes Bell had put out right before he had relieved Swarnes on the radios. The four Marines looked like they were trying to divine the

contents of the boxes. Each night, sometime between midnight and dawn, Bell put out twice as many C-ration boxes
as there were Marines in Tango Niner; he mixed them up
and laid them out upside down—the box lids said what
was inside the boxes. Each man in the platoon would then
pick two boxes blindly—the rule was, you touch it and it's
yours. The reason for the blind picking was that some
meals, such as turkey loaf, were passable if not good,
while others—ham and limas were the worst offenders—
were meals such as you might offer only to someone you
wanted to see starve to death. By picking blind, each man
had an equal chance at the better meals and everybody had
an equal chance of getting stuck with the ham and limas. It
was merely coincidence that the men who picked first
seemed usually to get the better meals while the slugabeds
who picked last got more than their fair share of ham and
limas. Sure.

   More than half the forty-six boxes Bell had put out were
gone by the time Randall, Lewis, Dodd, and Anderson
made their picks. Randall looked at his and shrugged; his
meals were probably all right. Lewis grimaced at his; he
most likely had gotten stuck with one of the ham and
limas. Anderson smiled. Dodd's impassive expression gave
no indication of what he had gotten.

   Bell watched as Lewis sweet-talked Dodd, trying to
trade boxes. Dodd deadpanned his refusal; the rules were,
he reminded Lewis, you're stuck with what you pick out.
Dodd went into the rifle squad's tent to get his canteen cup
and field stove, then joined Randall and Anderson at one of
the tables to eat before stripping down and lying on his cot
for a few hours' sleep. Lewis swore and went into the tent
to sack out without eating. The other three men ate slowly
and talked little. When they finished, they cleaned their

mess kits by wiping them out with clean cloths and headed for their cots.

Bell let them go, didn't approach to say anything. He lugged the two radios back to the command hootch and set Swarnes's folding chair in the entrance of the radio room, then strung the headset close enough to hear anything coming over it while he sat in the entrance and watched over the hilltop until Swarnes woke up and relieved him.

Camp Apache came slowly awake as the day warmed up. The tropical sun beat down fiercely enough to heat the air until it was too warm to allow sleep for men who weren't sleeping the sleep of the exhausted. Hempen, Mazzucco, and Vega were the first ones up. They went through their morning ablutions, and by the time they sat at one of the tables to eat, both corpsmen were up and had joined them. The machine gunners and mortar men started to rise. Bell saw Burrison wander, blinking, out of the bunker where he'd spent the night. Zeitvogel and his men got up. Bell started wondering where Swarnes was.

An infrequent visitor would have thought it was an ordinary morning in the compound. The men staggered awake in irregular waves and slowly, methodically went about doing whatever it was each man did on rising. But Bell could tell it wasn't an ordinary morning; he sensed an electricity in the atmosphere. While everyone moved languidly, none of them slouched. The sleep-thickened voices the Marines greeted each other with had an unaccustomed briskness. The movements of toothbrushing, shaving, eating, and drinking coffee were crisp and economical. No one had sleep-fogged eyes. They were talking in hushed, excited tones about what it was they were going to do and who was going to do what part of it.

Bell let everybody do whatever he wanted to; he waited until everyone was up and fed and starting to jerk with anticipation of what would come next. He and Burrison had done their initial planning during the night while Swarnes was sleeping. Nobody could know yet. "Ready?" he asked the young lieutenant after he finally saw everyone except Swarnes.

Burrison nodded. "As ready as I'll ever be."

Bell rose from the chair, moved it out of the entryway, and stepped outside. "Big Louie," he shouted, "Tex, Big Red . . ." his voice trailed off. Slover, Randall, and Robertson were striding side by side toward him up the last slight grade to the highest point of the hill where the command-hootch tent stood. All three carried loaded rifles and had cartridge belts around their waists and light packs on their backs. He had a big hint that they knew what was happening from the fact that they were all wearing regulation soft covers instead of their normal bush hats and were wearing rank insignia pinned on their collars. A heavy-looking sea-bag hung lightly from Slover's left hand—and he was wearing a shirt. The big man *knew* they were going to Da Nang.

"We're ready any time Scrappy is, Jay Cee," the big man said. "Trading goods," he added, hefting the seabag.

Bell planted his fists on his hips and leaned slightly forward, mock glaring at the trio. "If I didn't know better I'd say the three of you knew you were going with him," he said slowly. He looked through them for a second, then changed his mind. "*I* don't know any better. What the hell makes the three of you think you're going anyplace?"

Slover grinned. "A little bird told us to be ready for something different this morning."

A little bird named Swarnes? Bell thought furiously. He hadn't seen Swarnes leave the bunker yet, and even if the radioman had been faking sleep, how and when could he

have gotten word to anyone about who was going to Da
Nang?

The three men in front of him stood grinning and waiting until Randall finally said, "Can I have the keys to the
car, Pop?"

Bell gagged.

Slover sneered down at Randall. "You sure you know
how to drive?"

Randall looked up at the massive man. "I got an A in
driver's ed in high school."

Slover snorted. He hadn't finished high school and
wasn't sure his school even had driver's ed.

"Drop the seabag and come with me." Bell turned into
the tent. Swarnes was sitting on his folding chair in front of
the radios, his nose buried in a skin book, the radio headset
hanging on its nail near his right ear. He looked like he'd
been there for hours. Wondering where the radioman had
come from, the sergeant shook his head and led the others
into the tent's middle room, where Burrison waited for
them.

Burrison made the briefing as brief as he could: He and
the three of them were going to Da Nang—Bell was staying behind in command of Tango Niner. Burrison's job at
Da Nang was arranging for logistical support and transportation. He'd visit his good buddy Ensign Lily and Lily's
buddy, Lieutenant (j.g.) Reeves, a helicopter driver. Slover
was to visit Chief Petty Officer Ossie Slover, his cousin in
the Seabees, to secure maps and any special equipment the
mission was going to need. Burrison handed the big man a
shopping list. Randall would get any information of intelligence value he could from his girlfriend, Bobbie Harder.
Robertson was coming along as an extra rifle just in case
they ran into any trouble along the way and had to fight

their way out of it. Nobody had any questions; they were all ready to go.

None of the Marines who weren't going crowded around the jeep when the four men piled into it; they were all too anxious about what was going on not to be cool about it. Burrison sat in the passenger seat, and Randall—he'd taken that route several times already—drove. The big men sat in the back with the seabag on the floor between them. They'd removed the rank insignia and changed their soft covers for bush hats for the trip; they'd change back into proper uniform when they reached Da Nang. Slover planted a foot on the seabag to keep it from bouncing out and tried to look menacing. He intended to look too mean for anybody to dare try to take anything from them along the way. He certainly looked mean enough for that seabag to not even think about bouncing out of the jeep.

Randall flipped the ignition switch on the navy-blue jeep, checked the gas gauge, and shifted into first. He rolled it sedately through the main gate, down the bull-dozed road to the foot of the hill, right toward Hou Dau, and around Hou Dau hill to the south. He slowly picked up speed going through the thick woods south of the village's main hamlet. He was doing a probably unsafe 40 mph by the time they reached the cane fields to the east.

Burrison looked to his right and watched the band of big trees that bordered the Song Du Ong River. He thought he could pick out the place where he had first been involved in an ambush that had killed VC. A little beyond there was the small road that cut off to the left, toward Bun Anh village. Randall glanced at the lieutenant and wondered if he was thinking about the time they had been ambushed on that road, the first time Burrison had issued orders under fire—and been right. Eventually the bulldozed road emptied onto a rural highway, a hard-packed, one-lane affair lined by trees, and Randall had to reduce speed because of local bicycle and foot traffic. At one point he had to slow to a crawl around an overloaded bullock cart going the other way.

Passing through a small hamlet, Randall had to slow down enough to keep from running over any of the tiny children who suddenly appeared around the jeep, mobbing them, wanting the Marines to stop and play with them, but he didn't stop. If it hadn't been for the palm trees, thatch hootches, and the black pajamas worn by the people, the hamlet could have been an Appalachian homestead. The place was adorned with inoperative vehicles: An orange Vespa sat on sunbaked bricks in lieu of cinder blocks where its wheels should have been; an orange Rolls-Royce front was separating from the pickup truck bed welded to its back; serious body cancer had almost completely claimed a bus that had once been pale blue, white, and yellow. Only a pink and fire-engine-red and sky-blue flatbed truck seemed marginally capable of automation. That truck's one eye, centered over its grill, seemed to stare balefully through a cataract. The Marines smiled wanly at the vehicles. And here they'd thought the denizens of this vehicular mortuary were in bad shape the first time they saw them.

The roadway wound its way through an area of low hills and rice paddies until it finally reached Highway 1, the main coastal route through Vietnam. They had to stop and wait while a long convoy of olive-drab trucks packed with Marines with thousand-yard stares trundled by on its way south to an operation or to a new location for the Marines to hold against expected enemy onslaughts. While they waited, they examined a newly painted sign someone had erected to mark the entrance to the road they were leaving. The sign read "Indian Country," with a west-pointing arrow under the words. The I was dotted with a bullet hole. A weather-beaten, many-times-holed piece of plywood lay on the ground below the sign. Once it had hung there; now it was too badly worn and shot up to be legible.

The last truck of the convoy rolled past, and Randall gunned the jeep across the southbound lane into a gap in the northbound traffic. National Route 1 was a sorry, narrow two-lane road, badly eroding at its edges. Highway 1 desperately needed to be widened and repaved, but that couldn't be done. There was no alternate route for the military, commercial, and refugee traffic that flowed along it like a river bucking its own tide to use during repairs. Besides, everybody knew the Communists would come along behind the road workers and destroy any improvements as soon as no one was watching.

Landward of the highway, rice paddies sparkled with all the emerald in the world. Seaward, sand shimmered blinding white to the pale green water of the South China Sea. Many-colored caravans of civilian vehicles—Lambrettas, Vespas, motorbikes, and minuscule buses—creaked and rattled and coughed up and down the highway, attaching themselves as often as they could to military convoys, for the protection of the 50-caliber machine guns many of the trucks had mounted. Most of the buses and cars and bikes were top-heavy, piled high with people of all ages from ancients who looked to Western eyes like they might have already been mummified to babes suckling at breasts. Dogs and chickens and piglets lived precarious existences on the vehicles; household goods and farm produce tottered and constantly threatened to cascade off and create a massive traffic jam. Peasants who lived in the shanty settlements along the highway trudged and trotted along the road's beaten edge, barely missed by the cars and buses and bikes; wicker baskets swayed from yokes slung on their shoulders.

Traffic stuttered and roared and stop-goed at a terrifying more or less twenty-five miles an hour. Eventually the highway emptied its northbound traffic into Da Nang, South Vietnam's second largest city. Randall found his way to the base. A short distance from the gate he stopped long enough for everyone to pin on his rank insignia and don his regulation soft cover.

Not as sharp as the bush hats, Randall thought about the regulation hats, but they beat all hell out of those silly-ass baseball caps the Army wears.

A Marine MP at the gate suspiciously eyed the navy-blue jeep before saluting Lieutenant Burrison. He didn't believe for even a second that the jeep legitimately belonged to them, but he knew how the black market worked and understood quite well that if they were ballsy enough to drive an obviously stolen jeep *onto* the base, there was probably no way it could be traced to its rightful owner. It just wasn't worth the paperwork he'd have to do if he stopped them for it. He looked into the back of the jeep.

"What's in the seabag?" he asked.

"Personal effects," Slover rumbled. The muscles of his right arm rippled; the M-14 he held loosely in his massive hand somehow looked like a toothpick.

The MP didn't bother to look around. He knew there was only one man there to back him up. Fucking grunts, he thought. He turned to Burrison and said, "Sir, it's regulations. You'll have to have your people clear their weapons before I can let you aboard. Bolts to the rear, safeties on, no magazines in the weapons."

Burrison nodded. "You heard the man. Clear them." He waited calmly while they obeyed.

"Your sidearm, too, sir," the MP said. "Chamber clear, safety on, no magazine."

Burrison shrugged and pulled his .45 from its holster. "As long as we don't have to check our arms anyplace," he said. "We've been out in the field too damn long and feel naked without them."

"I don't know about that, sir," the MP said. He stepped back and gave a wave-through salute. Randall drove by.

Burrison glanced at his watch. "Sixteen hundred," he said. "Let's split up and get started." He looked around for a landmark. "Tex, think you know where the old Three MAF headquarters is?"

"Sure do." Randall drove, turned left and drove on a road that paralleled the long jet runways. He stopped in front of the rambling wooden structure that once had housed the III MAF headquarters.

"We'll meet back here at eighteen hundred," Burrison said. "Big Red, you go with Big Louie. Tex, I'm taking the jeep." He looked at Slover. "Don't worry, I'll take good care of the seabag."

CHAPTER SIX

Da Nang

Slover snarled at the departing jeep. He had wanted to arrive at the Seabee area in splendor, but RHIP—rank has its privileges—and the officer got the jeep. "Later, pano," he said to Randall. "Let's go," he told Robertson. A pair of F-4 Phantom jets roared on the runway, sounding like the warbirds they were, and took off. The trio of Marines ignored them.

The Seabee building where Chief Petty Officer Ossie Slover worked was behind a row of warehouses. The big black man led his big redheaded partner to it without getting lost along the way. As he had once explained it, "No way one Slover can't find another, once he knows where he's at." But Big Louie didn't find his cousin Os this time.

"Chief Slover decided to knock off early today," a gangly seaman explained to them. He recognized Slover from having seen him once before and knew he was related to the chief. Evidently everybody had decided to knock off early that day, the Marines thought—the seaman they talked to was the only person in sight. "What you should do if you want to see him is you go someplace where peoples are friendly to Marine field grunts and have yourselves a good old time tonight, grab some chow, chug a few brews, maybe take in a flick, then come back tomorrow around ten hundred hours. Now, the chief checks in around oh eight hundred, but what he does then is he goes into his private office over there and he starts drinking pots of coffee, try to make himself human again, and he just ain't the kind of man no one never wants to see before he gets about three pots of good Navy coffee into him, and it takes until about ten hundred hours for him to do that. Then he can rightly see straight again and he can talk to peoples and understand straight what they're saying and not get all pissed off and kick them out of his office—hell, even our own CO don't never come in to see the chief before ten hundred hours or ask him to go see him, neither."

Slover opened his mouth to say all right, they'd come back in the morning, but the seaman misunderstood and held up a hand to stop him while he kept talking. "Now, no way I'm going to tell you where he is now even if I know where he is, and I think I do know where he is. You see, where he is, is where he is every day after he knocks off, he's at a club for chief petty officers and he's getting drunk and all the rest of them is getting drunk right along with him, so it won't do you no good to try to find him to talk to him tonight. I can tell just by looking at you, you two are a couple of badass field grunts and I bet the two of you can do some heavy-duty ass kicking any time you feel like it, but it's not a good idea for you to go where a bunch of chief petty officers are drinking and getting drunk. I don't care how big and badass you are or how drunk they are, fifty or sixty drunk chief petty officers can rightly swab the deck with your young asses."

Robertson stood gawking at the seaman. He'd never before heard anybody use so many words to say "He's not here; come back in the morning."

Slover, on the other hand, had heard that speech before —or at least a variation on it. He slumped deeper as the seaman talked. He didn't want to be rude about it, but finally he realized the sailor wasn't going to stop talking as long as he had an audience. "Let's go," he said to Robertson, and turned around and walked off. Robertson eagerly followed.

"Think he talks like that all the time?" Robertson asked when they were outside. He glanced back over his shoulder to see if the sailor was following them—he still could hear him talking.

"I do believe so," Slover said, shaking his head. "I think he spends every night alone in that place, and when he gets a chance to talk, he talks." They turned the corner of a warehouse, and the seaman's continued babbling was finally blocked from their hearing.

Elsewhere, Randall had better fortune.

The beefy gunnery sergeant sat in self-imagined splendor before the rattling air conditioner that labored to cool half the large office his desk presided over. The air conditioner did cool off the day somewhat, but what it mostly did was drown out the noise of jet aircraft landing and taking off from the nearby airstrip. The gunny reached one mighty paw for the cold half-smoked stogie that rested in his elephant's-foot ashtray. While he played the flame from his Zippo over the ash end of the cigar, he watched the parade of militariana passing by the window at his side. When the cigar was lit he puffed on it a couple of times to make sure it was going well and said, "You expecting that boy you're sweet on to come calling?"

Bobbie Harder jerked her head up from the papers she was going over. The pen she was marking them with slid from her suddenly limp fingers, rolled along the desk top, and clattered to the floor. "Tex?" she squealed. "Do you see Tex?"

The gunnery sergeant puffed again on his cigar and took it from his mouth, holding it in front of his eyes as though examining something rare and valuable. "Unless you've been holding out on old Gunny here, girl, if there's others you haven't told me about, yep, that's the boy I mean."

Her face lit up with excitement. She almost stumbled over the words when she said, "Gunny, I've told you a hundred times, he's not a boy, he's a twenty-year-old Marine corporal."

"Ayup, that's what I said a hundred times."

The door to the office burst open, and Tex Randall rushed in. "Bobbie, I wasn't sure I'd catch you. I was afraid you'd already left for the day."

"No, Tex, I'm here until sixteen thirty." Her husky voice clashed with the prosaic words.

Randall pushed through the gate in the slatted fence that separated the desks from a waiting area. She was standing when he reached her and grabbed for her hand.

The gunny sat staring at them and sucking on his teeth. They weren't consciously aware of his presence, but something told them to hold back; they didn't throw their arms around each other, which was what they wanted to do. The gunnery sergeant muttered something under his breath about moonstruck puppies and thought lascivious thoughts about how firm Bobbie's round tits and ass must be and thought something angry about how he'd never find out for himself. Not as long as she had this twenty-year-old boyfriend who had the habit of carrying a rifle every time he came into the office. He glanced at his watch: twenty after four. Close enough for government work, he thought.

"Quitting time," he boomed parade-ground style. "Get the fuck out of my office."

Randall flinched at the loud voice; Bobbie jerked like a puppet on a string.

"Bu-but, Gunny," she said, looking at the wall clock, "it's only twenty after."

"Girlie, my timepiece says sixteen thirty," he said around his cigar. One finger tapped the face of his wristwatch. "I'm the official timekeeper around here, and I say it's quitting time. Go!" The last word was almost a bellow.

Randall grinned and said, "Thanks, Gunny. Nice seeing you again." He waved at the senior NCO as he dragged Bobbie through the gate and toward the door.

"Wait, Tex, I have to get my things." She pulled her arm free from his grasp and dashed back to her desk. Randall stood seemingly calmly waiting for her; inside he was jittering. He grinned at the gunny. The gunny exhaled a fog bank of cigar smoke and glared back.

"Let's go." Bobbie had returned to Randall, clutch bag in one hand. Her eyes sparkled at him. She grabbed his hand with her free one and pulled him out into the afternoon blast furnace.

At his desk the gunnery sergeant steamed amid billows of smoke. Gawd, how he wanted that girl. And she had to take up with this damn grunt corporal! There were a lot of ways a gunnery sergeant could fuck with a corporal. But when that corporal spent most of his time killing people who were trying to kill him, and he was in the habit of being armed when he walked into your office, you damn well had to be careful how you fucked with him. And fucking with his girl was one bodacious bad thing to do. Damn, he couldn't even risk copping a feel.

Outside, Randall withdrew his hand from Bobbie's. It wasn't that he didn't want to hold hands with her—he wanted to hold hands and a lot more—but holding hands in uniform was the same as being out of uniform, and he didn't want the kind of grief he could get if he ran into an officer or senior NCO while he was holding hands with his girlfriend. Bobbie understood. She wrapped her right arm around his left. His right hand was free to salute, and he could maintain a military posture.

"Oh, Tex, I'm so glad to see you," she whispered.

He nodded dumbly. It was a month since he'd last seen her. His throat thickened so that he was afraid he wouldn't have a voice if he tried to talk.

Bobbie shook her head; the brisk movement sent the rich brown hair that cascaded over her shoulders swirling around. She knew she had a powerful effect on the young men she met in Da Nang, yet it never failed to amaze her how she could make them blush all the way through their deep-baked bronzes. But she had met Tex last October, and they'd been lovers for three months now. It seemed to her he should have been over that by now, but he obviously wasn't. "Let's find a geedunk and have a Pepsi," she said. "You can tell me what brings you to Da Nang." She looked up at him, and her eyes sparkled. "If you can find your voice."

A brilliant red suddenly flushed Randall's sun-browned face. He swallowed and nodded. "Yes, let's do that," he croaked.

Her laugh was all the most beautiful wind chimes in the entire world.

Shortly they were seated at a Formica-topped table in a corner of a geedunk, tall cups of soda with ice between them. Randall had turned down her offer to have dinner together right then; he didn't know what was going to happen when he rejoined the others in an hour and a half. They made small talk for a while, oblivious to the stares of the utility-clad Marine clerks who crowded into tables near them the better to see the beautiful woman. The clerks wondered how the obvious grunt had managed to hook up with the beautiful girl, where she worked, how they could find her and get close once the scuzzy grunt went back into the field. Hell, if she was taking up with a grunt, who knew what she'd do with a man who kept himself clean with daily hot showers. Finally, Randall became aware of the unabashed stares directed at his girlfriend and turned to stare back. When he stared back, the others turned away. His stare was the cold-eyed stare of a man who'd killed more men than he'd ever want to count and who expected to kill more before he was through.

Randall and Bobbie finished telling each other how much they missed each other, then got into the business of why he was there.

"I need every bit of information I can get about the A Shau Valley," he said, "especially Marine activities in it: recent, current, and planned and anything between there and Camp Apache."

Bobbie's eyes opened so wide that there was a wide circle of white all the way around her irises. "Do you know what the A Shau is?" she asked in a hushed voice that was all she could use unless she screamed.

He nodded solemnly.

"Tex, what are you guys planning?" She knew about Tango Niner's unauthorized raid on the Vietcong communications center in the hills west of Bun Hou.

He shook his head. "We aren't planning anything. It's just that we've heard some rumors, and we need information nobody wants to give us through official channels."

"Why? Why do you need that information?" His explanation didn't satisfy her. She knew her man too well, and she knew how independent Tango Niner could be. She was terrified that one day Randall would do something brave that he wasn't supposed to do and it would get him killed. That had already happened to one man she knew of in his CAP. She'd dated a lot of men—that was inevitable for a woman with her looks and social graces—but Randall was the one she liked the best. She didn't want to have to mourn the man she secretly hoped to marry someday.

Randall looked deep into her eyes and chewed on his lip while he thought about how much he should tell her. This was the woman he loved. He decided he had no choice but to tell her the truth; he thought if he ever lied to her about anything, he would lose this most wonderful of women. "Almost two years ago the Vee Cee came to Houng's home in Hou Ky. They, they. . ." He hesitated, uncertain how to tell her. "They did things to his family." That felt like a satisfactory way to say it. "They left his wife and daughter to die, and they took his son to work as slave labor in their camp. The other day Houng found out where the Vee Cee are holding his son."

"In the A Shau."

He nodded. "We need all the information we can get so someone can go in there and get Houng's son out."

Her eyes widened again. Randall saw fear in them, fear for him. "When you say someone, you don't mean someone else, you mean so you can go and get him."

He nodded numbly. "If we can't get anybody else to do it, yes, some men from Tango Niner will go. Bobbie—" He folded a hand over hers, and his voice became hushed and earnest. "—we need to know as much as we can so the men who go in there can come back out again alive."

She yanked her hand out from under his and shook her head violently. "No," she said, her voice sounding rusty like a too long unused gate hinge. "I'm not going to give you any information. If you don't know enough, you won't do it. I'm not going to tell you something that might help you kill yourself." Her eyes blazed with that last remark.

"If nobody else will do it, Tango Niner will," he repeated, leaning across the table and tapping the point of his forefinger on the table close to her to emphasize his sincerity. "I might be one of the men to go, and maybe I won't. I don't know yet. If we have to do it, we will use whatever information we have, even if it isn't enough to ensure success. It's something that has to be done. Period." His voice softened, and his eyes pleaded; he awkwardly reached his fingers to lightly touch her arm. "Will you help us, please?"

Tears brimmed her eyes, too many for her to blink away. Her throat thickened until it felt too painful to speak. She nodded, then jumped up and ran away, wiping away unwanted tears.

CHAPTER SEVEN

1800 Hours

They met as planned in front of III MAF headquarters and went to a geedunk, one that served officers as well as enlisted men. There was no other way they could sit down to eat together. In the field a general and a private could sit on the same log at the same time to share their C-rations. In garrison—and Da Nang was garrison—they weren't allowed to eat or drink in the same place. Unless it was a civilian-run concession.

Robertson's eyes bugged at the sight of the establishment. "Goddam, I'm in the wrong MOS." MOS stood for Military Occupational Specialty, what a Marine's job was. "I didn't know pogues got to eat like this. Shit, man, this is almost just like back on the block in The World." He looked around. "All we need is some girls in bobby socks."

"I don't think they wear bobby socks anymore, Big Red," Burrison said.

Robertson didn't care what they didn't wear anymore. He thought all the place needed to be just like back on the block was some girls.

They sidestepped through the cafeteria-type line, Robertson first, Randall, Slover, and Burrison bringing up the rear. Force of habit. Marines going through a chow line in the field did it in reverse order of rank—Slover was senior to Randall. Robertson ordered two deluxe cheeseburgers, a large french fries, a malt, and a large Coke.

"No Coke," said the man behind the counter. "We got Pepsi."

"A large Pepsi, then."

Randall ordered the same.

Slover's grin seemed too big for his face; he was already salivating over the meal. He ordered five deluxe cheeseburgers, two fries, a malt, and three large Pepsis. The counterman looked at him as if to say, "Sure, and who's going to help you eat all that?" But instead of saying anything he filled the order. He'd been working there long enough to know that when dumb grunts came in out of the field and got their first chance to eat in a geedunk, they usually ordered more than they could eat and tended to get angry if anybody tried to tell them their eyes were bigger than their stomachs. Slover, however, had eaten in one of those geedunks before and knew how much the trays could comfortably hold; he didn't want to overload the tray. He also knew he could come back for seconds when he finished his first trayful.

Burrison cocked an eye at the big man, but he suspected Slover could probably eat that much and more. He placed the same order that Robertson and Randall had.

They found a table that wasn't too close to anyone else. It wasn't because they wanted privacy, though they did want privacy for their conversation. They took the isolated table because they knew they looked like field grunts, and anybody they sat too near to would get up and leave. And anybody who wasn't too offended by field grunts would leave because one of them was an officer, and most pogues thought it was bad luck to be too close to officers when they were off duty.

Slover and Robertson talked about not finding Chief Slover. Randall said Bobbie was going to help. Then his throat lumped up and he decided against telling them about the emotional scene when he had tried to persuade her to help. Burrison filled them in on his short meeting with Ensign Lily.

Lily leaned back in his swivel chair and propped his feet on an open desk drawer. A mug of strong Navy coffee steamed between his hands. "You know, Burrie, you really should drink this java black; it'll put some hair on your chest." The kid-faced eager-beaver-looking jarhead sitting across from Lily looked like he didn't have any hair on his chest, or anywhere else on his body. But Lily knew Burrison's childlike appearance was deceiving; Burrison was the leader of one tough band of Marines, even though he looked more like somebody's kid brother.

Burrison set his mug down on the corner of the desk after sipping it to make sure he'd put enough milk and sugar into it to soften the blow to his digestive system. "No thanks. I've seen your coffee eat spoons. I have to cut it with something so it won't do the same to my insides."

Lily laughed.

"How's your friend Reeves doing?"

"Kind of grumpy. Whenever his helicopter breaks, nobody will lend him one." He laughed again. "Somehow, word seems to have gotten around about that Huey's need for substantial body work when he brought it back." Four months earlier Reeves had had to fly out to Camp Apache when his helicopter was down for repairs. The only one available was a Huey that belonged to an Army accounting team visiting Da Nang to inventory Marine equipment—they were looking for material stolen from the Army off the docks at Cam Ranh Bay. "Nothing official, of course, but he's been shot up so many times, he's having trouble getting copilots and crew chiefs willing to fly with him. Some of the other helicopter drivers in his squadron say he's working on becoming a Vee Cee ace." He laughed harder and splashed some coffee on himself. After swearing and brushing at the wet spot until it was cool, he turned serious. "You need somebody to drive you somewhere?"

Burrison grinned wryly. This was the hard part. If he got past it, he was home free. Maybe. "The A Shau Valley."

Lily whistled. "Ain't going to be easy, talking him into this one."

"What's been happening lately with the Lily and Reeves Vee Cee and NVA War Surplus Company?"

Lily smiled appreciably. "Damn little. Since you and your people got the Song Du Ong valley cleaned out, there hasn't been much coming our way. That's a good hook. Reeves wants souvenirs badly enough, that might convince him to do it."

"I need to talk to the man."

Lily rolled his eyes up in thought. "I think we can find him at the club tonight. Between the two of us I'm sure we can make a good enough appeal to his avaricious side to convince him." He smiled in anticipation of all the new trade items the Lily and Reeves VC and NVA War Surplus

Company could get from a mission into the Vietcong stronghold known as the A Shau. He could smile because he knew he wasn't the one who had to go in there.

So that was what they had to show for their first two hours in Da Nang. Slover couldn't do anything more until ten o'clock the next morning, so he went back for three more cheeseburgers, another fries, and two more Pepsis. Randall sulked; he didn't know whether to go to Bobbie's quarters and try to sweet-talk her into forgiving him or let her have the night to think about the matter. Burrison had some time to kill. Robertson was just along for the ride. They made small talk until Burrison made his farewells so he could meet Lily to track down Lieutenant (j.g.) Reeves.

Slover belched contentedly and rubbed his stomach. "I think we should find us a 45 club and pop a few brews, bros," he said. A "45 club" was one for corporals and sergeants, pay grades E-4 and E-5, hence a "45" club.

"What's the matter, Big Louie, don't you like me anymore?" Robertson asked. As a lance corporal he wasn't allowed in a 45 club.

Slover assumed a look of offended dignity. "What do you mean, 'anymore.' I never did like you, Big Red." He reached into his shirt pocket and pulled out an extra pair of metal corporal's chevrons. "Put these on; nobody will know."

"What if they check ID?" ID cards had the bearer's rank on them.

"You dumb shit," Randall said. "This is why you're never going to make corporal; you're too damn dumb. You're a field grunt; you got promoted in the field and haven't had a chance to get a new ID card yet." He pulled his own out of his shirt pocket and handed it over. In the space designated for rank it said "L/Cpl." "I got my second stripe almost a year ago," he continued. "So far I haven't had the chance to get a new ID card. If some pogue bouncer doesn't like it, tough shit. I'm a corporal, and I get to go into any 45 club I want to. You will be, too, as soon as you put on those chevrons."

Robertson looked around furtively and tried so hard to be inconspicuous about changing the rank insignia on his collars that nobody in the geedunk could help but see him do it.

They found that nobody bothered to check IDs at the 45 club. That didn't make any difference to Robertson, not at first. He felt uncomfortable in the 45 club. It was full of sergeants and corporals who he knew would want to kick him out if they knew a lowly lance corporal was desecrating their sanctum. And he didn't want to think of what they might want to do to him before they kicked him out. And afterward, busting him back down to private would probably just be the most minor thing they'd do.

"How the hell is anybody going to know, Big Red?" Randall demanded when Robertson voiced that fear.

Robertson shrugged tightly and shook his head. "I donno." He was certain NCOs had some kind of secret password they used among themselves to make sure no officers or junior enlisted men tried to sneak into their private groups, a password they'd just slip into a conversation. After a few beers, when nobody challenged him, he started to relax. A few beers after that he became cocky enough to get loud. A few more beers and Randall and Slover hustled him out before he started something.

Lieutenant (j.g.) Reeves took a sip of his drink and looked down into it. He screwed up his face and held the glass in front of his eyes to peer through it. "How the hell can anybody water down a Mai Tai?" he asked. "Basically all a Mai Tai is, is rum with a little bit of orange juice so you don't taste how hard it's hitting you." He lowered the glass to the table top. "Why would anybody water down a Mai Tai? Sort of defeats the purpose."

Burrison put his beer down and wiped foam from his upper lip. "They've seen drunken sailors in this club before and don't want to see them again," he said. "They only let you come in here because if they didn't you'd go into Da Nang city and get so blasted in a skivvy house they'd have to throw you in the brig for twenty years—if they could find enough of you to lock up after the Vee Cee got through with you."

Reeves snorted. "Bullshit."

"Truth."

"How's your bird doing?" Lily asked before the other two could take it any further. The three sat closely enough at the small wooden table so they could talk without shouting. The crisp voices of young Navy officers and a few Marines bounced off the walls, almost drowning out the slurred voices of others who had happy-houred away their dinner time. Laboring air conditioners filled any gaps in the background noise and filtered out the roars of jet aircraft on the nearby airstrip.

Reeves shrugged. "It's up. But I don't know for how long. The collective's acting funny, and I'm going to have to let my crew chief hand it over to the next-echelon repair people. Who knows how long they'll want to keep it."

Lily laughed. "They'll probably want to keep it forever as an illustration of how good some pilots are at making anything that's not supposed to go wrong with a helicopter go wrong with one."

Reeves glared at him.

"When's it going to the shop?" Burrison asked.

Reeves grimaced. "Probably sometime next week. That means I'll be grounded for the duration." He shook his head furiously. "They'll have me flying a damn desk, doing paperwork twenty hours a day until my bird is up again. They'll make me coffee-mess officer!" His voice rose sharply, and his eyes widened with indignation. "Do you know what a coffee-mess officer does, for Christ sake? He's responsible for keeping the coffeepot filled with fresh coffee and making sure everybody pays up! I'm a pilot, goddammit, not a steward. I'm supposed to be driving helicopters."

Lily patted the air and made shushing noises. "Calm down, good buddy," he said. "People are looking at you."

Reeves hunched over his drink; his eyes flicked from side to side, looking for anyone watching him. "Goddamn fucking coffee-mess officer," he snarled in a lower voice.

The three officers small-chattered for a few minutes more, and then Lily said, "Burrie's got a proposition for you."

Reeves looked at the Marine suspiciously. He'd made many trips out to Camp Apache, unauthorized trips. They were all profitable, of course, but he still hadn't lived down the time he had borrowed that Army Huey and brought it back with holes in it. "Tell me about that dam you were going to build," he said.

"Dam? What dam?" Burrison asked with all the innocence he could muster.

"The dam you said you were going to build when you had me ferry all those damn explosives out into the hills."

Burrison somehow dredged up more innocence. "When did you do that?" He turned to Lily. "Do you remember anything about taking explosives into the hills?"

Lily did his best to look innocent as well. He didn't know what had been done with those explosives, but he had never believed Tango Niner was going to build a dam on the Song Du Ong, not with everything being delivered to a hilltop that far from the river. "Explosives? What explosives?" He leaned close to Reeves. "Have you been holding out on me, good buddy? Do you have another source of supplies for the Lily and Reeves Vee Cee and NVA War Surplus Company, a source that I'm not getting anything from?"

"Reeves and Lily," Reeves said, and hunkered lower over his glass.

"Well, I never," Lily said, pulling back and assuming a posture that indicated offended trust. "Here I thought we were friends, I thought we were in this together. You've been holding out on me, haven't you? In your mind the Lily and Reeves Vee Cee and NVA War Surplus Company is strictly for your benefit."

Reeves flinched at the accusation. "Reeves and Lily. And I'm not holding out," he said. "You know what explosives I mean." His eyes darted from one to the other. "But if you say we didn't do that . . ."

"There were never any explosives. The Lily and Reeves Vee Cee and NVA War Surplus Company doesn't deal in contraband or black market."

"Reeves and Lily. And it wasn't contraband or black market, it was a great humanitarian gesture."

"What was—don't answer that." Lily shifted close to Reeves again, friendly once more. "Now, good buddy, it might have escaped your attention that of late the Lily and Reeves Vee Cee and NVA War Surplus Company . . ."

"Reeves and Lily."

". . . has been running short on stock."

"Damn Skippy. We ain't got nothing for the past month, and the month before that was nothing but a bunch of Vee Cee flags and those fake Vee Cee commando daggers." His eyes narrowed suspiciously. "I've got this uncomfortable feeling those Vee Cee flags were made by people working for you, and I know the so-called commando knives are rice knives." The comments about the souvenirs were directed at Burrison, who once more looked his most innocent.

"The pipeline has dried up. Burrie and his boys have done such a good job of convincing the bad guys that the Song Du Ong floodplain isn't a healthy place for them, they've taken their goodies cart and gone someplace else."

"Yah?" Reeves looked at Lily from under lowered lids. He didn't like the way this was beginning to sound.

"What that means is if the Lily and Reeves Vee Cee and NVA War Surplus Company is going to stay in business, Burrie and his boys have to go where the goodies are."

"Reeves and Lily. Now wait just a goddamn minute," Reeves swore. "What do you have in mind here? You want me to fly them to goddamn Hanoi or someplace?"

"No, no, no. Nothing like that."

"The Ho Chi fucking Minh Trail, then." Reeves's voice rose with each word. Burrison flinched because the Ho Chi Minh Trail was awfully close to the truth.

"Nothing so dangerous, good buddy," Lily said placatingly, patting the air again to quiet the pilot.

"All right, then, what?" Reeves lowered his voice.

"They need a favor, something that can only be done by one of the very best and bravest helicopter drivers in all the naval services."

"I don't think I want to hear this."

"Burrie and his boys have to pay a visit to the A Shau Valley."

"Oh, no, you don't. I'm not going to have anything to do with this. This is insane. You're out of your fucking mind if you think I'm going to the A Shau."

"It's essential to the future of the Lily and Reeves Vee Cee and NVA War Surplus Company."

"Reeves and Lily."

"They need one quick hop into someplace near the valley, someplace where there aren't any bad guys. Then, when they're through with what they have to do, you pick them up again someplace else where there aren't any bad guys."

"No way, José."

"If we don't do this thing," Lily said half-plaintively, "then we'll have to kiss the Lily and Reeves Vee Cee and NVA War Surplus Company good-bye."

"Reeves and Lily. Go in where there aren't any bad guys and come out where there aren't any either?"

"That's right."

Reeves looked at the two, mulling it over.

"I think the Lily and Reeves Vee Cee and NVA War Surplus Company can get some really choice goodies out of this one," Lily said.

"Reeves and Lily. You're sure?"

Burrison nodded.

Reeves stretched his hand across the table to shake. "On your word as an officer and a gentleman?"

Burrison took the offered hand. "On my word."

"Reeves and Lily," Reeves said for the umpteenth time.

"Reeves and Lily," Lily agreed.

CHAPTER EIGHT

March 9, 1967

Chief Petty Officer Ossie Slover sat leaning back in his swivel chair. His feet were planted firmly on the concrete floor, and his knees were spread in the manner of men whose legs were far too thick to comfortably cross. He folded his hamlike arms across his pork-barrel chest. The coal of the cigar stub he held clamped between the middle of his lips glowed like some fearsome misplaced third eye. His forehead was deeply canyoned in a glower. Everything about him radiated the fact that he was not happy to see his father's sister's son.

"I want you to tell me the truth this time, Little Louie." His voice rumbled out from somewhere deep; it sounded like the hideous, godlike voice that came from the bronze idol Baal must have sounded—and it brooked no competition from the air conditioner that chugged and clanked in the background. "No bullshit, Little Louie, not again. I want it straight from jump street." Several months earlier

Slover had gone to his cousin Os to trade for explosives for Tango Niner to use to destroy a Vietcong communications center—the same explosives Burrison and Lily had told Reeves hadn't existed. Cousin Os didn't believe him, so Slover came back with a story about how the explosives were actually going to be used to make a dam. Ossie Slover liked that story and dreamed grandiose dreams of winning a Navy Commendation Medal or some such for his assistance. His dashed dream had left a very sour taste.

Robertson swallowed. He had never before heard anybody call Big Louie Slover "Little Louie." For that matter he'd never met a man big enough to get away with it. He'd seen Louie Slover in combat many times and knew him to be fearless. That physical fearlessness evaporated in the face of Ossie Slover, and the big man, dwarfed by his huger cousin, squirmed on his chair. Robertson swallowed again and hoped the sweat he felt beading on his forehead wouldn't get any worse.

"Cousin Os," Slover said, sounding like his throat was parched, "I told you the truth from jump street last time, you didn't believe me. That's why I had to lie to you."

Chief Slover grunted. It sounded like approaching thunder. His cigar glowed brighter; the clouds of smoke that bellowed around his head looked like the clouds that surround an erupting volcano.

Robertson swallowed again and squeegeed the edge of his hand across his forehead.

Slover squirmed more but spoke in a stronger voice. He wasn't going to let himself be intimidated by his cousin this time, nossir. "This is straight scoop, Cousin Os, we're going to send a patrol into the A Shau Valley. I shit you not."

The glowering canyons on Chief Slover's brows gradually changed to interested valleys, and he listened intently

to his cousin's story about why Tango Niner was going to
make its foray into the heart of a Vietcong stronghold.
While the narrative unfolded, so did he. He slowly planted
one elbow on his desk and leaned his Saint Bernard head
on its fist. He balled up his other hand on his hip—a hand
that looked big enough to pick up a basketball from the top
and have enough left over to get a start on a second one.
He didn't interrupt and only broke his reverie once to light
a fresh cigar from the butt of the old one. Then he rolled
his new cigar to the corner of his mouth, where it looked
less threatening.

"Straight scoop?" Chief Slover asked when it was over.

"Straight scoop, Cousin Os," Slover stated.

"I need to think on this. Come back at sixteen hundred
hours." He levered his monstrous bulk out of his chair—
the chair creaked its relief but stopped shy of promising to
hold up against the next assault on its integrity—and
walked out of his office to look like he was doing some of
the work he was supposed to do. ["Walk,"—it was not a
very adequate word to use to describe his method of loco-
motion, but it would have to do.] His torso shifted mightily
from side to side as though he was clumping, sending huge
trees crashing to the ground with each shoulder thrust, yet
his feet glided so silently, they seemed nimble.

Slover and Robertson looked at each other and wiped
the sweat from their faces. Despite the air conditioner, their
shirts were soaked through.

"Goddamn, I'm glad that man's on our side," Robertson
whispered.

"Are you sure he is?" Slover asked.

Tex Randall had a less frightening but equally upsetting
time with Bobbie Harder. She'd cried the night away, she
told him when he came to her office, and the red in her

eyes showed the truth of what she said. The gunny point-
edly ignored them, but Randall knew if he stayed too long,
the gunny'd get upset. Bobbie agreed to meet him for
lunch; he blinked when she called it "noon chow." He was
waiting outside when she came out at noon. He had picked
up bread and cold cuts so they could find a secluded spot
and have some privacy to talk while they ate. She led him
to an open-air pavilion, where they had a good chance of
being undisturbed and not overheard.

"Tex." She had thought it through and decided not to
beat around the bush, let him have it full. "If you go on
this mission and get yourself killed I'll never forgive you."
Her voice showed the strain of what she had to say. "I'll
never forgive you for doing something so dangerous and
irresponsible, and I'll never forgive you for refusing to
give me a chance to even *try* to talk you out of it."

"Bobbie, stop that," he said softly, pain in his eyes. "We
don't know that I'm going." He started to say again that
they were trying to get enough information to persuade
someone else to do it, then decided to drop that pretense.
She hadn't believed him when he had said that yesterday,
and he knew she wouldn't believe him today. And he knew
they weren't trying to persuade someone else; no one else
was going to do it. "We haven't decided who's going yet. I
might not be one of the men picked."

"Maybe nobody has been picked yet, but you're going,
Tex. I know that as well as you do." Her red-rimmed eyes
blazed at him. "I know who's who in that unit of yours so
well I could probably tell you right now who will go.
You're going on it, and I wish you'd stop lying to me about
it."

He didn't say anything. She was probably right.

"Why can't you be honest and just get somebody else to
do it?" She held up a hand. "Don't tell me, I know, nobody

else thinks it's important enough to run an operation just to rescue some farmer's kid—I don't care who Houng is to you." She held up her hand again to stop the objection he was about to make. "To nearly everybody official he's still just some farmer. If nobody else thinks it's important enough, why don't you just let it lie? Why do you have to risk your lives for something you might not be able to do?"

"Bobbie." He tried to keep his voice from cracking and wasn't completely successful. "There are some things a man just has to do. If he's going to be able to look at himself in the mirror every morning, there are things he has to do for friends. If he doesn't, he's not worth much as a man."

She listened, appalled at the risk he was willing to run, the danger he was willing to put himself in. A faint trace of wailing underscored her voice when she finally spoke again. "I'm going to help you. And the only reason is you're right: Every bit of information you have before you go in increases your chances of coming back out all right. What do you need to know?"

He told her.

She hiccuped, from trying so hard not to cry again. "How can I get you intelligence on enemy deployments in the A Shau?" she demanded. "I'm not in intelligence. And what do I know about what kind of operations the Marines have planned?"

"You have friends in G-2 and G-3. You could find out from them." G-2 was division-level or higher intelligence; G-3 was operations.

"How am I supposed to do that? Do you know what kind of security clearances you need to work in those places? Yes, I have friends in G-2 and G-3, and they're very security-conscious. Some days they won't even tell you their names because they aren't sure what they know that is classified and what isn't."

"I don't know how you can get them to tell you, but you're resourceful and intelligent. You can find a way if you want to."

She stared at him hard, her jaw clamped tight, for a long moment before she said, "Tex Randall, I'm beginning to hate you."

Less frightening, but just as distressful.

At 1600 hours Chief Petty Officer Ossie Slover handed over to Corporal Louis Slover and Lance Corporal John Robertson military topographical maps of the A Shau Valley. The maps already had marked on them known or suspected VC and NVA locations in the valley. He also gave them two hundred yards of detonation cord, a hundred pounds of C-4 plastic explosives, an over-the-horizon radio, a dozen tear gas grenades, and a half dozen U.S. Army fatigue baseball caps. In exchange Louie Slover gave his Cousin Os four AK-47 assault rifles and two SKS carbines—one with sniper sights.

"We tested them all, Cousin Os," Slover said. "They all work fine, not one misfire in a hundred rounds out of each of them."

Chief Slover looked at the offerings and grunted. "That's good for a down payment, Little Louie," he said. "I'll expect the second installment inside two weeks."

Robertson emptied his pockets of VC hat and collar insignia and added a small bag of loaded AK-47 banana magazines.

Chief Slover grunted again. "That cuts your payment schedule by one. Det-cord don't grow on palm trees, you know." He looked at them levelly. "And you ain't got no idea what I had to give up to get them CS grenades." All it

had cost him was one fifth of Seagram Seven—the baseball caps had cost another fifth of Lord Calvert—but he
didn't think they needed to know any of that.

Louie Slover nodded dumbly and loaded the equipment
into two seabags. He promised to come back with more as
soon as he could make another trip. Then he and Robertson
hefted the two weighty seabags onto their shoulders and
headed back to their transient barracks.

Chief Slover watched them walk away. He didn't really
like taking such unfair advantage of his cousin, but blood
was blood and business was business, and it was bad business to mix the two; it made for bad blood. Besides, he
really wanted to be able to buy that cottage when he re-
tired, the one with a fireplace, so he'd have a mantelpiece
he could use to display that bush hat he'd gotten from Little Louie's Sergeant Bell. After he had that bush hat
bronzed. Besides, what Little Louie told him they were
going to do was so far out of line, if they got caught and
the explosives and other equipment he gave them ever got
traced back to him, well, he was damn well going to get
enough out of the deal to make up for what he'd lose when
he got busted for his involvement. He looked at the rifles
again, picked one up, and clumsily held it to his shoulder.
Fucking little gooks, he thought, can't even use a weapon
big enough for a normal-size man to handle properly. He
held the rifle out and peered at it. It should be worth, he
calculated, a couple of hundred dollars or more to some
blue-water sailor who'd been to sea six months and had all
that good pay burning a hole in his pocket. And if it didn't
fire as well as Little Louie'd said, that was okay, too. By
the time that blue-water sailor found out, he'd be so far
away he'd never find Chief Slover ever again. Anyway,
they were going to have a crackdown on war souvenirs
some day and when they did wasn't nobody gonna get no

AK-47 back into the US of A nohow. Chief Slover was satisfied.

When they were out of sight, Robertson said, "Maybe you're right; maybe he's not on our side."

"We probably could have got twice as much for one AK from the Army Corps of Engineers," Slover agreed.

"Except there ain't no Army Corps of Engineers around here."

Slover and Robertson, still carrying their seabags—no way they were going to let them out of their sight—met Lieutenant Burrison at the same geedunk they had met at the day before. Randall didn't join them. He wanted to be where Bobbie Harder could find him, so he waited in the transient barracks until it was almost closing time at the mess hall near it. He waited that long in case Bobbie called him or came to see him. He thought they might eat together someplace private on the beach as they had the last couple of times he had been in Da Nang. When he finally went to the mess hall, he sat near a door where he had a view of the front of the barracks—just in case she showed up. When he was through eating, he went back and lay down on the bunk assigned to him. He was too distracted to read anything, and after he only grunted at the few men who tried to engage him in conversation, the other Marines in the barracks left him alone.

A couple of hours later Slover stopped Robertson when the two of them were on their way back to the barracks. They were actually on their way to a flick but were making the side trip to see if Randall wanted to go with them. The reason Slover stopped Robertson was that he saw Randall standing by the driver's side of a jeep. He recognized the driver: Bobbie Harder. They stood, trying to look inconspicuous, next to a Quonset hut and watched. They watched her hand him a small packet, and they watched while the two talked a little longer. They watched Randall scramble around to the other side of the jeep and climb in when she gave a flick of her head, and they watched the two drive away. Slover and Robertson nodded at each other; they were certain she had given Randall the information they needed. They were right.

CHAPTER NINE

On the Beach

Randall sat upright and quiet while Bobbie drove the jeep along the beach. She drove below the surf line so the water lapping on the beach would wipe out the tire tracks. He kept his head straight ahead, though his eyes were constantly moving from side to side, watching for signs of danger ahead and to the land side. He looked everywhere but at her. Put a rifle in a man's hands, stick him in the boonies, and leave him there to hunt down and kill other armed men who are hunting to kill him, and he learns pretty quickly to swivel-neck constantly and to eyeball everything. It's a survival mechanism that takes years to get over. Tex Randall was such a man. It was a strain for him to keep his head to the front, but he concentrated and managed it. But no way was he going to stop eyeballing everything.

Bobbie Harder didn't talk during the drive, either. Nor did she swivel-neck or eyeball; she had never had the need to learn to do so. With Marble Mountain clearly in sight, she turned away from the waterline and parked the jeep in a small alcove in the dunes that bordered the beach. Randall recognized the alcove; they had been there before. Wordlessly, Bobbie got out and climbed to the top of the low dune. She sat cross-legged and spread the wide skirt of her light dress over her lap to drape gracefully on the sand at her sides. She tucked the dress down between her legs and left her hands folded there. She stared at the darkening sky out over the South China Sea. Randall climbed the dune and sat next to her. He stopped straining and started swivel-necking. He even looked at Bobbie.

They sat for a long time without talking and without touching. Suddenly she twisted around and threw herself on him, almost knocking him over. He wrapped his arms around her and gently kissed her cheek; he tasted salt from tears he hadn't seen.

"I don't hate you, Tex," she said. "I love you too much to ever hate you."

"I love you, too," he said, his voice breaking on the words.

"If you get killed on this mission, I'll never forgive myself for not finding some way to stop you from going." Tears rolled down her face.

He lifted her face and kissed the tears away. "I won't get killed," he said. "The information you gave me is going to keep me alive. I promise."

"How good is your word?" she asked harshly. Then her mouth found his and no more words were possible.

They fumbled and poked and prodded and pulled and managed not to tear anything getting each other's clothes off. They intertwined and rolled down the dune, unmindful of the sand that stuck to their sweat-glistened skin. For endless minutes their bodies meshed and became one writhing, gasping beast. They both gave all the pleasure they were capable of giving, and each took every bit of pleasure the other offered. Their sweat mingled, their tongues played until there was no separating their saliva, he thrust deeply into her, and their loin juices flowed and merged. She convulsed in a mighty orgasm; he spasmed a brief moment later. She bucked again in secondary peaks that slowly ebbed until she was as sated from their efforts as he was. They lay still for a long time, their fulfilling passion and fury replaced with tenderness.

After that endless time known only to lovers who truly care, she pushed softly at his shoulder and he rolled off her. She breathed deeply, filling her lungs for the first time since she had first flung herself on him. Her fingers brushed over her belly and his, and they felt the sand stuck to both their flanks.

"Wait here," she gasped, and was on her feet, running naked back up the dune and over it. He thought her silhouette with the starlight glinting off the sweat that coated her was the most beautiful thing he had ever seen. She was back in seconds, appearing like Venus rising on her half shell above the dune. Towels flapped in her hand. When she reached him, she dropped the towels and grabbed his hand. "Come on," she said, husky-voiced, and pulled him to his feet. They ran to the water splashing gently on the beach and dove into its cleansing waves. They played like children or otters in chest-deep water. But they didn't yell or scream in glee; they didn't want to attract any attention.

After they played for a while and washed the sand from every inch and crevice of each other's body he grabbed her and pulled her tightly to him. He put his hands on her buttocks and pulled. She lifted with him and wrapped her legs around him; he was already erect and slid easily in. He walked them to where the lapping water merely dampened the sand and easily lay them down. Their lovemaking this time was less furious than before but no less passionate. They lingered over it, and it took more endless minutes than it had the first time. At last they collapsed together.

Once more they entered the water. This time they didn't play, they merely washed each other. Then they walked back to the place of their passionate fury and used the towels to pat and caress each other dry. They climbed back to the top of the dune where they had left their clothes and slowly dressed. Hand in hand they returned to the jeep and headed back.

She stopped in front of the barracks and looked at him dry-eyed for a long moment. "Come back to me, Tex. Come back safe and whole."

"I will, Bobbie. I promise."

She kissed him softly and said, "Go."

He got out of the jeep and went into the barracks. Bobbie watched until he was inside, then shifted into first and slowly drove away. She could hardly see through the mist that filled her eyes.

Slover and Robertson were in their racks snoring away the many beers they had drunk at the 45 club. Randall lay down on his own, but it was a long time before he was asleep.

In the morning the four Marines got into their jeep. Slover drove this time; Randall was far too distracted. Slover looked at the two seabags in the back of the jeep and said, "You people better be glad I'm as good a night fighter as I am. I scoped the situation out and found a place we can drive out of here without any nosy MP wanting to look in those seabags and finding contraband."

Burrison looked at him.

"Who you trying to bullshit, night fighter?" Robertson

said. "You don't hardly ever go outside after dark, Big Louie."

"Watch my smoke," Slover said. "I'm gonna show you how I drove back in Paramus. You better believe neither the cops or nobody else never caught Big Louie Slover when I was behind a wheel."

They tacked themselves onto the end of a truck convoy heading south, empty now, probably on its way to pick up a company or battalion at the end of an operation. They reached their cutoff and turned onto the road that led eventually to Camp Apache. The "Indian Country" sign marking the small road had a couple more bullet holes in it. A wag someone had turned loose with a red marking pen had drawn a flaming arrow through the words.

They made it back to the Marine compound in Bun Hou without incident.

CHAPTER TEN

March 10, 1967

Things seemed quiet at Camp Apache. Anyone visiting who had never been there before—or at least hadn't visited in the past couple of months—would have thought everything was quiet and easy. The Marines and PFs were apparently calm and relaxed; they joked a lot and played goof-off games. However, a very perceptive visitor might have wondered why the Marines didn't seem bored being so far from home with not much to do; he wouldn't have wondered about the PFs, since they were already home doing what they normally did. Such a perceptive visitor might have wondered about the undercurrent of excitement, the feel of electricity in the air. Of course, had that visitor gone into the command hootch and seen the calm anticipation of the men reading over the materials brought back from Da Nang and noted what those materials were, he would have known immediately there was more going on than met the eye.

The air of calm anticipation lasted only until Lieutenant Burrison, Sergeant Bell, and the corporals finished going over the maps Chief Slover had given them and the papers Bobbie Harder had provided.

"This looks like Reeves was right," Burrison said softly, awed at what the documents told him. "We want him to fly us into Hanoi." His gaze slowly swept through the commander's quarters, briefly stopping at each of the men in it.

Bell whistled through his teeth, and the others were silent for a long moment.

After a while Zeitvogel shrugged. "Piece a cake," he said.

Hempen nodded sagely. "Just goes to prove what I say," he said. "Man gets to be too tall, he hits his head on things, high trees, mountaintops, low-flying aircraft. Knocks dumb into him." He nodded again. "Ain't nothing dumber than a roundball player." He ducked out of the way of the slow roundhouse the tall man threw at him.

They had known that the A Shau Valley was in enemy hands. It was only a couple of miles east of Laos and the Ho Chi Minh Trail. They knew already that a year earlier the Army had had a Special Forces team with a company of Vietnamese irregulars encamped in the valley. The North Vietnamese had sent a regiment to take out the camp. There were more than four hundred defenders when they were attacked. It took two days of fierce fighting, but the NVA finally overran the camp, inflicting heavy casualties on the defenders. A Marine helicopter squadron was sent in to pull out the survivors. The fighting around the extraction was so heavy and required so much bravery that the commander of the extraction squadron, who was shot down and had to fight on the ground overnight, was awarded a Navy Cross, the country's second highest decoration. Allied forces had not since tried to reoccupy the valley. That much the Marines of Tango Niner already knew.

Here's what they now knew about the A Shau that they hadn't known a day earlier: The A Shau was a major infiltration route, maybe the most important one in all of I Corps. The VC regimental headquarters was only a small part of the enemy installations in the valley. It was suspected but not yet verified that the enemy had built truck roads in the valley, that it was a major supply depot, that it was a major communications center, and that there was a division or more of NVA in it. The NVA had a perimeter security system on the lookout for aircraft; the sentries fired their rifles when they saw something approaching in the sky.

"A piece of cake you say, Stilts?" Bell asked.

"Sure. Them gooks got that place tied up so tight, no way they'll think anybody's dumb enough to sneak in there to rescue some kid. They won't be looking for us. Hell, their security is probably so loose, we can walk in and walk out and not even snoop and poop and nobody'll have any idea we're there."

Burrison shook his head. "By the time we get close enough for Reeves to drop us, every little bad guy in that valley will know someone's on his way."

"Be easier to get into the Ho Chi fucking Minh Trail," Slover said somberly. "Not as many bad guys per square yard there."

"Can't go to the Ho Chi Minh Trail," McEntire said. "It's in Laos; Laos is a neutral country."

Zeitvogel jumped on that. "What's a neutral country?"

"Huh?"

"Come on, Wall," Zeitvogel said, "define neutral country."

"It's one that isn't involved in a war," McEntire said.

He looked around at the others to see if any of them could give him a clue to what Zeitvogel was driving at; the question had confused him.

"The Laotians let the Vee Cee Hanoi run all their men and supplies through their country," Zeitvogel said. "You gonna sit there with your teeth in your mouth and your bare face hanging out and tell me Laos is neutral?"

"Stilts is right, Wall," Hempen said, jumping in before McEntire could frame an answer. "You ever listen to Radio Free Cambodia? You must, you're in the compound every night and don't have to use your ears to listen for Charlie sneaking up on your young ass like we do out there." He waved his arm to indicate the floodplain beyond the hill. "You hear what they say on Radio Free Cambodia? They call us the bad guys and tell us not to fight, to let the damn commies take over this country."

"But what's Radio Free Cambodia got to do with Laos?" McEntire asked, more confused.

"Short Round's right, Wall," Zeitvogel said, glad for the reinforcement he had been given. "Remember one thing, my man, ain't nobody in the whole fucking world neutral on this war. Except the farmers and fishermen out here in the countryside. All they want is for everybody to go away and stop fucking with them."

"As you were, people," Bell interrupted. "This little sidebar has gone on long enough. We've got an operation to plan, remember?"

They returned to the problem of how could anybody get into the A Shau, rescue Houng's son, and get back out again without getting killed. They compared Houng's hand-drawn map with the topographical maps Slover's Cousin Os had given them, matched the features on the one against the features on the other, and decided the place they were going was just a few hundred meters north of the southernmost end of the valley on its west side. Chief Slover's maps showed an NVA battalion headquartered at that location. The VC regiment Houng's information said was there wasn't shown as being in the valley, not on the maps and not in the packet of information Bobbie Harder had given Randall.

"Houng's information is probably more accurate," Slover said. "We got ours from my Cousin Os. What the fuck does a squid know about enemy deployment unless it's aboard ship?"

"I bet Force Recon hasn't been there in quite a while," Bell muttered.

They pored over the maps and rifled through the packet of papers, abstracts of intelligence reports, and notes on operational plans. There was precious little of current use, not without someone sending in a reconnaissance in depth, and there was no indication anywhere that anybody planned to do that in the next few days. And a few days was all they had; they had to plan and execute the operation before Lieutenant (j.g.) Reeves's helicopter went down for overhaul. They poked at the maps and traced lines on them with their fingers and talked and agreed and contradicted each other. They read and reread the notes and copies of confidential reports and took notes. And they talked. After several hours they were certain it could be pulled off by a very few men who were extremely good at what they did—if they got a few breaks along the way. The big problem was, they didn't know how.

Then the daily hot meal bird came in with their evening chow and some mail. Nothing special arrived in the mail except McEntire's *Playboy* magazine. Everybody got in on the discussions, even the PFs who visited the compound to share their meals with their Marine friends so they could eat some of that exotic American food. So what if the

American food was too bland to eat as a regular diet. It was varied and—according to the Marines, though this didn't seem quite possible for food so tasteless—nourishing. The Marines, for their part, weren't as eager to share the food of their Vietnamese friends. The variety was small and quickly boring, but it tasted good enough—except the PFs insisted on smothering everything with that gawdawful homemade *nuoc mam* sauce hardly any of the Americans could stomach. The sauce was milk-gray and stank like the rancid fish oil it was fermented from. And its taste, well, they say variety is the spice of life. Some of the Marines thought if you needed a concoction like that to spice up your food, your taste buds were probably burnt out and it had to be overpowering so you could taste it at all.

Around sunset the first of the night's three regularly scheduled patrols went out for the beginning of the sixty-sixth consecutive boring night on the Song Du Ong flood-plain.

Bell and Burrison waited until it was one of their turns on radio watch before they discussed one of the most important aspects of the operation—who was going on it. They waited until they were certain Swearin' Swarnes was sound asleep.

"You do understand who goes will have a major impact on exactly how this operation is run, don't you?" Burrison asked softly. Swarnes was breathing quiet and evenly in the background.

It was about midnight. They knew without discussion that there was no need for either of them to physically check the lines; a phone check at midnight would be enough. They made the check and then continued their discussion.

"What I was thinking exactly," Bell agreed, picking up

where they'd left off. "Billy Boy's obvious. He's our best man at snooping and pooping and night movement. Most of the time when he talks Vietnamese, his accent is so bad he doesn't sound like it, but he's got maybe the best understanding of the language of our Marines. Being able to understand what the enemy's saying if we get close enough to hear them might be damn important."

"And he's one silent killer," Burrison added.

"You got that right."

They sat facing each other just outside the entrance of the night bunker. Bell had lugged one of the radios to the entrance and strung its handset out to where he could easily hear anything that came over it. Burrison had brought along the field phone that was connected by wire to each of the defensive positions around the perimeter.

"All-Marine or mixed?" Bell asked.

Burrison breathed deeply. This was something he'd thought about but hadn't decided on. "Both ways have their advantages."

"Yeah. I think we need at least one of the fay epps on it, though. If we get into a situation where somebody has to confront the bad guys face to face, no way they'll buy one of us as a Vee Cee. Got to have at least one fay epp."

"Not Houng."

"Not Houng," Bell agreed. "He's too involved."

Stars glittered from horizon to horizon, turning the night sky into a blaze of brilliance, a sight that dazzled men new to the tropics. But Bell had been there for a year, and Burrison was no newby. They ignored the glory of the heavens.

"Stilts is one mean mother in a fight," Burrison said. "And he's mature enough to know when not to pick one."

"Good choice."

"Short Round's a sneaky little bastard who can take care of himself anywhere."

"And avoid a fight when it's better to. That's three."

"How many do you think should go?"

"Got to be small, otherwise there's too great a risk of discovery. We've got three and still need to designate a leader. Four's the minimum for safety. We don't want to send many more than that. And we still have to pick a fay epp."

Swarnes let out a muffled snore as he rolled over on his cot.

"Tex."

"Scrappy, I could almost think you were reading my mind when I was picking them out."

The young lieutenant's smile was clearly visible in the starlight. "We still need a leader and a fay epp," he said.

Bell nodded. "Once we pick all the Americans, we can let them choose the fay epp."

"Sounds fair. Now the leader. This is the tough one, because I think we're going to disagree on it."

"Shit, Scrappy, you've been so good at picking the rest of them, I'm surprised you haven't realized I'm the best man to lead it."

"See what I mean?"

Swarnes's sleepy voice drifted out to them. "We'll settle this the American way tomorrow." They heard coins jingle in the bunker. "Coin toss. Now, keep it down and let a sleeping man stay that way."

"Bullshit, Swearin' Swarnes," Bell snapped.

"No way, Swarnes," Burrison said. "You go back to sleep and stop listening to what's none of your business."

Swarnes made sleeping noises.

CHAPTER ELEVEN

March 11, 1967

"Ladles and gennlemans," Swearin' Swarnes announced in his best sports broadcaster voice to the Marines and PFs gathered around him in the middle of the compound, "Moreens and Pop'lar Forces. You NCOs and ossifers are included, too. What I got here is a genu-wine US of A quarter dollar, a two-bit piece of American coinage." He held his quarter up between thumb and forefinger for inspection and twirled it to show both faces. "This side, with the visage of the great first American president on it, is called heads." He stopped twirling the quarter to display Washington's profile, then flipped it around and continued. "This here other side with a brazen American eagle spreadlegged, and not at all modest about it, mind you, on it is called tails.

"What I'm going to do here is I'm going to throw this genu-wine US of A quarter dollar into the air. Whilst it is in the air one of these two gennlemans, either Lieutenant

Burrison or Sergeant Bell, will call out heads or he will call out tails, whichever he chooses. If the coin lands with that side what he called facing up, he wins the toss and he gets to make the decision. Edgies are a misdeal and we have to toss it again." He added in a lower voice, "Wins or loses, depends on how he decides and how you look at it."

Bell and Burrison stood facing each other in front of Swarnes.

"You realize, don't you," Burrison said, "this isn't a very military way of doing this." His eyes sparkled with excitement.

"That's only because you don't want to do it the right way," Bell replied. His eyes were just as bright.

Burrison shook his head. "It's not that I don't want to do it the right way, it's that you don't want to obey orders." A smile cracked his face.

Bell snorted. "You haven't given any orders." The corners of his lips twitched.

"Hell, Jay Cee, I don't want to give any orders and have you disobey them; it'd be terrible to have to bust your ass." He was smiling openly.

"Right," Bell said in a tone that said "bullshit." He smiled widely, too.

"Are you two about through there?" Swarnes said in mock disgust.

"Whose turn is it to call it?" Burrison asked. His body twitched with the tension.

"I think it's mine," Bell said. All of him trembled in anticipation.

"I'm the official coin tosser here," Swarnes said. "My recollection, if you're taking turns, is it's Jay Cee's turn to call it. Are you ready?"

They both nodded.

Swarnes took a referee's one foot forward, one foot

back stance and said, "Here goes. Jay Cee, call it in the air." He flipped the quarter high into the air. The silver disk tumbled, and the brilliant sun sent sharp shards of light glancing off it.

Bell squinted at the coin, watched it arc upward, and waited for it to reach its tumbling apex before calling out in a loud, clear voice, "Tails."

Everyone waited bate-breathed while the coin completed its sharp parabolic arc. It hit the ground, bounced onto the edge, wobbled, and fell flat.

"Stand back!" Swarnes barked, and held a hand in front of each of them. "No fair peeking until *I* seen it." He dropped down onto all fours, elbows splayed wide, and lowered his face to within inches of the quarter, peering at it with one eye and then the other.

"Well, what is it?" Bell and Burrison both demanded. They dropped down and put their heads close to his, trying to see the quarter themselves when he didn't immediately answer.

Burrison slowly rolled back until he was sitting on his heels. Bell saw him and did the same. The sergeant looked smug, the lieutenant stern.

"These coin tosses are rigged, you know that, Jay Cee?" Burrison said.

The sergeant sucked on his lower lip and slowly shook his head.

"I didn't hear that scurrilous defamation on my character, Lieutenant," Swarnes grumbled. "I run a clean coin toss."

"Then how come Jay Cee always wins?"

"Just the way the ball bounces." Swarnes often got his metaphors mixed when talking about chance.

They stood up as Swarnes announced in his loudest voice, "And the winnah is . . ."

"Shut up, Swearin' Swarnes," Zeitvogel said; the tall man suddenly appeared, towering over the radioman.

"Come on, Jay Cee, let's get this show on the road," Randall said from Zeitvogel's side.

"Dammit, Jay Cee, I'm a growing boy," Hempen said. "Why for you want me to go and do some kind of happy horseshit like this? I should be eating regular meals and getting plenty of sleep so I can grow up big and tall like my Uncle Stilts here." He reached his hand above his shoulder to slap Zeitvogel's biceps.

Lewis stood with them, looking as fierce as he could. The left end of his mustache swooped out in a rakish swashbuckler, and the right end drooped Pancho Villa style. "Shitcan the grab-assing, Jay Cee," he said. "We got to pick us a fay epp."

Bell and Burrison looked at each other, then turned and stared at Swarnes. How could he have told anybody who was going? They'd kept close watch on him all morning and knew he hadn't had a chance to talk to anyone.

Swarnes shrugged and didn't even try to look innocent.

"We're carrying AKs," Bell told the Marines who were going with him. "No American weapons. If we do get into a firefight, I don't want every bad guy in the valley to know where we are by the sound of our weapons." The M-14, which most U.S. Marines still carried at that time, made a distinctive *boom* when it fired; the AK-47 carried by the North Vietnamese and many Vietcong had a higher-pitched *crack*. Anyone listening to a firefight could tell which side was which by the sound of their fire.

"What about this?" Zeitvogel asked, and patted the .357 magnum holstered on his hip. Bell had an identical hand-gun—that was why Zeitvogel had picked the one he carried.

The sergeant considered the question for a few seconds, then said, "Weapon of last resort."

Zeitvogel grunted, satisfied. He'd never used his magnum in combat, but before he got it there had been a couple of times he would have if he'd had one.

Bell himself wasn't going to carry one of the Chinese-manufactured assault rifles Tango Niner had so many of. He picked for himself an SKS carbine. He had qualified as high expert, the highest qualification, on the rifle range and strongly believed in the principle of aimed fire—he thought it was much better to shoot one round and put it exactly where he wanted it than to spray an area with an automatic rifle. The SKS somewhat resembled a small M-1; it was four or five inches shorter than the M-14 and weighed about two and a half pounds less. A bayonet was permanently attached to the SKS and could be swiveled back when not needed. It was accurate at longer range than the AK-47, but not as far as the M-14. Bell didn't think the difference in range would be that important; he expected to have very short sight lines where they were going—the A Shau was more heavily forested than the Song Du Ong floodplain.

"Let's test them and pick the best ones we've got," he said.

They still had more than two dozen captured AK-47s that hadn't been turned over to Marine authorities or used for trading purposes. Every Marine in Tango Niner grabbed one of the Kalashnikovs, and they trooped down the hill to the open land south of it. By the time they reached the improvised firing line southeast of the hill most of the PFs were straggling in from the west. They had earlier been sent to scour that area, to clear it of civilians and warn everybody in Hou Ky hamlet to stay away from the area southwest of Camp Apache for the next two hours.

There were two lines of targets, empty cardboard C-ration cartons with bull's eyes drawn on them, downrange from the firing line, hanging from communications wire strung between the posts. One row of targets was one hundred meters distant, the other two hundred. Bell set up another target three hundred meters away.

The Marines had played around enough with the captured weapons to know how they worked, but none of them had ever seriously tried to fire one for accuracy. Each of the four men shooting assumed a prone position on the firing line. They fumbled with the unfamiliar weapons, trying to get comfortable with them. The blocky wooden stocks weren't as sleek as the M-14's and didn't slide quite right into their shoulders. The folding leaf–type rear sights were set far forward on the stocks instead of behind the breech as they were used to with most American rifles. The thirty-round banana magazines the AKs were loaded with instead of the twenty-round straight box magazines of the M-14 felt odd. It seemed strange to have the gas piston cylinder above the barrel instead of below it, concealed and protected by the forestock. And it was ten inches shorter than the rifles they were used to. Bell stood in back of the four men so he could act as range master.

"Short Round, you first," Bell said. "Semiautomatic, slow fire. Let's find the range on this piece." He picked Hempen because, like him, Hempen qualified as high expert.

Hempen jacked a round into the chamber and turned the safety-fire selection lever to semiautomatic. The lever made a loud *clack-clack* as he rotated it. "Goddamn, I hope I never have to take this sucker off safety when somebody's close." The AK-47's biggest flaw as a combat weapon was how much noise its safety-fire selection lever made when moving from one position to another.

"With any luck that'll never happen," Bell said. "Put one downrange." He lifted a pair of field glasses to his eyes and focused on the left-hand hundred-meter target. Hempen carefully aimed and squeezed the trigger. "What target you aiming at, Short Round?" Bell asked when he didn't see a hole in the target.

"One on the left. What do you mean, which one? How the fuck do you think I made Expert if I don't fire at my own target?"

Bell didn't look at him. "Put another one downrange at the one-hundred-meter target."

Hempen looked up at him, shrugged, aimed, and squeezed again.

Bell lowered the glasses. "You sure you're firing downrange? You sure didn't come close to that target."

Hempen glared up at him. "If I didn't get two dead center in the black, either this rifle's a piece of shit or the sights are way the fuck off."

"Jay Cee," Burrison interrupted, "if it's the sights, we need a bigger target."

Bell agreed. They set up a target on the side of Camp Apache's hill. That way if the sights were off and the bullet missed the target, at least they could see its impact and know how far off it was and in what direction. This time it was easier; the sights on the weapon Hempen was firing were way off. When he made the correct adjustment, he put three rounds in a tight group in the middle of the bull's eye. Bell and Burrison decided to have the four men sight in all the rifles that way before shooting at the fixed-range targets. Gunfire rang out through Bun Hou. For one of the few times in recent memory it wasn't the manic cacophony of some men being successful in their attempt to kill others, other men unsuccessful in their attempts to survive this most primordial of human contests.

It took a half hour to see how the sights were set on each of them and make the necessary adjustments. Then they started firing at the hundred-meter targets. They fired slow and easy, three shots to get the exact setting for a hundred meters, then three more to see how tight a group they could make. Some of the rifles were too loose or their bores were too badly worn, and nobody could get a tight group with them. Bell tagged those for trade use. He knew there were plenty of airedales and squids and pogues who would never know the rifles they got couldn't shoot straight, and it would never matter.

Finally they were down to five rifles that all seemed to fire straight and didn't have any jams with the few rounds they put through them. They exchanged the shot-up C-ration cartons they'd been shooting at for fresh ones. The fifth rifle was for whichever PF they chose to take with them.

"Just like qualday, people," Bell announced. "Ten rounds slow fire; try to put every one in the middle of the black." He looked around to make sure everyone was still behind the firing line and that the four shooters were ready. "All ready on the right, all ready on the left," he said, the words of every range master in the world when it was time for the shooters to open up. "All ready on the firing line. Fire when ready."

The four shooters started cracking rounds at the targets. They had all been through this kind of known-distance shooting often enough to know exactly how to go about it. Slowly, carefully, zero in on the aiming point, take a deep breath, relax, exhale half of the deep breath, take up the trigger slack, squeeze the trigger. Each of them had a note-pad open to a page with a bull's eye drawn on it near his elbow. After each shot the shooter marked where he thought the bullet should have hit. They took most of the

ten minutes allotted for the slow fire. When they were
through, they walked to the targets and examined the hits.
Nobody was off much between where he thought his
rounds hit and where they actually did. They marked the
holes with grease pencils and returned to the firing line for
twenty rounds of automatic fire.

"Remember, people," Bell admonished them, "keep
your bursts short. Short bursts are at least as effective as
long sprays, and they conserve ammunition." He looked
around and, satisfied with the disposition of everyone,
began the range master's incantation, "All ready on the
right. . . ."

On command, the four shooters opened up. Short
bursts, mostly three rounds. They aimed and shot and
didn't take time to plot their shots. They were done in less
than two minutes. Every one of them found the automatic
fire surprisingly easy. Because the barrel of the AK-47 was
lower within the mass of the rifle, it didn't kick as much as
they were used to with the M-14 and was much more con-
trollable in automatic fire.

After that they went through the whole ten rounds slow
fire, twenty rounds automatic fire at two hundred meters.
By that point each of them had fired about seventy-five
rounds and they had a much higher regard for the enemy's
weapons.

Then it was Bell's turn with the SKS. He had paid attention to the problems the other men had had with the
unfamiliar weapons; he'd had to, because as range master
it was his responsibility to make sure everything was done
safely. Because he paid such close attention, he had fewer
problems of his own. It took him twenty rounds to feel
secure that he could put his rounds where he wanted them.

Back on the hill Bell supervised his four Marines in
loading five magazines for each of the five AKs. One

hundred fifty rounds per man. He himself loaded ten strip-per clips for his SKS. They were more heavily armed than the typical Vietcong or North Vietnamese soldier going into combat. It was typical of Americans to carry more ammunition; they seemed to believe there was an inex-haustible supply of bullets. The other side knew every round had to be laboriously hauled down the Ho Chi Minh Trail or hand-loaded locally. The hand-loaded rounds weren't as reliable as the others.

"Who you plan on bringing as the fay epp?" Zeitvogel asked while they were cleaning the rifles. "You want my little pano? Be a good trick if I can talk him out of his BAR." The PF the Marines called "Pee Wee," a man so short he could walk under Hempen's outstretched arm without ducking, was Zeitvogel's favorite PF. Pee Wee car-ried a Browning automatic rifle that he refused to relin-quish under almost any circumstances. The twenty-pound BAR was several inches longer than Pee Wee was tall.

Bell shook his head. "Pee Wee'd be a good choice for most operations, but for this one I want someone more sophisticated, someone bigger and stronger than him."

"Collard Green maybe?" Randall asked. Collard Green was older than most of the PFs; that might make him more sophisticated. Plus he was a squad leader, more experi-enced and knowledgeable. He got his nickname because of his constant distressed facial expression and the slightly greenish tint to his skin; he always looked like he was less than one burp away from throwing up.

"Maybe." Bell looked like he was thinking about it.

"Who's it going to be, Jay Cee?" Lewis asked. The right side of his mustache curled up in a graceful arch that would have touched his eye if it had been long enough; the other slithered down and away from the corner of his mouth.

"Huu did you say?" Hempen asked Lewis. "Sounds like a good idea, Billy Boy." He leaned toward Lewis and said solicitously, "Damn, you don't get many of them, Billy Boy. You feel okay? I mean you didn't hurt your brainbox or nothing, did you?" Lewis swiped at him, but Hempen was expecting the swing and easily blocked it.

"Yah, Huu," Bell said. "Anybody object for any reason?"

Do Chot Huu was a former Vietcong who had surrendered to Tango Niner. He had surrendered on the condition he could join them. He had seen with his own eyes that the American Marines were not the beasts the Communist political cadres said they were. Instead, he saw the American Marines giving free medical attention to the people and saw them paying good prices for everything they took from the people—and they never seemed to take anything without permission. He knew how those foreigners who looked so much like the hated French treated the villagers: like decent people, like friends and neighbors. And he saw the Vietcong murder innocent peasants. What he saw changed his mind about who was right and who was wrong in the war. Maybe the government in Saigon was not very good, maybe it was oppressive, but it wasn't murderous like the leaders of his former comrades in arms. And maybe, if enough of the Americans were like the ones here, and if the Americans had enough influence on the Saigonese, maybe the Saigon government would turn out to be far better than anything the Communists had to offer.

The Marines going on the operation into the A Shau agreed readily on Huu.

CHAPTER TWELVE

March 12, 1967

The evening chow bird arrived shortly after they finished selecting and zeroing in the rifles, and Lieutenant Burrison hitched a ride partway to Da Nang on it. The Marines of Tango Niner who stayed behind somehow managed to survive their sixty-seventh consecutive night of utter boredom. Each of the patrols even managed to have an unbroken string of a least one man awake at all times, and at least four of the perimeter positions around Camp Apache had someone awake every time Jay Cee Bell or Doc Rankin or Swearin' Swarnes made a comm check.

The helicopter Burrison rode out on didn't go all the way to Da Nang. It went to one of those small, company-size fire bases that punctuated Highway 1 north of Chu Lai to drop off mail before continuing to the Ky Ha helicopter facility at Chu Lai. Burrison hoped to hop a flight north from there, but he wasn't able to get anything until the next morning. Someone at the Marble Mountain helicopter facility was driving over to the other side of the Da Nang River and gave him a lift. It was time for noon chow by the time he found Ensign Lily, so he joined him for lunch, then had to entertain himself through the afternoon until Lily got off work and the two could track down Lieutenant (j.g.) Reeves. Burrison had a map of the target area with him.

"You're out of your fucking mind, you know that, Burrie?" Reeves stated when he examined the map. "And those people of yours are even dumber." He shook his head. "Oh, well, they don't call you jarheads in deference to your high mental faculties; they call Marines jarheads in deference to their lack of plain, everyday smarts."

"I'm just going to consider the source and not get pissed off at that," Burrison said, smiling.

Reeves snorted. "The fact that I make my living driving a helicopter while you go running around the boonies with people shooting at you is proof enough which one of us is smarter. And if that isn't enough, you want to go into the goddamn A Shau Valley without at least a whole Marine regiment backing you up." He shook his head again at the insanity of it all. "You're fucking dinky dau, Burrie; you done went and gone Asiatic on us."

"And you're too chicken to even get anywhere near the A Shau. That's why you're only a squid and I'm one of Uncle Sam's Misguided Children."

"USMC." Reeves nodded this time. "Uncle Sam's Misguided Children. You sure as shit got that right." He made to say something more, but Burrison cut him off.

"Ever hear of Cyrano de Bergerac?"

"What's that got to do with anything?"

"His nose. He could say anything he wanted about it, but God help any other dumb son of a bitch who did."

Reeves gave a surprised smile at that, then returned to

what he had been about to say. "No way a helicopter driver's chicken. Driving a helicopter's so hairy, you got to be able to think with your balls to do it."

Burrison burst out laughing, startling both Reeves and Lily. "That's right, Reeves, think with your balls, not your head. Thinking with your balls all the time gets you in trouble and keeps you there until it kills you." He laughed again, harder this time, until he had to shake his head violently to stop the laughter.

Reeves wanted to say something but thought first—with his head. He knew Marine officers were gentlemen by act of Congress, same as he was. But Marine officers were trained to kill, and he thought someone had to be at least a little unstable to go into that line of work. Granted, the bright-eyed, bushy-tailed Marine officer across the table looked more like a Boy Scout than a killer, but he wasn't a Boy Scout trained to help little old ladies across the street. No telling when some dumb jarhead might decide to prove he was king of the hill. So he said instead, "Exactly how do you want me to help in this death wish drama of yours?"

Burrison got serious. He bent back over his map and started tapping out locations. "Here's our objective," he said on one tap. "This place is close enough to walk there in a day and doesn't seem to have any bad guys in residence." He tapped another. "That's where I want you to drop us." He didn't think it was the best time to tell Reeves he wasn't going himself. He didn't want the Navy officer to ask why. He might have to explain the coin toss, and that would cost him the upper hand he had now. "Then there's this other place over here." He tapped the map a third time. "It's again about a day's march from the objective and also doesn't seem to be occupied. That's where we want to be picked up."

"When do you want to do this?" Reeves was also all business.

"When does your bird go into the shop?"

"Five days."

"Then we go either tomorrow or the day after, preferably tomorrow. I want an extra day just in case there are any problems and it takes us an extra day to reach the extraction point."

Reeves stared at Burrison hard but didn't hold the stare when Burrison mentioned possible problems in reaching the extraction point.

"Can you do this for us?"

Reeves looked down for a long moment. He looked like he was examining the map, but his eyes were unfocused while he thought. Finally he nodded. "Barring any unexpected problems at this end? Yeah."

Unexpected problems at that end was something nobody wanted to talk about—or even think about. If Reeves got shot down, or there was a change in schedule and his bird went into the shop earlier than expected, or he got a sudden emergency mission, or any of a number of other possibilities, the Tango Niner rescue team was going to be stuck way out deep in Indian Country on its own. Totally on its own.

"Tomorrow or the next day," Burrison said. "Which?"

Reeves swallowed. "Let's go for tomorrow," he said. "That way if I run into a problem on the day we're supposed to go, we've got a day's slack."

"Then I better get back to Camp Apache." The Marine lieutenant stood up and held out his hand. "See you tomorrow." He turned and left.

"We're in it this time," Lily said quickly to Reeves, then followed Burrison out. He had a jeep and drove him to

Marble Mountain. "Luck," he said, and shook Burrison's hand.

Burrison asked around and found a helicopter heading his way. It got him to a battalion headquarters advance fire base minutes before sunset. The fire base had an artillery battery in it; one platoon in that battery was 155mm howitzers. Camp Apache was eight miles away, just in range of those 155s. Burrison found the communications center and talked the duty communications officer into letting him use one of the radios to call Camp Apache. He had Swarnes put Bell on the horn. They talked and agreed that Bell would come in the jeep to meet him a mile southwest of the fire base. What the hell, both Burrison and Bell thought, Charlie don't live here anymore, it's safe to drive around at night. When he signed off he thanked the comm officer.

The comm officer looked at him blankly. "You going out there alone at night?" he asked in a flat tone that almost wasn't a question.

Burrison nodded.

"You're out of your fucking mind, Lieutenant. It's dangerous out there."

"I don't know why it is," Burrison said in a voice that could have been discussing the weather, "but people seem to be awful solicitous about my well-being these days. You're the second person in the last couple of hours to tell me that. But I've seen my share of the boonies, and I've killed more than my share of bad guys. To my way of thinking, it's safe out here." He waved his arm to indicate the area surrounding the fire base. "The only danger I'm in is if I run into a patrol of your people. Hang loose, Lieutenant."

"Good hunting, Lieutenant." the comm officer, who had never been outside the perimeter wire at night, waited until Burrison was far enough away not to hear him and murmured, "And you're going to need all the luck you can get."

Burrison didn't run into any friendly patrols, so maybe he had the luck. The only other thing he needed was a little patience to go along with the certainty he had that Bell wouldn't get lost driving around at night. It wasn't a half hour, it was forty-five minutes before they met. Burrison gratefully climbed into the jeep. Lewis and Dodd were along as extra rifles—just in case.

"Good to see you, Jay Cee. Let's get ready to put this show on the road tomorrow." Despite the darkness Burrison could tell Dodd was pleased with himself. Lewis seemed to be sulking.

While Burrison was away Huu test-fired the AK-47 he would carry. Then everybody gathered around inside the compound while Lewis practiced with the Ninja throwing stars he carried, a present from his younger brother. He propped a six-foot-long board against a bunker and paced off twenty feet to mark his throwing line. He opened the plastic-wrapped package he carried in the inside pocket of his utility shirt and unfolded the lightly oiled cloth in it to expose the three stars. After refolding the cloth inside the plastic and replacing the package inside his shirt, he stood half facing away from the board, with two of the stars in his left hand and the other in his right. Everyone gathered around to watch. There was a lot of cheering and encouraging shouts, except from Dodd. The draftee stood there with everybody else, but as usual he looked like he was somewhere else—or at least like he wished he was somewhere else.

With an air of disdain, Lewis ignored his audience. He pointed his left hand at the board, held his right hand by his shoulder, and twisted his body away from it. He suddenly uncoiled, and his right hand shot forward. The star flashed through the air and thunked into the board. In the same motion he took another star from his left hand, coiled back, thrust forward, and threw. The third star was on its way almost before the second one hit the board. The three were in such a tight group, they almost touched.

"All *right*, Billy Boy!" Robertson shouted.

Dodd didn't seem to notice or wasn't impressed.

"Charlie, stand by for a new asshole," Vega said, a wide grin spreading across his face.

"Shit, 'stand by,'" Hempen snorted, and looked at Vega. "That's the problem with newbies, no sense of history."

Lewis glared briefly at Vega from under lowered brows. He balled his fists in front of his face while he walked to the board to retrieve his stars. When he reached for them, the right end of his mustache draped up and over the ball of his nose and the left side zigzagged over and down under his lower lip. He worked his jaw to build up saliva and spit a long spume in Vega's direction before returning to his throwing line.

"What'd I say wrong?" Vega asked the world at large.

"Charlie already got his new asshole," Randall said. He stood next to Vega; his arms were folded across his powerful chest.

"Twice," Zeitvogel added from Vega's other side. Lewis had thrown the stars in combat twice. The first time had been when he and Robertson and two other Marines had come across a VC mortar squad that was getting ready to fire on Camp Apache in broad daylight. Lewis had killed two of them with his stars to set off the attack that killed the entire mortar squad. The second time was at night, when he had killed two VC sentries at the entrance to a hidden communications center. Both of those incidents had happened before Vega joined Tango Niner.

Back at his throwing line, Lewis stood with his right side toward the board and held one star in his left hand, the other two in his right. He threw them left-handed. *Thunk, thunk, thunk.* They hit almost as close to each other as the first three had.

Dodd didn't seem to be paying much attention, but his eyes followed Lewis's movements, studying them. When Lewis went to get the stars, Dodd walked to the rifle squad's tent. He emerged from it as Lewis threw the stars again, one right-handed, one left, one right. Dodd arrived at the board at the same time Lewis did.

"Anybody can do that," Dodd said softly. Something was in his hand.

"The hell you say," Lewis snapped.

"Yes they can," Dodd softly said again.

"Fuck you, Dumbshit." They called Dodd "Dumbshit" because he was the first Marine any of them had met who was a draftee. They agreed that being drafted into the Marines was the dumbest thing they could imagine anybody doing.

Dodd shrugged. "Try this," he said. He picked up the board and propped it on its side, balanced on protruding sandbags. Three playing cards and a box of thumbtacks were in his hand. He tacked one card to each end of the board and the third one two feet from one end. "Hit them." He stepped away from Lewis and gazed at him. Dodd's face held the absent expression it usually did.

Lewis scowled at the three cards, then stomped back to the throwing line. He threw right-handed, left to right. *Thunk*, the first star took off the corner of the deuce of clubs. *Thunk*, the second hit the center of the ace of spades. *Thunk*, the third missed the ten of diamonds by an inch. He glared at Dodd.

"I wouldn't have missed the last one if you'd spaced them right," he snarled.

Dodd shrugged again. "The bad guys don't maintain an even interval," he said.

Lewis retrieved his stars and threw again. This time all three hit the cards. He held his chin up and threw a "So?" look at Dodd. "Think you can do it?" he demanded.

Dodd nodded and chewed on his lip. Lewis retrieved his stars and thrust them into Dodd's hands as though saying "Show me." Dodd turned the stars around in his hands, looking at them as if they were alien artifacts, strange things he'd never seen before or had any idea about the uses of. It was true he'd never handled them before. He examined the short blades radiating from the central hubs. He thumbed the edges of the blades and pressed the tip of his finger on their points. He hefted them one at a time, feeling their balance. He held one between the forefinger and thumb of his right hand and swung his arm without releasing the star. The way he stood, flat-footed, without turning his body, the swing was an awkward movement. Apparently satisfied, he nodded to himself. He turned sideways to the board and bent over, peering at the targets. Slowly he stood straight with his hands together in front of his chest, then looked away from the board. Abruptly he lifted his left leg and leaned back, then he pivoted on his right foot and flung his right arm and entire body toward the target. He came down balanced on his left foot; his right hand crossed his left knee.

Swish, the star flew through the air. *Thunk*, it impaled the ace of spades. He stood straight again, hands at his chest, and went through the motions again. *Swish, thunk*. The second star split the ten of diamonds. Dodd turned and stood with his back to the board, glanced at it over his shoulder, looked to his left with his hands at his chest, then spun and threw the third star at the deuce of clubs. *Swish thunk*, the star clipped the card.

Lewis stood arms akimbo and glared at Dodd. He blew upward, and the end of his mustache curling over his nose wavered and fell forward. "What was that happy horse-shit?" he demanded.

"I pitched Little League and high school," Dodd said, and shrugged modestly.

Lewis briskly rubbed the lower part of his face. When he stopped, the left end of his mustache resembled a beef-eater's bush; the right end was simply unkempt and needed to be combed.

"How good were you?" Zeitvogel asked, a certain respect in his voice.

"All-county three years running."

"Were any of the opposing coaches on your draft board?" Robertson asked, grinning.

Dodd looked at him blankly. "I don't know. Maybe. Why?"

Robertson grinned wider. "That could explain why you got drafted into the Crotch," he said. "They wanted to get revenge on you for making their teams look bad."

A bulb seemed to light behind Dodd's eyes as he considered that. The light dimmed, and he shrugged again. The shrug seemed to say, "It doesn't matter." If an opposing coach had managed to draft him into the Marines for revenge, he knew the revenge would work. Ever since the day he hadn't been able to talk his draft board out of drafting him into the Marine Corps, he'd known he wasn't going to survive the experience—he was going to be killed in action. He was just a nice pudgy surburban kid, destined to be an insurance salesman, or an accountant, or a used car salesman. He knew he wasn't the stuff heroes were made of.

"You took too much time to throw them, Dumbshit," Lewis shouted. "You would of been killed after the first one, you took so long to throw the second star."

Dodd looked at him, basset-eyed. He knew he took too much time between throws for combat, and besides, the pickoff move was pure showing off. "But I never threw them before," he said flat-voiced. "Let me try again."

Lewis started to object but was overwhelmed by the others shouting for Dodd to try again. Lewis made a slight gesture of resignation and nodded.

Dodd retrieved the stars and faced the board a second time. This time around he didn't go into a full windup, just threw as fast and straight as he could. Each star hit a card.

Everyone congratulated Dodd, and there was a lot of backslapping. Except for Lewis. He stood off to the side and scowled. That was why Dodd seemed pleased with himself and Lewis seemed surly when they picked up Burrison.

The Marines and PFs of Tango Niner endured their sixty-eighth consecutive uneventful night.

CHAPTER THIRTEEN

March 13, 1967

The pilot and copilot of the helicopter that flew that day's hot meal out to Camp Apache had made many trips out there before. They were experienced pilots who had seen many strange things while flying around the war. There wasn't much that startled them. On their flight back from Camp Apache that day they saw something unusual enough that they talked about it between themselves.

"Now, where do you think that Navy bird's going?" the aircraft commander drawled. It seemed to be an occupational hazard of pilots that they all drawled. Probably had something to do with poorly developed frontal lobes or childhood head injuries.

"Unless he's lost," the copilot drawled back, "only place he can be going is where we just come from." Copilots were aircraft commanders in training; they drawled, too. He looked over to the pilot. "Why would he be going there?"

The pilot shrugged eloquently. The movement of his shoulders moved his hands on the cyclic and collective, and the helicopter swung about and dipped and staggered. He brought it back into trim before answering. "You weren't with me on Christmas Day. We ferried some split-tails out here so they could have dinner with Tango Niner. Some of them were Waves. Maybe they've got boyfriends there and that bird is bringing some of them out to see their men." He shrugged again, though less eloquently, and it didn't affect his control of the aircraft.

The copilot continued looking at him. He hadn't flinched when the pilot had momentarily lost control of the bird. "Women going into Indian Country to visit their boyfriends? You shitting me?"

The pilot grinned and glanced to his left. "I wouldn't shit you, you're my favorite turd."

The copilot didn't swing at the pilot, which was what he wanted to do. Instead he seemed to ignore the remark but set a corner of his mind to plotting a revenge for some time when the pilot wasn't driving a helicopter he was riding in.

The pilot continued. "I don't care how deep in Indian Country they are, hell, this area is safer than Da Nang. At any rate, Da Nang's been rocketed since the last time these grunts did any shooting."

The copilot grunted. It didn't seem to him to be a likely explanation, but it did make a kind of sense, and he couldn't think of any other reason for a Navy bird heading toward Camp Apache that made any kind of sense at all. He dwelled on it for a moment, then said, "Maybe I'll request transfer to one of those new CAGs."

The pilot glanced at him but didn't say anything. He wondered how his copilot had managed to come up with that idea. What kind of nut would want to give up flying to become a mud Marine?

The copilot was thinking that no matter how dangerous it sometimes got in the Combined Action Companies and Platoons, if they got the Navy to fly roundeye nookie out to them, they might be damn good units to be in. Flying a helicopter was the most fun he'd ever had doing anything —next to sex. Sex narrowly edged out flying. He decided to think on it more.

Seeing a Navy helicopter flying out to Camp Apache was unusual enough for them to talk between themselves about it, but it didn't strike them as odd enough to mention to anybody else, so they never did.

Of course the Navy helicopter they saw wasn't flying Waves or any other roundeye women out to Camp Apache. It was Lieutenant (j.g.) Reeves on the first leg of his highly unauthorized flight to drop a few good men onto the fringes of the A Shau Valley. As he flew along, Reeves wondered about his sanity. There was no question he'd physically survive; he wasn't going far enough to risk getting shot down. What was bothering him was what would happen if anybody ever found out about it. Like what if the crew of that bird he had just passed decided to ask someone about the Navy helicopter they saw headed to Camp Apache? He thought the hard stone of Portsmouth prison would probably erode away to sand before he ever got out.

Minutes later Reeves pointed the nose of his helicopter at Big Louis Slover and came in fast. The first time he'd come into Camp Apache he'd made that final approach slow to avoid kicking up hard debris that might injure the shirtless man with the orange Ping-Pong paddles. Later someone had explained to him that Slover didn't mind the little pings and nicks he got from whatever might get kicked up by a fast approach, but he hated like hell getting the thick coating of dust and having his eyes and mouth filled by the heavy dust kicked up by a slow descent.

Slover's sheer size was intimidating enough that Reeves came in fast ever after—he didn't want anybody that big mad at him.

J.C. Bell, carrying a thick roll of det-cord around his shoulders, boosted Tex Randall—who was carrying a radio on his back—Stilts Zeitvogel, Short Round Hempen, Billy Boy Lewis, and Do Chot Huu—all of whom had their faces, necks, arms, and hands splotched and striped in camouflage—into the cabin and climbed in behind them while Burrison got into the cockpit to talk to Reeves. Reeves nodded and waited for the Marine officer to get out before he took off. He climbed to five thousand feet and headed northwest. He handed the controls over to his copilot for a few minutes and scratched under the back of his helmet. He wondered what on earth Burrison had been talking about when he'd said he lost the coin toss. Nobody based command decisions on games of chance. Did they?

Below, the land became increasingly hilly. A dense rain forest blanketed the hills, softening their contours, but the ground was so rugged, not even the jungle could conceal that fact from the air. Brilliant flowers grew in many of the treetops, creating a riot of color. Here and there, and never too close, were occasional small clearings in the jungle: isolated homesteads and tiny hamlets.

When they were still a few miles east of the middle of the A Shau, Reeves took the controls again and banked sharply into a dive to the left. The dive was sudden and sharp enough that it would have thrown his passengers around the cabin if they hadn't been belted into their seats. It wasn't until the crew chief, using hand signals, explained to them that this was a dive, not a drop, that the Marines stopped thinking they'd been shot down. Huu didn't know what any part of a helicopter ride was supposed to be like, never having flown in anything before, so it didn't bother him—he was like a young kid on a roller coaster for the first time.

Reeves pulled out of the dive less than a hundred feet above the treetops between two steep ridges and flew below the level of the hilltops. He zigged and zagged and jinked and followed the narrow valleys. Years later, when "nap of the earth" became the state of the art in military flying, Reeves boasted to his fellow helicopter pilots that he had been in on its conception. He never did tell them it was on an unauthorized flight. Once you ironed out the zigs and zags and jinks so you found a straight line, you saw that Reeves flew in a direction that was mostly south but a little west as well. At length he located the small clearing that was the drop zone. It wasn't much of a clearing, just a bare spot on the side of one of the gentler hills in the area, made when lightning had struck one of the jungle giants and toppled it and it had knocked down several of its less gigantic neighbors. A Huey could have zipped right in, dropped its cargo, and zapped right back out again with no trouble. The bigger, less agile UH-34 was another matter. Reeves closed slowly with the opening. The changing contour of the land under him significantly altered the shape of the air pillow his main rotors created for the aircraft to fly on, and he had to be careful he didn't slide off it. The sun was falling behind the western mountains, and the slope Reeves aimed at was in shadow, which made the approach trickier.

Helicopters fly because their rotors create an air cushion that they then slide around on top of—but it's a controlled slide. Alter the size, shape, or density of that air cushion too quickly and the pilot can lose control and the helicopter can fall off it. That's the aerodynamics lesson for today. It sounds just as probable as what they say about how the curved upper surface of a wing has less air pressure on it

than does the flat undersurface and that's what makes air-
planes fly. Just don't tell the little guy with the rattles and
incense who lives inside the engine cowling that's what
they say. If you do, he's liable to stop his incantations and
the airplane will fall down go boom.

It didn't take many long minutes for Reeves to close in
on the clearing enough for Bell and his team to jump out on
the upper side of the slope, it just felt like it did. Reeves
nodded a fare-thee-well at the men he was leaving behind,
then shot off. He returned by a different route. In seconds
the roar of his helicopter shrank to a distant hum and then
was gone. Five Marines and one PF were very, very isolated. And they felt that alone.

Bell didn't see Reeves nod. He was the last man off the
bird and looked at Lewis and pointed uphill even before his
feet touched the ground. Lewis scrambled toward the crest
of the ridge, eyes and ears as open and receptive as they
could be. Randall, Zeitvogel, Huu, and Hempen followed
in that order. Bell brought up the rear. Lewis turned left at
the top and went fast, taking advantage of the day's last
light. The ridge wasn't rounded like a hilltop. It was flat on
top, and its sides were jaggedly torn away only feet from
the centerline. Small and midsized trees crowded each
other on the crest and tightly bound the narrow game track
that followed it. Larger trees couldn't root on the top; the
ones that tried were snuffed out by the dense root systems
of the trees already growing there. The ones that tried it
near the edge overbalanced and fell down its sides, taking
chunks of rock with them—part of the reason for the
jagged edges.

Fifty meters along the trail Lewis stopped and waited
for the others to reach him. Bell didn't speak but used hand
signals to communicate. The six men sat in a tight circle,
their backs together. They listened for two minutes for the

sound of pursuit or any noise that would indicate someone else was nearby. They didn't hear anything but their own breath and the excited pounding of their hearts until the birds restarted their startlingly loud roosting cries.

The sergeant snaked the map out of the inside pocket of his shirt and withdrew the compass from his left breast pocket. He tapped Hempen and Huu at his sides to let them know he was going and then broke away from the circle. He went to the west side of the ridge and tried to find a landmark he could use to locate himself on the map. No luck. The trees made the landscape look pretty much the same from where he was. All he could make out was the overall ups and downs of the terrain. He hoped Reeves was as good at navigation overland as Burrison had assured him. Bell matched what he could see with where he was supposed to be. It looked more or less right, but he couldn't tell for sure. If Reeves had put them down in the wrong place, they were a long way from their extraction point and had little assurance they could even find it. He returned to the others.

Randall was listening to the radio handset. His eyes flickered briefly in Bell's direction, and he nodded curtly. After listening a little longer he murmured, "Roger, Blue Danube. Wait one." He looked a question at Bell.

"Near as I can tell we're right where we're supposed to be," Bell said.

Randall returned to the handset. "Blue Danube, Waltz. We are at Checkpoint Alpha and ready to move. Over." He listened again, nodded, hung up the handset, and flipped the power switch off to save the batteries. "Reeves reported he didn't see sign of any enemy activity or civilian dwellings after he left us, and he's gone back. We're on our own now," he said to Bell.

"Let's go. I want to reach the next ridge before we stop, and it's going to be night in a few minutes."

Lewis again took the point, followed closely by Randall. Bell inserted himself third in line, and the others stayed in the same order they'd been in before. They went so fast, Hempen didn't have as much opportunity as he would have liked to watch his rear—not that it mattered. There really wasn't anyone close to them.

Night came so fast, Lewis almost stumbled over its edge. He stopped until he felt Randall slap his hand onto his shoulder and started again at a much slower pace, each foot probing the ground to make sure he was still following the game trail. The six men continued on, linked hand to shoulder, hand to pack, hand to belt. They had to let go to clamber down when they reached the end of the ridge. The night wasn't hot in the mountains, but they sweated anyway. Climbing down that ridge, they made much more noise than they wanted to. They hoped no VC or NVA were within a couple of kilometers.

They didn't know the jungle, though, those Marines and the PF with them. They lived and fought in the rice paddies and the lowland scrub forests. They didn't know how the jungle could muffle sounds so they didn't travel more than a few meters or how the jungle could reflect and magnify sounds so a noise could be heard a long way off and sound as if it were coming from a different direction. Jungle was a frightening place to be in if nobody in the group was familiar with it. No one heard them and came to investigate. At least no one came to investigate in the right place.

They reached the bottom of the ridge, and Lewis waited in the pitch darkness for Bell to come forward to point out a direction to him. Then he had to rely on whatever biological gyroscope he had to keep him going in the right direction: The jungle was too dense for more than the faintest light from the moon and stars to filter down and ease the eye-blindness they all felt too powerfully. Lewis thought the bottomland sloped gently down to a stream and then gently back up to the next ridge; at least that was what the map said it did. He thought if he walked downhill until he hit water and then went uphill until he reached someplace steep, he would probably be all right. Everyone else knew about and trusted his uncanny sixth sense that told him whenever someone was nearby, a sixth sense that had saved American and Vietnamese lives more than once and had cost many bad guys theirs. They figured maybe that same sixth sense could guide him to where they were supposed to go.

The bottom did what the map said it did—it sloped gently down for fifty meters to a rapidly running streamlet that burbled over smooth rocks, then rose another fifty or so meters to the next ridge. There was no game trail to follow there, but there were plenty of bushes and small trees to grab and pull up on. It took an hour in the dark for them to climb the hundred meters to the top. They were drenched with sweat and panting heavily when they reached it. Bell moved them a short distance south along the crest before deciding to stop for the rest of the night.

"One-third watch," he told them. He looked at the luminous hands of his watch and divided the remaining time until dawn by three. "Two-and-a-half hour shifts. We go again at first light." Five hours' sleep each. Not much, but they were all young and healthy and had gone on less sleep often enough in the past. Five hours was enough. They could catch up on their sleep when the mission was over. "I'll take last watch. Who wants first?"

* * *

On the Song Du Ong floodplain the Marines and PFs of Tango Niner were experiencing something different from what they had for the previous sixty-eight nights. It wasn't enemy activity, it was the sixty-ninth consecutive quiet night for them. Every man of Tango Niner was fervently hoping no member of the platoon would run into any trouble that night.

CHAPTER FOURTEEN

March 14, 1967

Strange noises, jungle noises: slithers, pads, wet snaps, buzzes, creeps, crawls, caws—and always the *fukyoos*—made sure the men on watch stayed alert and disturbed the sleep of those not on watch. Bell didn't have any trouble waking the sleeping men when the first light drifted down through the treetops.

"Chow down cold," he told them softly. "Do what you have to do fast and cover it. We move out in fifteen minutes."

They knew they were in enemy territory there. It wasn't Bun Hou, where the Americans not only owned the day, they owned the night as well. It was the real Indian Country, where Charlie didn't just own the night, he owned the day. Scattered sounds were an indication of night-filled bladders emptying. Nobody bothered dropping trou, so there wasn't anything to cover. They could hold it for the two days they expected to be out here. What morning throat clearing there was was as discreet as possible. No one even considered striking a match to a heat tab to warm up his morning C-rations; nobody had brought a heat tab along. For a brief moment there was the muffled sound of John Wayne can openers scraping on cans, opening them wide. They ate quietly.

"Box 'em up," Bell said when they were through eating. Can openers scraped again, opening the bottoms of empty cans. There were minor metallic creaks when the cans were flattened. The refuse of all six meals went into one box. Zeitvogel took that one box and tucked it in the bottom of his pack. When they moved out, the only sign they left of their visit was crushed leaves. They would rebound fast enough; in a few hours only the best woodsman would be able to tell somebody had spent the night there.

Bell spent a couple of minutes at the west edge of the ridge trying to pinpoint his location on the map. He swallowed nervously and thought again that he hoped Reeves had known what he was doing when he had put them down. He'd have to pay close attention to where they'd been and keep adjusting his assumed position on the map. This was the first time he'd ever been in a jungle, a place where the vegetation covers the land so thoroughly that its shape can't be seen; this was the first time he'd had serious trouble matching the landscape to a map. It scared him, made him fearful of getting lost. Every fiber in his body screamed he was in no place to get lost. He returned to the team for one last chore before moving out.

Randall hadn't shrugged into his pack yet; it lay on the ground with the radio strapped onto it. Bell knelt by it, removed the whip antenna, screwed in the thirty-foot wire antenna, and handed the other end to Huu. The wiry PF scrambled up a tree with the antenna end held firmly between his teeth. When he was as high as he could take the wire, he called softly down. Then Bell flipped the power switch on and held the handset to his face.

"Blue Danube, Blue Danube, this is Waltz, this is Waltz. Over," he said, cupping the mouthpiece with his free hand. The radio crackled at him instantly. Swarnes must have been waiting for his call. "Danube, Waltz is at Checkpoint Bravo and moving. Over." Swarnes's voice faded as he rogered the message and signed off. Bell hoped they wouldn't have problems transmitting and receiving when it came time to be extracted. He called softly to Huu to come down and unscrewed the antenna and started rolling it back up while the PF was climbing down. He didn't reattach the six-foot antenna, just slipped both of them into the bag between the radio and the pack.

"Let's go," he said quietly. He looked at Lewis, raised his right hand to his shoulder, and dropped it to the south.

Lewis nodded and stepped out along the trail. They went in the same order they had the night before. Slower this time; Hempen was able to walk backward half the time, making sure nobody came up behind them unannounced. They followed the ridge to its southern end, then down its shoulder to another one it joined, and up that one. They didn't follow the next ridge all along its top to its far end. Bell had Lewis follow a gently sloping outcropping that sprouted on its west side halfway along its length. That spur reassured him—it was the only ridge with such a spur showing on his map. They climbed sweating, panting, bleary-eyed up another ridge to the southwest before Bell called a break. "Go easy with your water," he warned. He didn't want anybody getting stomach cramps from drinking too much too fast when they were overheated. He was the only one who didn't collapse onto his back or double over heaving for breath. The leader could never do that, at least not until after the end of the mission. Bell sat leaning against a tree. He wiped the heavy sweat from his brow and breathed slowly and deeply until his trembling limbs calmed. He let a thin stream of water from one of his canteens trickle down his throat. The canteen was encased in a cut-down sock to muffle the sound if it was bumped and so light wouldn't reflect off it—both canteens carried by each Marine were in socks. He saw with satisfaction that the others drank just as carefully. Before he put the canteen away he shook it. Nearly empty, almost half his water gone, and they weren't nearly halfway through. He pored over his map again. Yes, one more ridge and the map showed a blue line indicating water. He didn't say anything to the others about it; he didn't want them drinking their fill now and not being able to replenish if that blue line was dry—or too tightly covered by the enemy for them to get to it. Or if they were not where he thought they were. He looked at his watch and back at the map. He wanted to reach their objective while there was still enough light to make some sort of visual reconnaissance from a safe distance. He stood up. The others rose, and they set out again.

Rotting vegetation squished under their feet. It was slippery and had them sliding on the slopes they went down and up, tried to make them fall. Vines dragged and dangled and crept everywhere, tried to trip them, catch them, hold them, imprison them. They forced their way through the living and decaying mass of flora that wanted to prevent their passage. At least it was mostly single-canopy jungle on top of the ridges and double on the bottoms, not triple-canopy.

Tropical rain forest trees mostly grew straight up in long trunks as high as they could before branching out, as many of their leaves as possible exposed to whatever sun and rain they could find. Not all tree species could grow to the same

height; some grew maybe fifty feet without branches and
then spread out. Their spreading branches formed a canopy. Others grew to a hundred or more feet and spread out
to make a second canopy above the first one. Still other
trees topped out at more than two hundred feet and created
a third canopy. Each canopy blocked out a measure of
light, cutting down the growth of whatever was below it.
Two canopies blotted out more than one, three more than
two. The ground under triple-canopy jungle was evening
dark no matter how bright the sun above the treetops, as
dark as under the band of heavy trees that lined the Song
Du Ong River. But men under the trees along the Song Du
Ong always knew there was openness and light not all that
far away. It didn't take long under triple canopy to convince men that endless twilight had fallen. And no matter
how clear the sky above was, there was a constant light
rain under the triple canopy.

The trek was harder on Lewis than on the others because he had to find a way through the tangle and always
be the first to breast the obstacles. He refused to let anyone
else take a turn at point. He knew they trusted him to find
where they were going. He wasn't as sure as the others
were of his ability to know distance and direction, but he
was, by God, going to give it his best shot.

His sixth sense didn't fail. He froze along the ridge crest
that was the last before the one where Bell hoped to find
water on the other side. Maybe he heard something, maybe
he smelled something. He didn't know. All he knew was
that something wasn't as it should have been. The others
saw him stop and froze in place as well. They were already
sweating profusely; they couldn't sweat more. Their sweat
became acrid; it stank of fear. Without looking behind him,
Lewis took two careful steps back and stopped again to
wait for Bell.

"What is it?" the sergeant whispered in his ear.

"There's somebody up ahead. I'm going to check it out." He dropped his pack and slid into a narrow space between bushes along the side of the trail and disappeared.

Bell looked back. Everyone stood still, staring at him. They knew why Lewis had stepped off the trail. They wondered what he was going to find, and it scared them. The five men on the trail waited.

Shit, Lewis thought, this is like the worst alley I ever been in. He told the other Marines he had learned night movement and evasive tactics running white lightning when he was a kid. They knew he'd never left his native Bronx before enlisting in the Marine Corps and wondered about that. It was true, though, that he had negotiated many alleys that others thought impassable, had made it through without being caught by anybody chasing him or leaving a trail that could be followed. He soft-footed through the jungle, sidestepped, high-stepped, slide-stepped, whatever it took to avoid stepping somewhere that would make noise. He twisted his body to one side and to the other, contorted it in double-jointed ways to evade the leaves, branches, and vines that wanted to stop him, delay him, shake, rattle, or roll his passage.

Twenty-five meters along he found what he was looking for. His mouth and throat went dry when he realized how close it was. His sixth sense didn't operate at the same distance in the jungle as it did in more open land. He was only a few feet away from a broad trail, six feet wide and well tended. A loop in the narrow game track the Marines followed brought the two so close at that point that they almost touched. A column of armed men in dark blue uniforms trooped quietly on soft-shoed feet along the wide trail heading in the direction Lewis had come from. He stayed where he was, hidden in the deep shadows, hidden behind leaves that would erase him from the sight of casual glances. Leaves that would do nothing to stop bullets if somebody saw him. He counted.

After minutes that seemed like hours the last man in the column trooped past. None of them had looked in his direction; they had all kept their eyes straight front. There was no reason for those North Vietnamese soldiers to look to the sides, to be on the watch for danger—the land belonged to them, and they knew it. Lewis waited a moment longer to see if anybody else came along. No one did. He slithered closer to the trail and looked both ways along it. It extended straight, murky in the half light, for as far as he could see in both directions. He slipped away from it, all the way to the game track. The track curved away from the straight trail. He walked back along it to where the others were waiting for him.

"Speed trail," he murmured to Bell, his head close enough to the other's that he could speak almost inaudibly. "It goes straight; this one curves away from it. I counted a company of Vee Cee Hanoi going along it. More went by before I got there." Speed trails were concealed highways for pedestrians and bicycles.

A muscle twitched in Bell's jaw. He nodded a nod that was no more than a slight bobbing of his head. He turned to the others to tell them what Lewis had seen. There is no such thing as an invisible man or a shrinking man. Randall, Zeitvogel, Hempen, and Huu nonetheless seemed to lose substantiality and size when they learned that more than a company of NVA had passed that closely.

Bell huddled with Lewis over the map for a moment. He pointed out where he thought they were, and Lewis agreed. A short distance farther the map showed a place where the ridge side wasn't as steep as it was for most of its length. Lewis nodded his understanding, his confidence in being able to find the gentler slope; he pulled his pack back on and led off.

Along that ridge for a while, down its side, up the next, along it for a time. They saw no more indication of enemy presence or activity. Bell stopped the short column so he could examine his map again. There should have been a small stream at the bottom of the ridge they were on. Then two more ridges and they'd be at the south end of the A Shau Valley. If his dead reckoning was on target. He pointed Lewis downslope without saying anything. During the break he noticed others shaking their canteens, concerned. They were sweating a lot more than they had anticipated, and their water was going faster than planned.

Halfway down Lewis heard the first soft burbling. He stopped and looked back. They needed water, needed it badly, he knew that. But he also knew that this deep in Indian Country, where there was running water there might well also be bad guys.

Bell pointed downhill.

Lewis swallowed and continued. The bottom between that ridge and the next was narrow, and the trees and brush grew right to the edge of the stream. Lewis took a cautious step, felt nothing but air under his foot, and pulled back. He leaned forward and looked down. There was the stream. He knelt at its side and waited for Bell to join him. They listened carefully and peered through the leaves without moving any of them. The stream was eight feet wide and ran fast; it had to be shallow. And fast-running water had a better chance of being free of parasites. The interbranching trees on both sides formed a tunnel's sides and top around the stream. Brush had been cleared away under the trees on the other side: another speed trail. No one moved on it.

"I'll pass the canteens to you, you fill them," Bell said.

Lewis nodded. He lay flat parallel to the stream. One-handed, he pulled one canteen from his belt and unscrewed its cap. His other hand held his rifle, finger on the trigger. He reached out as far as he could and submerged the canteen. Its gurgling was almost completely covered by the burble of the stream. He brought the full canteen back, but before he could recap it Bell dropped a tiny pill in it. Halazone, a water-purification tablet. No point taking any chances with the water. Lewis drank deeply from his second canteen before he filled it; the halazone had to be given a half hour to do its work before he could drink the fresh water. He held the canteen to take the pill before he tried to recap it. It took about ten minutes to fill all twelve canteens. By the time he finished the last one Lewis was feeling very edgy and wanted to get away from the stream.

Bell carefully poked his head through the curtain of foliage and looked both ways along the speed trail on the other side of the stream. He motioned: Let's cross it here.

Lewis held his head back for a moment. He didn't know why he wanted to get away from the place; there didn't seem to be anybody nearby. He stood in a low crouch and gingerly lowered one foot into the water. It went in to mid-calf. The streambed was covered with small, rounded rocks, slippery rocks that could trip up a man who didn't step on them right. He turned back and mouthed the word "careful," then faced the opposite bank and teetered across. The other bank was chest high. He clambered over it and looked both ways along the speed trail. He looked up and saw how dense the treetops were—no way the trail could be spotted from the air. On the other side he saw a small space between two bushes and eased himself through it. The next ridge started its climb bare meters from the speed trail. Randall joined him half a minute later. The rest arrived one at a time. A good way to cross an open space was for everybody to rush across at once; it lessened the time a not very observant enemy had to see you. Bell sent them across one at a time because of the slippery streambed. It took almost three minutes for all six to reach the brush on the other side.

Bell was the last to cross. He pointed at Lewis and pointed uphill. Lewis nodded and started to climb. The lower part of the ridge side was overgrown with brush and vines and was curtained by the tree branches that draped against it. Above that was a fifteen-foot-wide stretch of bare rock that looked like it ran nearly the entire length of the ridge. That part of the ridge face was steeper than that which they had already climbed and steeper than the tree-grown face above it. Lewis swallowed hard when he reached the bare area. The only alternative to going across it was backtracking to the other side of the stream. He wanted out of that valley badly, and he knew better than to cross open spaces. He looked at Bell. Bell nodded. Lewis swallowed again and darted uphill; the others came in a rush behind him. Before Lewis reached the higher growth, after all of them were exposed on the bare rockface, there was a shout and a rifle fired behind them and to their right.

CHAPTER FIFTEEN

Over the Top

"Go!" Bell snapped. "Go, go go go-go gogo." His voice was low, but it rang with urgency.

They scrambled faster and in seconds were under the cover of the trees. They didn't stop. Bell kept them going twenty feet deeper into the trees. He stopped them when there weren't any more shots. Two voices were shouting on the trail, and more voices were heard under the shouters.

Bell looked at his men. They were all facing downhill, their rifles ready to open up at anyone coming at them. "Stilts," Bell said to the man closest to him, "let's take a look." He loosened his feet from where they were dug in to keep him in place and slid downward on the seat of his pants. He held his rifle in his right hand and grabbed saplings with his left to control his slide. Right before he reached the lower edge of the wooded area he twisted his feet and jammed the edges of his boots into the dirt to stop his slide. A thump and a grunt announced Zeitvogel's arrival at his side. Miraculously, no debris tumbled down the hill from their hasty slide.

Carefully they peered down the slope. Directly below them the trees formed a carpeted wall they couldn't see through. To the left there was a break in the trees, and through it they saw movement on the trail. They sat and watched. One of the yelling men was in sight. He was waving his arms and shouting at someone just out of their view; a pistol was in his hand. At his feet they saw a body sprawled, blood pooled around its head. Two other men squatted closely over the body. The body and the two squatting men were dressed in American-style fatigues but were too small to be American. The uniforms and size told them the corpse and two men must be ARVN, soldiers of the Army of the Republic of Vietnam. The shouting man screamed something Bell had trouble understanding because of the shrillness of his voice, pointed his pistol menacingly, then shouted orders in a parade-ground command voice. Two more fatigue-clad figures came clumsily into sight and did something to the body, then picked it up. They moved clumsily because a short length of rope ran from one man's neck to the other's. The watching Marines realized that the two men squatting were linked to the neck of the corpse by ropes. The shouter stepped aside and gestured; a short column of men then trooped along the speed trail. Most of them were dressed in fatigues; ropes linked their necks, and they were unarmed. A few others wore khaki uniforms and pith helmets. They were armed and prodded their prisoners with bayonets fixed to the muzzles of their rifles. Bell saw a red splotch on one prisoner's shirt.

Bell and Zeitvogel stayed where they were long enough for the POW column to pass beyond them. It wouldn't do

to move too soon and risk accidentally rolling a rock or
something downhill to announce their presence.

Then Zeitvogel asked, "Were you able to understand
any of that?"

Bell nodded. "Enough to know the dead man tried to
make a break and the officer was chewing somebody out
for not keeping close enough tabs on him. He paused
briefly before adding, "And those POWs are being taken to
the A Shau before they get sent someplace else."

Zeitvogel stared unfocused for a moment, then said,
"You thinking the same thing I am?"

"Probably. Diversion."

The tall man nodded thoughtfully.

"Let's go." They scuttled back up to where the others
were waiting. Bell told them in a few words what they had
seen. Then they moved on.

Bell thought about the situation. That prisoners of war
were being held in the A Shau was information that Marine
intelligence evidently didn't have. If his patrol could somehow find a way to free the POWs—preferably a noisy
way—that could create enough of a distraction to help the
Marines get away. Hell, he thought, that's a basic maneuver for revolutionaries. When you try to take over a city,
you take the radio or TV station so you can get your message out to the populace, and you bust open the jail and
free the prisoners to make more confusion and give the
authorities more problems to deal with so they have fewer
resources available to use against you. . . . Maybe, just
maybe.

They reached the top of the ridge and found it was different
from the others they'd walked along. Some cataclysm must
have come to it; its floor was almost bare of accumulated
dirt and the detritus of erosion. Not as many bushes and

trees were able to find root there, and what trees there were, were smaller. It was a thicker woods than the scrub growth in much of Bun Hou but was much thinner than the jungle. They didn't go very far before Lewis stopped and looked at something to his left.

"Holy shit," Bell whispered when he found out why Lewis had stopped. A hole had been dug in the crumbling rock near the lip of the ridge top and reinforced with sandbags. It looked like it had been in use recently: None of the sandbags was rotting; no sand had spilled from them into the bottom of the hole; few leaves had drifted into the hole; no animals were nesting in it. The ridge top was too hard to show footprints, so Bell couldn't tell anything that way. No equipment was in the hole, but a communications wire led to it. The bare copper ends of the wire were dull but hadn't turned green yet. All signs indicated that the position had been manned recently, hadn't been vacated for more than a few hours.

Bell stepped into the hole and whistled softly. In it he saw what he could not see standing above it. Channels of brush had been skillfully cleared downslope from the hole to expose the speed trail below to clear view from it. His practiced eye told him that nobody on the trail would be able to spot the observation post from down there unless he knew exactly where to look—and maybe not even then. This is a major difference between us and them, he thought. We cut and plow cleared areas so our view isn't obstructed, but everybody out there can see where we are. Charlie doesn't give himself fields of fire as good as ours, but he can't be seen until he's ready for it. He wondered why the OP wasn't manned—not that he was complaining, of course. He looked to the side, where they came up the side of the ridge, and was doubly glad the OP was unmanned. He thought he saw the open area they'd crossed.

He was sure he saw the very break in the trees he'd watched the POWs train through.

"Be alert, people," he said sotto voce. "We can run into Mister Charlie any time now. Unless we see him before he sees us, we're fucked."

The others nodded and looked into the thin trees around them, hoping they wouldn't see anybody. They didn't.

"Go," Bell told Lewis. He climbed out of the hole and looked back in it to make sure he hadn't left anything behind, not even a footprint, to show it had been visited. Lewis led off.

It was midafternoon by the time they reached a place where the A Shau Valley spread out before them. The valley floor for as far as they could clearly see to the north was a rolling plain, though it seemed to roll more violently in the southern end than it did farther north. It seemed somehow quiet there, not that it was, just that there weren't as many birds crying and insects buzzing or lizards *fukyoo*ing. Other noises, human and mechanical noises, were an undercurrent, but they were not close and didn't immediately register on Bell's consciousness.

Bell oriented himself to the valley and his map. Then he lay prone and focused his field glasses on a compound a kilometer away. It was exactly where Houng's information said it was supposed to be. From ground level he could see the bunkers and tents under the trees, bunkers and tents invisible to anyone looking down from above. Men in the black pajama uniform with red armbands of the Vietcong moved about the compound. There didn't seem to be barbed-wire barricades around it, though Bell did see what looked like pointed stake walls here and there, barriers that probably had been placed to funnel an attacking force into prepared killing zones. He wondered what kind of booby traps might be in place.

"Looks like we're here," he said to his men, who had gathered close around him.

Randall tapped Bell on the shoulder and pointed to the right. The sergeant swung his glasses in that direction, and suddenly the human and mechanical noises he'd earlier ignored seemed to leap about fifty decibels. His stomach sank. Trucks were trundling from place to place, some of them out in the middle of the valley rather than under what cover the edge of the forest offered. A distant bulldozer belched smoke as it built up earthwork defenses. Here and there he spotted an antiaircraft gun pointing skyward. It was the first time he'd seen heavy equipment and weapons larger than a 60mm mortar or 50-caliber machine gun in the enemy's possession. They must feel very confident of their ability to hold and move about this valley if they have all this big stuff here, he thought. He watched five trucks rumble in convoy across the valley. The A Shau must be the VC-NVA equivalent of Da Nang, he thought. And I'm leading a six-man team into it. I must be fucking dinky dau.

He shifted his glasses to the left. A few soldiers were escorting some prisoners across the bottom of the valley a kilometer away. Probably the same ones we saw earlier, he thought.

"Keep an eye on them," he told Randall. He wanted to complete his eyeball reconnaissance and wanted to know where the POW train disappeared to if it went out of sight before he returned his attention to it. Several minutes of careful looking in a sweep to the south revealed no enemy positions in that direction. Bell lowered his glasses and chewed on his lower lip for a long moment, lost in thought. They could go around the south end and hope they didn't encounter any hidden forces, or they could wait until after nightfall and go straight across. Waiting was probably safer, but it was so much better to get closer to their objective while there was still enough light to see; maybe they could spot Houng's son and find out exactly where to locate him when it was time. The slave laborers might be locked up early, and they wouldn't have a chance to spot him if they waited until sundown. Bell decided that if they didn't go right away, they'd probably have to hole up all day the next day to locate the boy.

He huddled with the others. "I didn't see anything in that direction—" He pointed to the bottom of the valley. "—but that doesn't mean nobody's there. That's where we're going now, get close to that camp across the way while it's still day. With any luck we'll spot the kid and see where he's kept overnight so we'll be able to get him out of there. Questions?"

"What if we run into the big bad bear on our way?" Hempen asked.

"If he's there, we'll spot him before he sees us and we won't run into him," Bell said with more confidence than he felt.

Right! the others thought but didn't say.

"Look," Bell said, as much to reassure himself as to give his men confidence, "we know the big bad bear's here; he doesn't know we are. The odds are on our side."

Then Randall had something else to say. "They're going in."

Bell looked where the husky corporal had pointed. The guards were directing their prisoners into the trees a couple of hundred meters shy of the camp. Bell looked through his glasses and couldn't see where they were going; nothing was visible under the trees. He grinned wryly. "There's a big bad bear who's in the way. You just know we're going to spot him before he sees us."

Uh huh, the others thought.

There were high mountains close to the west of the A Shau, the Annamese Cordillera that formed the spine of the Indochinese peninsula. At that point the Annamese Cordillera was the border between South Vietnam and Laos. Moisture-laden clouds swept in from the South China Sea and precipitated some of their moisture as they gained altitude over the rising ground. The higher they had to rise to go above the land under them, the more rain they dropped. When they reached the mountains, they had to drop a lot more of their moisture in order to make it over. All that additional rainfall east of the mountains gave the jungle trees more of what they needed to grow; the A Shau was ringed by double- and triple-canopy jungle that climbed up the mountains. In normal triple-canopy jungle, the jungle giants take too much of the nutrients from the soil and prevent enough sunlight from reaching the ground for any undergrowth to take root and flourish. But around the A Shau Valley, the sun shone under the trees and bushes and weeds and saplings grew ariot. The only clear way through the forest was on paths, the same paths used by the VC and NVA. Breaking a trail through the brush would make too much noise and attract the attention of anybody nearby. That wouldn't do at all.

"Huu," Bell said. As soon as he had the chieu hoi's attention he slapped his own upper arm.

Huu nodded. He took a strip of red cloth from his tube pack and pinned it onto his upper sleeve. Then he put his bush hat in the pack and pulled out the U.S. Army baseball cap and put it on.

"Everybody," Bell said, and removed his own bush hat.

He tucked it into the top of his pack as carefully as he could but thought it was going to get crushed anyway and he'd have to buy a new one when they got back to Camp Apache. He took the olive drab baseball cap from his hip pocket, flipped it open, and pulled it as far down on his head as it would go. The other Marines also changed hats. He looked at them and mentally shook his head. It was a very flimsy disguise. If someone caught only a fleeting glimpse of them, the hats resembled a hat the NVA wore and might throw them off enough that they might not notice the Marines' skin color or size. Hah, he thought, next someone's going to try to sell me a bridge. Well, Hempen and Lewis maybe, they were small enough at a quick glance that someone expecting to see only Vietnamese might mistake Hempen for a fat Vietnamese or Lewis for a tall one. They both had deep tans. He and Randall, not a chance; they were both too big. Randall was blond besides. Between Zeitvogel's height and dark brown skin, no way, never. But the baseball caps were all the disguise they had.

"Huu," he said. The former Vietcong already had his AK-47 slung muzzle down over his shoulder. He nodded curtly and led the way to the nearest trail leading south. The others trailed a short distance behind. If Huu met anybody coming along the trail he at least looked like a Vietcong and, having been one, could talk as if he belonged in the A Shau. As long as nobody asked what unit he was in or who his commander was. If he met someone, the Marines following him would hear him talk to whoever it was and try to get out of sight off the trail.

The heavy jungle growth hemming them in on both sides could have panicked the Marines if any of them had been claustrophobic. Instead, walking openly on a trail in the enemy's territory made them feel naked and helpless.

Huu set a brisk pace. He walked erect and looked confident; he didn't try to step softly. Stepping softly was for interlopers; this was where he was supposed to be. His confident walk was what saved him from the observation post he didn't see.

"Comrade, you come from a strange direction," an unexpected voice said to him from a clump of bushes.

Huu almost managed to completely hide his surprise at hearing the voice. A short distance behind him, hidden beyond a twist in the trail, the Marines froze when they heard Huu speak. "Comrade, you hide in a strange place," he said. He looked closer and smiled when he saw the telltales: a branch that was broken in a strange way, a row of grass stalks that grew in too straight a line, bamboo sproutlings that were to evenly spaced, clumps of leaves that were too artfully arranged. "I thought nobody was here because you didn't challenge me earlier." The way he said that implied he knew someone was in the blind but thought the sentry was asleep instead of watching.

"No, comrade. I was watching to see how close you would come without seeing my hiding place." The voice implied the hidden speaker didn't think Huu had seen his hiding place at all. A section of brush swung open; it hinged where the branch was strangely broken. The too straight row of grass, the too evenly spaced bamboo, and the too artfully arranged leaves moved on a latticework of split bamboo. A small space, densely surrounded by thorn branches, was cleared behind them. Most of the ground of the cleared space was dug out. A man stood to his waist in the hole. There was enough distance between the open door and the front of the hole for a man sitting in the hole to aim his rifle through the gate. The blind was a very well hidden observation post, and the thorn branches would do an excellent job of preventing anybody from slipping close enough to silently kill the watcher without being heard by him in time.

The Marines listened intently to the conversation. Bell and Lewis knew the language best, but it was hard for them to understand what was being said because the sentry spoke in a dialect with which they weren't familiar. Lewis slung his rifle and reached inside his shirt to pull out his small plastic-wrapped package. Silently he opened the plastic and unfolded the oily cloth it protected. He withdrew one of the stars from the cloth and repacked and replaced the package. He tapped Bell on the shoulder and gestured with the star. The sergeant's chest heaved in an inaudible sigh. He nodded and mouthed, "Only if the Vee Cee is about to fire his weapon."

Lewis nodded somberly and crept along the trail until he could see his Vietnamese friend through the foliage without being seen. He had a tense wait.

"I have been here a long time without relief, comrade," the VC sentry said. "Have you come to relieve me? I have not eaten since morning, and my water is nearly gone." He shook his bamboo canteen to demonstrate how little water was in it. "And only a low beast would foul its own nest." He wiggled so as to relieve the pressure on his bladder.

"No, comrade," Huu said, "I am not your relief. Would though that I was. I'm sure your sacrifice in this matter is much appreciated and you will soon be properly relieved. For myself I am delivering a message to the commander."

"Oh?" the sentry asked, his face blank and his tone neutral; his hand shifted almost imperceptibly on his rifle. Lewis saw the motion and prepared to step into the open and throw his star in one motion. "Do you know where to find Major Quoc?"

Huu thought fast; it could be a trap. "I do not know. Is Major Quoc your commander? My commander told me to deliver this message to the commander of the 314th Battalion of the Peoples Liberation Army, he did not tell me who its commander is." Confusion touched the sentry's face, and Huu smiled slightly. "Comrade," he said reprovingly, "did you just now test me? Is Major Quoc not truly your commander's name?"

The sentry smiled ruefully. "Comrade, you understand how it is. One never knows who might come along. You could be an inspector checking to see if we sentries are alert, or you could even be a spy."

Lewis relaxed.

Huu's eyes opened wide. "Comrade, a spy?" he asked, sounding amazed. "Here, a spy? Only the greatest of fools would think he could come here and not be detected."

The sentry shrugged. "I am only doing that job which the Peoples Army has assigned to me. I am but a fighter."

"I understand, comrade. Your life must be dull here, but we must all do our best for the Revolution and ask nothing for ourselves."

The sentry nodded again, glad that someone understood what it was like being a mere perimeter security guard. "You may continue, comrade." He held up his hand to stop Huu from leaving immediately. "Three hundred meters along is another sentry post. You will know when you reach it because it is marked ten meters distant by a bamboo pole stuck in the ground. That pole is there so inspectors will know when they are close to it and will not be embarrassed by being surprised by the sentry." He smiled.

"Thank you, comrade, this is good to know." Huu bowed to the sentry and took a step. He stopped and turned back to the closing gate. "One moment, comrade. Who is your commander?"

The sentry pushed his gate open again and answered,

"Lieutenant Colonel Dong. Be careful and most respectful; he is a harsh man."

"I thank you, comrade. Can you send a signal that I am on my way with my message?"

"I am a thousand times sorry, comrade. The only signaling method we have in these observation posts is to fire our rifles."

"I thank you ten thousand times, comrade." Huu bowed again and went down the trail out of sight.

Lewis eased away and, relieved, rejoined the others. He hadn't wanted to kill the sentry; sooner or later someone would have discovered the body and sounded the alert. But he would have if he had thought the guard was about to fire. That gunshot would bring others, and the risk of discovery would be immediate.

Bell breathed easier as well. "Let's find a way around that OP," he said. Lewis led the way back along the trail until he found a place where they could enter the brush without leaving too obvious sign of their passage. They were certain they would find Huu waiting for them somewhere farther along the trail.

CHAPTER SIXTEEN

Valley Boys

The bamboo marker pole was right where the sentry had said it was. And it was skillfully placed in a thin clump of bamboo where anyone who wasn't looking for it wouldn't notice it or would think it was a dead bamboo tree that had lost its leaves and branches. But Huu was looking for it, so he saw it right off. He soft-stepped back to the Marines. Lewis took the point again, as Bell had ordered when the Marines had met Huu beyond the first sentry post, and led them through the heavy brush in a fifty-meter arc around the observation post.

Lewis didn't know exactly where the VC watcher was; it might be more than ten meters from the marker to the OP, and he wanted to give it a wide berth. When they returned to the winding trail, Huu took the point again. Not long after that they finally reached the southwest corner of the valley, where there would be more traffic and their risk of discovery was greater. It was time to get off the trail.

Bell gestured to Lewis to lead them through. The wiry lance corporal nodded grimly and went into the thick brush. This was the tricky part: He knew where they were headed, but between here and there was where the guards had led their prisoners into the trees. They had no way of knowing how far in the POW train went. There could have been a jungle prison fifty meters inside the trees, or they could have simply followed a trail that led them all the way into Laos.

Lewis didn't so much break a trail as find places where bushes and saplings weren't growing too tightly together and eased between them. When a branch or vine blocked his way and he had to push it aside, he did so slowly and cautiously and held it for Bell to take from his hand so it wouldn't slap back into place. Bell handed the branch or vine to Huu, who gave it to Zeitvogel, who gave it to Randall, who gave it to Hempen, who eased it back into its place. Twenty-five meters in, the undergrowth thinned enough so that Lewis no longer had to move things out of his way. Here and there he could see far enough into the jungle that his line of sight was ended by the eternal twilight rather than blocked by foliage. Another twenty-five meters and the underbrush thinned so much that if he went much farther they would have to rely on the dimness and trees for concealment. He turned right.

Lewis's mind was blank, in a way. He didn't have any conscious thoughts, and nothing internal distracted him. He didn't think about anything, just let his senses open and absorb whatever was there to take in: air wafting against his face, neck, and hands. His ever-moving eyes saw the shapes, forms, colors, movements, and relative positions of objects; buzzes, cries, cracks, shuffles, and tinks were filtered by his ears; the myriad scents of the jungle—those confused him a bit, as he wasn't used to the scents of the full jungle. All that information was funneled into some deep subcortical recess of his brain where it was sorted, analyzed, shuffled, resorted, reanalyzed, and shuffled again until it meant something. That was how his so-called sixth sense worked. His conscious mind didn't know what was going on; like a data processor keying bits and pieces of information into a data bank, his conscious mind had no idea of the meaning of anything. His subconscious did all the work. It wasn't something he did deliberately, it was just something he did because it worked.

Heavy as air, massive as a pinfeather, weighty as a soap bubble, Lewis glided through the thin brush fifty meters from the trail along the edge of the valley. He zigged and zagged and went straight ahead now and again and backstepped two or three times. His erratic movement avoided pitfalls, noisemakers—natural and man-made—and booby traps. The others walked as near as they could in his footsteps. His conscious mind was barely aware of the brightbanded krait he sidestepped. The snake noticed him, though. It was startled by the sudden appearance of so big an animal, and it slithered quickly to a better protected hiding place—the venomous snake didn't realize it could kill the encroacher with one bite. It was gone before any of the other men in the patrol reached it.

After two hundred meters Lewis stopped and lowered himself to one knee. Bell came forward and knelt beside him. "Somebody's up ahead," Lewis said in the low voice used by night fighters who intended to live to fight another day.

"Think it's the prisoners?" Bell asked.

Lewis lifted his shoulders in a minor shrug. "Could be."

"Can we check it out?"

Lewis didn't answer immediately; he listened and looked for a moment longer. "Wait here," he finally said, and was on his feet and vanished into the brush.

Bell settled himself to wait. He hoped the wait wouldn't be long.

Lewis walked hunched over, evenly balanced over his gliding feet. Both hands were on his rifle; his right elbow clamped it to his ribs, and its muzzle looked wherever his eyes pointed. All the movements he made were deliberate; none were fast. He took full advantage of every iota of concealment the thin brush afforded. Thin was a relative term when talking about jungle undergrowth. This wasn't thin as in some places, places where you could walk in a straight line in any direction without encountering anything until you bumped into the bole of a jungle giant. This was the kind of thin where there were spaces between the bushes and saplings, and not all of them were thickly festooned with dense leaves or draped with trailing vines. Here and there the spaces abutted against each other and seemed to form lanes under the spreading trees. It was the kind of thin where you could see an enemy as far away as you could make out his dim form in the half light or not see him until you stepped on him or he shot you.

Lewis nervously passed the tip of his tongue over his lips. He moved slowly from bush to bush, shadow to shadow. Slow, slower, slowest. He stopped. He heard garbled voices. He lowered himself to a deep knee-bend crouch and duck-walked in the direction he thought they were. A few thigh-burning steps and the voices abruptly became clear. He leaned forward to a three-point stance and lowered himself to the ground.

A couple of spaces away, under the separating foliage, two soldiers were sitting under a tree, drinking tepid tea and talking. They talked soldier talk, the same as uniformed men the world around. Fortunately, they talked slowly the way people making an oft-voiced complaint do;

otherwise, their accents would have been too much for Lewis to understand. One was complaining to the other about the dull duty. He didn't say brave things about how he wanted to go into glorious combat against the American devils or the ARVN oppressors. Soldiers did talk like that when they were far from a fight and knew there was little possibility of getting into a fight, but not usually unless there was an officer or someone else they wanted to impress close enough to overhear. He complained about how dull and tedious life was under the trees guarding ARVN prisoners, prisoners he had to keep a sharp eye on when he watched them. He complained about missing his family and friends up north and never being allowed to visit any of the villages in or near the valley to get a good home-cooked meal. He sounded bitter when he complained that the cultural troupes never visited the small POW camp in which he was a guard, and he always seemed to be on duty when a cultural troupe performed close enough to allow men from his unit to attend. "Cultural troupes" were the Vietcong equivalent of USO shows.

The other soldier didn't complain. He made soothing sounds and occasionally said something in agreement, something about yes, it was boring duty; yes, it was sad they could not visit any villages; yes, he also missed his family and friends. His response to the cultural troupes made Lewis think this man got to see all the performances.

The Marine lay still and let the circle his senses were aware of expand. At some indefinable distance beyond the two soldiers he heard noises of other people. The two he'd been listening to must be off duty, he decided. He listened to the dull susurration of the more distant noises and thought about going closer to find out what they were. In order to get closer he had to pass and go deeper into the forest than the two off-duty men he was observing. He thought about it, then, glancing frequently in their direction, he crawled toward the other noises.

He gave the complaining soldier and his companion a wide berth but had to stop abruptly fifty meters beyond them. The brush under the jungle towers was cleared out, and the smaller trees had been cut down. A large open space, roofed by the jungle canopy, unfolded before him. Four peasant-type hootches were clumped together at the far end of the open area, some two hundred meters distant. Separated maybe twenty meters from them was a wooden house bigger than any of the thatch hootches. Light reflected off the windows of the wooden house, surprising the Marine—he wouldn't have guessed the Vietcong had any glazed windows. A twenty-foot-tall guard tower stood at the far corner of the clearing, near the four thatch hootches, and a rope ladder hung down from the tower. A searchlight was in the guard tower, swiveled up. There were several spotlights scattered about. Between the hootches and where Lewis hid at the edge of the clearing were about fifty bamboo cages. There was no fence around the clearing.

Each cage was a cube about three feet on a side, on stilts that held it two feet above the ground. Their doors seemed to be held closed by thongs and hinges of leather. Two men hunkered in most of them. A stench rose from pots placed under the cages. Lewis grimaced at the smell that suddenly assaulted his senses. Some of the prisoners squatted in the cages, and some lay curled in fetal balls. The cages weren't big enough in any direction for a man to stretch out at full length, either standing or lying; they were even too tight to allow comfortable sitting. The men Lewis could see clearly were gaunt. Their sole garments seemed to be filthy loincloths. The caged prisoners looked like their spirits were beaten. None of them turned their heads in the direction of the new prisoners who were herded together, standing side to side, belly to back along one side of the clearing.

Four guards stood around the tight group of prisoners. They held AK-47s ready and looked quite willing to use them. Two North Vietnamese officers stood in front of the prisoners. One of them was talking loudly in a high-pitched voice. Lewis tried to listen, but the Northerner's accent was too harsh and he talked too rapidly for the American to make out anything. From the shrill tone of the officer's voice and the expression on his face, Lewis imagined he was detailing to the prisoners all the horrors that would fall on them if they didn't do exactly as told. The North Vietnamese officer abruptly broke off and spun away; he marched to the wooden building at the far end of the clearing.

The other officer watched him for a few seconds, then snapped something at the prisoners and pointed at one of them. The prisoner he pointed at wailed but didn't move. A guard leapt at him and smashed the butt of his rifle into the man's belly, then hit him again, on the head, when he doubled over, knocking him to the ground. The guard kicked the downed man repeatedly. While the guard was kicking, the officer snapped another order and pointed at a different prisoner. The second prisoner took a reluctant step forward and was given another order. He started stripping off his uniform. A different guard grabbed his shoulders and yanked him to his knees. The guard tore at his clothes until the man was naked except for the trousers bunched around his knees. The guard then kicked him in his buttocks, knocking him on his face, and jerked at his cuffs until his trousers were off.

By then the first guard had finished kicking the other prisoner, who was shedding his uniform as quickly as he could. The officer spoke again, and the other prisoners shucked off their uniforms as fast as they could without breaking formation.

Lewis grimaced. He thought of standing there naked in front of the guards with other naked men pressed against him, and his skin crawled.

The officer nodded, apparently satisfied, and followed the first one. The guards proceeded to walk circles around the naked prisoners and point at their groins—which the prisoners weren't allowed to cover with their hands—and laughed.

Lewis didn't stay to watch the men's humiliation. It was getting late, and the patrol had farther to go before the sun set. He didn't go back the way he had come in; he looked for the trail that led from the valley floor to the clearing. He located it to his right and made a loop in that direction. He got to where he could see the path; it was about three feet wide, and its hard surface showed it was frequently traveled by many people. No footprints stayed on it. He stepped deeper into the woods, far enough that he could see the gaps in the foliage that indicated where the path was without directly seeing it—or, more important, being seen from it. The path didn't go in a very straight line, neither did it quite meander. Lewis thought it basically more or less just avoided the trees along a straight line from here to there. The trail went little more than a hundred meters before opening into the valley floor. After seeing where it went, he pointed himself in what he knew had to be the right direction and went to rejoin the rest of the patrol.

"Jay Cee."

Bell jumped at the words quietly spoken from a few feet away and spun toward the sound, his rifle muzzle aimed at their source. He saw it was Lewis and went limp. "You're going to get killed someday doing that, Billy Boy," he whispered. He wiped sweat from his forehead. The long wait for Lewis's return had made him nervous and jumpy.

"Nevah hoppen, Jay Cee. I'm too damn good."

"What'd you find?"

"POW camp in that way." Lewis pointed. "They got 'em in cages, Jay Cee, tiny fucking little cages. Like animals."

While they talked, the others gathered around to hear Lewis's report.

"How many?"

"Seventy-five, maybe more."

"If we open their cages, do you think they'll make a break, make the diversion we want?"

Lewis looked at Bell patiently, a teacher tutoring a slow student. "Two-man cages. Too many for us to open."

"How about some of them?"

Lewis looked through the trees in the direction of the POW camp. "Maybe," he said slowly. "Maybe the new ones still have enough grit to go." He chewed on one end of his mustache. The way the guards were cowing those prisoners, he wasn't sure any of them would dare take a step away even if an entire Marine regiment suddenly landed in the camp.

Bell filed away what Lewis said in a recess of his mind to think about later—what Lewis said and what he didn't say. There were more immediate things he had to deal with. "How do we get past it?"

"I didn't go beyond the camp, but we can get across the path easy enough."

Bell looked at him questioningly.

"No sweat, Jay Cee, easy."

"Any guards on it?"

"None."

"You didn't look too hard for them, did you?"

Lewis didn't say, "You know better than that, Jay Cee. I don't need to eyeball both sides of the trail to know no one's there." He didn't say it in words, but his expression made his thought clear.

Bell looked at him briefly. "Lead the way," he said. He glanced at the others; they were all ready.

Lewis led the patrol in a straight line to the path from the valley floor to the clearing the POW camp was in. The underbrush was thick enough that they got to within ten meters of the path before anybody but Lewis saw where it was. Bell stopped the patrol and went ahead with Lewis to look at it. From where they were hidden the path went straight for seven meters before turning around a tree at each end of the straight part.

Bell nodded. "I'll get the others, Billy Boy. You watch." He slipped back through the brush to bring the other four up.

Lewis waited patiently, absorbing all the sensory data available to him. The only indication he had of any nearby people was the five men behind him.

Bell didn't waste any time. He lined his men up and pointed each at a thin spot in the brush on the opposite side. He positioned himself once everyone was in place, looked both ways along the trail, and saw no one on the trail. He raised his hands to shoulder level and pushed forward. The six men sprinted the half dozen steps it took to get into deep foliage on the other side of the path. He listened intently and heard no sign of pursuit. The nobody he saw didn't see them, either. They headed on until Lewis stopped again.

"We're there," Lewis said when Bell stepped next to him.

CHAPTER SEVENTEEN

Over the Forest and into the Trees

It was more of the same for the next 150 meters. The trees grew high, higher, highest; the undergrowth grew thin, thinner, but never reached thinnest as Lewis led them deeper, away from the valley floor. It didn't seem like more of the same, though. It wasn't just Indian Country; it was *their* homeland, the enemy's headquarters. Here and there a voice called out; an occasional hammer rang or ax thunked; there was a constant undercurrent sound from revving truck motors. The sounds came from all directions; they even seemed to come from above. In war, men go out to kill each other deliberately; no man out to kill can escape the possibility of being killed. The sounds of enemy activity heightened the expectation of murderous action. Where the Marines were they weren't simply outnumbered, they felt like they were a piece of bloody meat in the middle of a swarm of great white sharks in a feeding frenzy.

When you're in a situation you know is extremely dangerous, adrenaline pumps madly throughout your system, creating the primordial fight or flight reaction. All sphincters tighten up, and blood is shunted away from places that need it less to places that need it more; the throat dries so internal moisture is conserved; the anal and urinary tracts contract so you don't leave spoor. Soldiers call this "the pucker factor." The pucker factor was very high in the patrol—so high that some small part of Hempen's mind wondered if he'd be constipated for the rest of his life.

That's the way it feels in the middle of the enemy's headquarters. But if you're careful enough, it's not really all that bad. The enemy doesn't expect a few men to come sneaking into the middle of his stronghold; he's not looking very hard at all for interlopers. Bell and his men didn't know it, but except for the sentries stationed on the approaches into the valley, there were very few sentries around. Most of those sentries were guarding armories or communication huts or supply dumps—places the commanders wanted to keep the common troops out of. Others were stationed at carefully selected spots where they could salute the commanders as they came by. They weren't guarding anything; they were just there to give the commanders the illusion their troops were alert—and to give the commanders the ego boost of being saluted. That was not the way it was officially, of course, but that was certainly the way the troops interpreted it.

So as long as Lewis didn't lead the patrol into anyone, they really weren't in much danger. Nobody was looking for them.

The ground climbed irregularly up and down, then folded back on itself. It went steadily up, not in a sharp incline but up nonetheless. Irregularities in the ground masked sounds from one direction or another, echoed them so they sounded as if they were someplace other than where they were. The pucker factor remained high.

There was a basic difference in the philosophy of massing troops in action here. When the Americans established a base, they kept their troops close together and cleared the land. That clearing made it very difficult for enemy troops to move about an American base unobserved—unless they came in unarmed, disguised as Vietnamese laborers. The North Vietnamese and Vietcong, on the other hand, spread their troops out and cleared only as much ground as their hootches and holes and tents and paths covered. There could be large areas within a VC or NVA base camp that almost no one ever entered. The enemy wanted to be hard to spot; that made their bases easy to penetrate—once you got past the outlying rings of sentries, that is. In the A Shau, where there were many units and each had its own area, there were very large spaces between them. It was even easier to penetrate deeply—once you got inside that outlying ring. The Tango Niner patrol was well within that outlying ring.

Bell called a halt at the bottom of a dip. He picked up a pebble and wiped it as clean as he could with his dirty fingers, then stuck it in his mouth to get some saliva working. "Where are we at, Billy Boy?" he asked, his voice harsh from his throat and mouth being too dry.

"Getting close, honcho," Lewis answered. His voice sounded more normal. He had put a pebble in his mouth earlier.

The others crowded around to listen.

"How close?"

Lewis tipped his head away from Bell, and his eyes went out of focus. He held that position for a few seconds, his mouth slightly agape, and let his senses absorb everything. Then he said, "Too damn close to talk," and climbed to the top of the other side of the dip they were in. He peered over it and slinked back down. He pursed his lips and lay a finger across them, then went back the way they'd come. As soon as a slight ground fold was between them and the dip they'd been in, he stopped. "We were right there," he said. His eyes showed white all around, and his voice trembled slightly. "There was a gook squatting down to take a shit. I almost could a reached out and grabbed his balls from behind." He gave an involuntary shiver. He didn't understand how he could have gotten that close to someone without realizing it.

"How come we didn't smell anything?"

"He was just squatting, hadn't dumped yet."

"There a latrine there?" Zeitvogel asked.

Lewis shook his head. Surely even the VC had designated places to take their craps. The man must have had some reason for going there. Maybe he was a guard and couldn't leave his station.

Bell looked into the trees and thought for a moment. He decided. "That way fifty meters, then back around." He pointed deeper into the forest.

Lewis looked and nodded. He headed out again, slower this time, trying harder to understand all the sights, sounds, and smells around him. He had to skirt a tangle of thornbushes before getting fifty meters deeper. Bell stopped him again and walked around the tangle, looking carefully at it from all sides. He nodded to himself, then set Lewis off again. Fifty meters, climb a scarp along the way, hang a right, another fifty meters using handholds along the side of a steep slope, hang another right, go downslope a few meters. And the VC regimental headquarters spread out before them.

It was tucked into a small valley on the west side of the

main valley. A shoulder of the western mountains came down there and bifurcated into a shallow V just before reaching the A Shau plain. It wasn't a big side-valley, just a little tuckaway, but it was well protected on three sides by the split shoulder. The ground under the trees was mostly cleared of underbrush. It was a tough position for a combat unit to attack, almost impossible for a battalion to reach without being discovered before it launched its final assault.

A thatch roof covered a large area, maybe twenty by thirty feet, at the point of the valley V. Awninged wall sections were swung up around its sides, increasing the covered area and opening the inside for ventilation. A lectern stood centered on the veranda that wrapped around its front. A red banner with words the Marines couldn't read hung between two poles behind the stage. A knot of about fifty soldiers squatted before the stage, listening raptly to a man in a tropical-weight suit talking at the lectern. Twenty-five meters downvalley along the right a smaller roof stood over a pit dug in the ground. A wisp of smoke from a banked fire under a large pot rose to the roof and filtered away to nothing through it. Three women puttered about, stirring, mixing—a kitchen. Another awning-sided roof stood on the other side of the main hootch. Under it were glass-doored white enamel cabinets, a six-foot-long stainless-steel table, a desk, and large glass jugs that stood on the dirt floor. A woman wearing a nurse's cap fiddled with the contents of one cabinet: the pharmacy-cum-sick bay. Farther down that side was a long, narrow roof. Several clerks typed and filed under it. A score of small hootches were grouped beyond it; strung hammocks were visible in their shade. On an area of beaten ground in front of the small hootches another group of soldiers was being led through calisthenics. Bell looked at the exercising soldiers and grinned wryly.

It wasn't a large headquarters, not by American standards. A Marine regimental headquarters was 250 to 300 officers and men. A Vietcong regiment needed only a commanding officer, a political officer, an executive officer, a few staff officers to do planning and take care of logistics, a doctor with a nurse or two, and a small number of clerks and cooks. Bell thought the soldiers being lectured to and exercising were a main force company either assigned to guard the HQ or on a form of R&R, away from the battlefield.

There were two other things in the cleared side-valley that caught the Marines' attention: A ten-by-ten-foot patch of ground was surrounded by a barbed-wire fence. Inside it was a six-by-six-foot bamboo cage, door open, leather ties hanging loose, empty. Two soldiers idly watched eight rag-clad, filthy people carrying heavy-looking baskets on yokes from one place to another. One of the bearers was much smaller than the others.

"Think that's him?" Zeitvogel asked, soft-voiced.

"I do believe so," Bell answered. He fished the photos from his shirt pocket and looked at them, then back at the small boy struggling under the weight of his burden.

Randall looked at the photos and the boy. "Too far away to tell for sure," he said. "But he looks like him."

"Let's go back to those thornbushes," Bell said. They went.

CHAPTER EIGHTEEN

The Plot Thickens

Bell examined the thornbush tangle again before saying anything. When he did speak, it was, "If we have to hide, I think we can hide in here." Then he stepped between two branches, dropped to his knees, and squirmed into the bushes. A few seconds later his voice came hollowly out. "Come on in, water's fine."

The others followed him. Hempen was the last; he twisted around to erase sign of their entry. All he had to do was turn one dead leaf back dry side up and push one thorn twig back in place. He thought no one could see that six men had just penetrated the bushes there.

It was hollow inside the bushes, an inverted bowl. There were breaks in the otherwise solid wall of foliage around them through which they could see the surrounding area. The floor of the hollow was covered with a dense bed of fallen leaves that muffled the sounds they made.

"When I was a little kid I visited some cousins in New

Jersey," Bell said in answer to the questions looked at him. "They showed me some broad-leafed bushes that were hollow inside, said they were old Indian hootches. We used them for teepees when we played cowboys and Indians, forts when we played soldier. This clump of bushes was shaped the same way. I thought it might be hollow inside." He shrugged out of his pack. "Let's chow down while we figure out what to do next." Somebody's stomach growled in second to that.

For a few minutes there were no sounds from the six other than the quiet scraping of can openers on C-ration cans and the odd muffled grunt of satisfaction as they wolfed down their first food since dawn. They looked at their food only enough to see what they were doing; mostly they looked through breaks in the leaves around them, watching for anyone coming near. When they finished eating, they broke down all the trash and put it into one box. Hempen stuffed that box into his pack.

Bell glanced at his watch. "We've got less than an hour until sunset," he said, "and a lot to do between now and then. Stilts, you take Short Round and Huu and scout the camp more, find out exactly where they put that kid. And make damn sure you see where they place their sentries for the night. I don't want to stumble over somebody before we're ready tonight and set off an alarm. Tex and Billy Boy, come with me. We're going up the hill a little to make a radio check, then back to that POW camp, see what we can do for a diversion if we need one. Questions?" He looked each of them in the eye. No one averted his gaze or said anything. "Here," he added, taking paint sticks from his shirt pocket. "Pair off and touch up each other's camouflage before going back out. It's starting to run on us." He waited while that was done, then finished, "We'll meet back here in forty minutes. Put your packs back on, just in case we aren't able to get in here. Let's do this thing."

A moment later they were crawling out from under the cover of the thornbush tangle.

Zeitvogel looked at the two men with him: Hempen, a foot and an inch shorter than he was, Huu shorter yet. "I used to think it was bad," he muttered. "Now look what I got. Shit, spot me the Lakers and I *still* won't have a team tall enough to take on and beat a girls' high school basketball team."

Hempen heard him and chuckled softly. "Shit, Stilts," he said, "it's easy for us to beat them. You stand over those darling little girlies and distract them while I walk face first into their cute little titties. Then, while they're all atitter about being face-groped, Huu can grab the ball, dribble up court, climb a ladder, and drop the ball right through the hoop." He shook his head in wonder at the vision. "Hey, if we try, bet we come up with some good rules for strip roundball. And win."

"Fuck you, Short Round."

Huu looked at them briefly. He had no idea what they were talking about.

Zeitvogel took his two men back to the regimental headquarters by a different route from the one they had used before. A small erosion gully ran down the shoulder-split. Zeitvogel ducked low and followed it—he almost bent double to stay below its top. Hempen and Huu didn't have to duck so low. Low bushes crawled along the top of the ditch. Some of their roots dangled in the air where erosion had eaten dirt away; fallen, rotting leaves mottled the floor of the gully. Camp noises could be heard through the brush. When they were close enough, Zeitvogel stopped his men and straightened slightly to peer through the bushes. They were near the kitchen. The cooks were serving the evening meal to the last of the soldiers. Voices bantered in jest. Camp dogs scampered around the eating soldiers, begging for scraps.

Hempen nudged Zeitvogel and pointed. The tall man looked. The eight laborers were crowded into the tiny cage surrounded by barbed wire. A bucket had been placed on the ground under the cage. One of the laborers squatted above it, and a thin stream dribbled out of him into the bucket. Two soldiers lounged near the barbed-wire fence watching.

"Bad case of the shits," Hempen mumbled.

Zeitvogel nodded. He wondered how long that man had had his diarrhea and what the VC were doing to stop it. Or if they were going to allow him to dehydrate until he was too weak to work, maybe until he died from it. He looked carefully and saw the boy; at least they knew exactly where he was, even if Zeitvogel didn't have a clear idea of how they were going to get him out of the cage and themselves safely out of the A Shau.

The last soldier was served his meal, and the cooks scooped rice and soup out of the pots for themselves. Then one of them scraped the remainder of the rice into the soup pot and the other stirred the mixture. They upended the soup pot and poured its contents into a large bowl. One cook shouted something. One of the soldiers watching the cage shouted back and ambled over. He was a burly man with a scar running diagonally across his face. He carried his rifle slung muzzle down over his shoulder. He picked up the bowl and carried it carelessly. Some of the liquid and rice slopped out; a camp dog ran behind him and lapped up whatever spilled. Back again, he roughly pushed open a gate in the wire fence. He shouted at the caged workers, and they all huddled away from the floor space over the honey bucket. The soldier said a few words that were indistinct at the distance Zeitvogel was listening from and shoved the bowl in through a slot in the cage wall. It wobbled briefly and came to an abrupt rest. Evidently there was a hole in the bamboo pole floor of the cage, a hole just large enough for the bowl to sit in. The soldier left the enclosure and closed the gate behind himself. He stared at the huddled workers for a long moment, then snapped a word. The laborers rushed forward and crowded around the bowl.

Huu watched them impassively. Zeitvogel turned his head away and made a show of looking for sentries. Hempen watched for a moment, then jerked his eyes away. He grimaced and clutched his stomach, hoping he wouldn't get sick. The caged men and boys had no utensils; they had to eat the gruel with their hands. Their captors made them eat where they fouled. The man with diarrhea continued to dribble through the bars of the cage floor. The eight shouldered and pushed at each other to get to the bowl but didn't hit; each was able to get his share. They ate silently.

As dusk approached the awninged walls of the main hootch were dropped and lamps were lit in it; a few winked on in the smaller troop hootches. An armed soldier settled into the pharmacy, another into the kitchen—protecting the medicine and food stores from pilferage by the troops. Two others, bantering, disappeared down the main trail toward the valley floor. One of the guards watching the cage strung a fishnet hammock between the fence around it and a nearby small tree; he lay in the hammock with one leg dangling out, foot brushing the ground with the motion of his rocking. The other squatted, watching the laborers.

Zeitvogel looked at his watch. He would have liked to stay longer to watch for more sentries, but they had to meet Bell. He tapped Hempen and Huu. "Let's di-di." They edged back into and across the gully, back to the thornbushes. They got there about a minute before the others did.

"What'd you find?" Bell asked Zeitvogel. He didn't

bother going back into the thornbushes. "You tell me yours, I'll tell you what we found at the POW camp. Then we got a problem."

Zeitvogel didn't have much to tell: a guard at the pharmacy next to the command post hootch, one at the kitchen store, two on the trail, two at the cage—maybe one of them sleeping. If there were any others, he had no way of knowing. No one in the camp had said anything Huu heard that would tell them what the camp routine was.

Bell's report wasn't encouraging, either. During the time he, Randall, and Lewis had watched, none of the prisoners jammed in pairs into the three-foot cube cages had moved. The dozen new prisoners, still naked, were tightly packed four to a cage. Some of them were crying. "I don't think any of those men will make a break for it if we let them out of their cages," he concluded. "The new ones are too frightened; the ones who've been there a while seem catatonic. The only guards we saw them post were three in the tower. They turned on some floodlights that seem to be on fixed mounts; they light most of the compound. One light is on a swivel, and they move it around." He looked at his five men, but his eyes seemed unfocused, his mind elsewhere."

"I think we should open cages if we can, anyway," Randall said. "Some of those poor bastards might have more left in them than it seems. Besides, they deserve the chance."

Bell grunted noncommittally.

Then Randall said, "Tell us about the radio, Jay Cee."

"Yeah, the radio," Bell said, his voice flat. Lewis had strung the wire antenna up a tree. Bell intended to just make a quick report, that they were at the objective and had located the target, would act tonight. Then, instead of listening to the acknowledgment of his report and signing off, he stayed on the radio for a long time, listening to a message. Randall watched emotions dance across the sergeant's face while he listened and, in the end, fall. When he finally signed off, he refused to talk about it. "Later," he said, "when we're all together."

Later was now. Time to tell them what he'd heard on the radio.

CHAPTER NINETEEN

Earlier That Day at Camp Apache

Swearin' Swarnes had poked his head out of his radio room and looked around early that afternoon. He spotted Burrison lounging on a beach chair overlooking the open ground south of the hill and headed toward him. He hitched up his trousers as he walked, tipped his bush hat far over his nose, tried to put a bowlegged roll into his gait like a cowboy who had just gotten off his horse, and staggered more like a sailor who'd been at sea too long and didn't have his land legs back. He wasn't concerned that a call might come over his radios while he was away from them. "If it's that fucking important, the goddamn assholes'll call the fuck back" was what he said about it whenever he left his radios unattended for a few minutes.

Burrison wore shorts and a pair of Ho Chi Minh sandals. He lay back as far as he could in his beach chair, exposing as much of his body to the sun as he could—except for his face. His bush hat was tipped far forward, shading his face. He had looked at a calendar and realized he was getting short, would be rotating back to The World soon. Time to get a tan, he told himself. He shaded his face because it was burned so dark by long exposure to the sun that it didn't need any more, but his torso and legs were, he thought, fish-belly white. He was dozing lightly and wasn't really aware of Swarnes's approach until the radioman spoke.

"Fucking company's coming, Scrappy."

Burrison leaned his head away from Swarnes and used one hand to tip the brim of his hat up enough to see him with one eye. He kept the other eye covered and closed. "Any idea who?"

"Goddamn railroad-tracker."

Burrison's mouth curved in the hint of a smile. "Careful how you talk about officers, Swearin' Swarnes," he said. "Most Marines don't wear rank insignia in the field. You never know when you might be talking to one. And some officers take offense if enlisted swine don't speak respectfully."

Swarnes looked at Burrison as though the young lieutenant were talking gibberish. "Not know I'm talking to a goddamn ossifer?" he said, amazed. "Scrappy, ain't you been in the Crotch long enough, you don't fucking know better 'an 'at? Man, it's just fucking like you can walk into a room full of peoples and other shitheads and know just by eye-fucking them right off who's a Marine and who's a dumbass squid and who's a sloppy civilian. You can sure as shit look at a man and know if he's a fucking ossifer or not."

"You sure about that, Swarnes?"

"No screaming shit."

Burrison used his free hand to finger where his right

collar point would have been if he had been wearing a shirt.

Swarnes looked at the gesture for a moment, puzzling over it. Then it clicked. "Ah, Lieutenant Burrison, sir," he said slowly, "Captain Hasford's on his way out here, ETA about one five minutes."

Burrison dropped his hat over his eyes again. "Thank you, Swarnes. That's all."

Swarnes didn't leave immediately but stood shuffling uncertainly from one foot to the other. Then he said, "Scrappy, uh, sir? Would you really of, uh, jumped on my shit about that? Sir?"

"Let's not find out, Swarnes. You're dismissed." The brim of Burrison's hat hid his smile.

"Aye-aye, Scrappy. Sir." Swarnes about-faced and sprinted back to the safety of his radio room, thankful he'd gotten away intact. He sat in front of his radios and talked to them. "That's the fucking trouble with being around a goddamn ossifer all the time," he said. "You might forget some swinging dick wears bars. When he wears any goddamn rank insignia a'tall. You can get your shitty ass in a sling most ricky-fucking-tick, you fucking forget some-goddamn-thing like that." He didn't seem to notice Burrison when the lieutenant came through his radio room on the way to his own quarters to put on a shirt before Hasford arrived.

Nobody told Big Louie Slover a bird was coming. Nobody had to, even though one normally didn't come in at that time of day. Slover was like everybody else in Camp Apache, bored. He was finely tuned to anything he could do out of the ordinary, anything to relieve the tedium. He heard the helicopter before anyone saw it closing rapidly from the horizon. It meant he had something to do. He strolled casually to his squad tent for the orange Ping-Pong paddles and was standing at the white circle, facing into the wind, before the helicopter finished its final orbit of the hill. The pilot aligned himself on Slover's orange paddles, pointed the nose of his grasshopper-shaped UH-34 at the big man's bare torso, and came in fast. The wheels of his bird's landing gear didn't take the weight of the helicopter before he was climbing again. One passenger jumped off at the bottom of the parabolic arc the aircraft described in its descent and climb. He was Captain Hasford.

Hasford ran to where Burrison stood waiting, off to the side of the landing pad. Slover, white dust coating his face and torso, joined them.

"Good afternoon, Skipper." Burrison greeted the captain with the title Marines usually use to indicate their company commander.

"Hello, Scrappy," Hasford said. He was smiling broadly. "Morning, Big Louie." He glanced quickly around. "Where's Jay Cee?"

Burrison blinked and swallowed, "Uh, he's up in the hills." He thought fast. This was something he and Bell hadn't thought about, what he should say if somebody asked for the sergeant—or any of the others who were with him. "He's gone fishing," he said, hoping the words didn't sound as flimsy as they felt.

"Fishing?" Hasford asked slowly. His tone implied he was thinking about that, not quite ready to believe it.

Slover thought as fast as Burrison did. "He just got a CARE package from his uncle," he said. "Had a fly rod in it. He went to try it out."

Hasford looked at the big mortar man, then to the west, disbelief clear on his face. "He went alone into the hills to go fishing?"

"Uh, no-o-o," Burrison said. "Not alone."

Hasford looked at the young officer. "Who went with him?"

"Stilts and Tex."

"Just the three of them?"

"Short Round and Billy Boy, too."

Hasford didn't say anything for a few seconds. Then, "You let your sergeant, all three fire team leaders, and your best night fighter take off into the hills to go fishing?" His voice rose at the end. He waved an arm at the south side of the compound, where there were several frame hammocks and lawn chairs sitting in a group, and headed toward them.

Burrison and Slover followed, exchanging worried glances. The lieutenant tried hard not to blanch. "It's been quiet around here lately," he said, his voice almost cracked. "I thought it would be all right."

"Seemed like a good idea at the time, huh?" Hasford said, the Marine expression meaning "You did something dumb."

"Sir." Burrison stood tall. "We haven't had any enemy contact for more than two months. We've had no indication of any enemy activity in those hills in just as long. I saw no harm in letting a few of my men go away for a couple of days' fishing."

"They're loaded for bear, sir," Slover added.

They had reached the hammocks and chairs. Hasford sat in one before continuing. "What if they run into a bear bigger than they're ready for? What if there's an accident and someone gets injured?"

"They've got a radio. They can get in touch if they need help." Burrison hesitated a second, then sat facing the captain. Slover sat off to one side.

"Are they carrying enough batteries to keep the radio on

all the time? Can you call them whenever you need to?"

"Nossir. They check in morning and night. Otherwise only if something happens."

Hasford stared at the hills. "Any fay epps with them?"

"One."

"Who?"

Burrison started. "How'd you know that?"

"What?"

"Oh. That's the name of the one who went with them, Huu."

Hasford's eyes bored into Burrison. "Somewhere along the line I heard a rumor you had your own chieu hoi," he said, cold-voiced. "Mister Burrison, I hope, I most certainly hope, the hills Sergeant Bell and the others have gone into are not surrounding a certain valley. And I hope what they are fishing for swims in rivers and is not a child."

"They are fishing, using a new fly rod that Jay Cee just got," Burrison said firmly. He knew he couldn't get in it any deeper than he already was.

"He's going to check in this evening?"

"Yessir."

"When he does, tell him to get his ass back here immediately and saddle up. His tour's over. He's going back to The World. Tomorrow."

"Aye-aye, sir." Burrison didn't try to say more than that. His throat suddenly went dry, and he didn't think he could.

Hasford looked around the compound. "That's not all. Do not tell anyone this yet." He looked hard at Slover to include him in the admonition to keep quiet. "You're not the only ones who know how quiet Bun Hou has been lately. G-5 has noticed as well." G-5 was the civil affairs and pacification staff. "At the end of the week Lieutenant Colonel Tornado is going to come out here and decommission Tango Niner. Higher-higher has decided Bun Hou no longer needs Marines. Everyone's going to be reassigned."

The news stunned Burrison and Slover. They stared almost uncomprehendingly at Hasford. The captain waited for them to recover.

"But, but," Burrison sputtered, "how can they do that? We live here; the people of Bun Hou depend on us. What are they going to do when we leave? What if Charlie comes back in as soon as we go?"

Hasford was ready for that question. "How good are your fay epps?"

"They're good."

"Damn good," Slover said.

"There you are. It's quiet here; the Bun Hou fay epps are good, damn good." He nodded at Slover. "If the bad guys decide to come back in here, the people of this village can protect themselves. We only have so many Marines in this war. We need to put them where the bad guy is so they can put a hurting on him; we can't afford to leave Marines in places where the bad guy isn't."

Burrison didn't say anything; there wasn't anything he could say. Hasford was right; whoever higher-higher was was right. Tango Niner had done its job. When a fighting unit did its job, it put itself out of work; that was the nature of the beast. Time to move on.

"Jay Cee's not the only one about to rotate," Hasford said when neither of the others spoke for a moment. "There are a dozen men left in this unit from when it was formed, you for one, Big Louie. All of them, including you, have tours that are up this month. Three or four others—including you, Lieutenant—are due to go home next month.

With that many leaving anyway, it makes a perverted sort of sense to decommission the unit, make a fresh start. Right." He didn't sound like he fully believed the last part of what he had said.

"By your leave, sir," Slover said, and stood up and walked away without waiting for Hasford to say he could leave. He trudged around the perimeter, looking out over the land. He stopped at various places along the way: the command tent, where Kennith Kelley had been killed while Slover and his mortar men were down by the river when Bell was leading the rest of the platoon on a raid on a hidden NVA bunker complex on the other side of the river. The south side of the compound where Steven Lam, Pancho Carrilo, and Terry Graham had been killed; the east side, scene of Gene Neissi's death. Three times Charlie had tried to overrun Camp Apache, and those men had died in its defense. Others were killed on patrols. He looked to the south, the broad expanse of land between the hill and the river. Down there "Mountain Lion" Monteleone had been killed during the day. Somewhere out there Kanaki Lanani, Leroy Robinson, "Beaver" Sulser, and "Junior" Johnson had been wiped out in an ambush. "Malahini" Webster had died just on the other side of the clear ground below the hill, the day before he was supposed to go on R&R. In another place, "Preacher" Langston had met his end. He looked to where they had held the fake firefight to cover "Jesse James" Wells's death. "Izze" Perez had died on the finger ridge coming down from the western hills. Storey, so new that most of the men in Tango Niner hadn't even known his name yet, died west of the hill. He was going to have to visit those places in the next few days, say a final farewell to his old friends.

Wall McEntire joined him during his circuit of the hill.

"How soon, Louie?" McEntire asked. He didn't need to say, "Do we leave?" Leaving was the only reason Slover would be walking around the perimeter that way, stopping at each place a Marine had died defending the hill, looking out at other places where they'd lost good men in the battle to free the village.

Slover shook his head. "You're not supposed to know anything about it."

McEntire saw where Slover had looked beyond the wire and understood what he was looking at. "We've been together a long time, pano," he said. "That's a good idea. Let's go say good-bye together." He had a lump in his throat.

Slover nodded. The lump in his throat was suddenly too big for him to speak at all.

The two corporals ignored the helicopter when it came back down to pick up Hasford. The pilot didn't particularly mind not being directed in. He assumed the wind hadn't changed since he had dropped Hasford off, so he came in from the same direction.

Slover and McEntire glowered at everybody who approached them; they didn't want anybody's company at that time. Except Jay Cee, Stilts, and Tex. And those three weren't there. They shunned everybody until Burrison joined them when the captain was gone.

"He wants to see a fly rod when Jay Cee gets back," Burrison said. "I think he means it."

Slover stood like a half-carved statue of a man too tired to continue. After a long moment he said, "Me and my big fucking mouth."

The problem J.C. Bell had was how to successfully complete the mission and get back to Camp Apache early enough the next day to get packed to leave. Completing the mission was no problem; he knew how to do that. Neither was getting back early enough the next day. All they had to do was scrap the rescue and head out immediately. Accomplishing both was a problem. Burrison hadn't told him about the fly rod or the pending decommissioning of Tango Niner. The lieutenant figured those were *his* problems.

CHAPTER TWENTY

Late That Night

In the darkness Huu fingered the medallion Cai Lin had given him to show her son as proof he had come from her. His fingers traced the design his eyes had studied the day before; one side of the bronze medallion was blank and smooth, and the other was divided into two parts, top and bottom, by an embossed line. Above the line a long, thin dragon snaked sinuously through a pagoda; below it a tiger slinked through a bamboo thicket. The medallion was large, more than two inches in diameter, and the design was easy to trace. Huu carefully replaced it in the small pouch he carried suspended from a thong around his neck so he wouldn't lose it. Unless the boy's mind was shattered from his imprisonment, there was no doubt in Huu's mind he would remember it and believe.

Then it was time to go.

"Synchronize watches," Bell said. "On my mark, twenty-two thirty hours exactly. Ready, one, two, mark."

Four watch stems clicked inaudibly, and their watches were synchronized. Not that the two groups would need split-second timing, but they did have to be close enough that each knew when the other was about to do a certain thing; those two things needed to happen very close to each other. "Let's go and do it." There was a rustle of cloth as Bell extended his hand. Randall couldn't see the hand in the nearly absolute blackness of the night, but he knew where it was and why it was there; he clasped it. Hempen and Lewis banged fingers as they clamped their hands on top of the other two. Zeitvogel nudged Huu to put his hand on the others. The tall man kept his hand until the last; it was big enough to wrap around all five of the others. Bell and Randall pumped once, and the others pumped with them. "Go," the sergeant said. The hands slid away from each other, and the tight knot of men dissolved into two smaller groups that faded away from each other.

Zeitvogel took the point and led Hempen and Huu back to the VC camp's kitchen, the same place they had watched from hours earlier. It was too dark, and the risk of making noise by stumbling over an unknown obstacle was too great. He followed the same route they'd used going from the camp to the thornbushes. Their skin crawled doing it; a basic rule of patrolling was not to use the same route going and coming. If the enemy spotted you or saw sign of your passage, he might set an ambush or put booby traps along your route, hoping you'd return the same way. Zeitvogel reasoned that if the enemy had seen them or sign of their presence, they would have made a full-scale hunt, not set a trap. That made it safe to use the same route. Hempen and Huu agreed with him intellectually. Psychologically, though, following the same route set their nerves on edge, made them cringe; their psyches screamed, constantly expecting their ears to be blasted by explosions, their bodies torn by bullets, rent by shrapnel. It didn't happen, of course.

They took their time getting where they were going. Zeitvogel's watch said 2255 when they reached the spot in the gully next to the kitchen. They eased up and looked through the brush. The kitchen was dark, but a few dim lights were spotted through the camp, silhouetting the kitchen stores guard. He nodded, not staying awake and alert. A small lamp cast a glow around the door of the headquarters building, illuminating the pharmacy guard who stood slackly between the pharmacy and the command hootch. The guard held his rifle by its barrel; the rifle butt leaned against the side of the veranda. A string of very dim lights led from the troop hootch area—showing the way to the head, Zeitvogel thought. A small fire burned in a brazier near the cage the laborers were kept in. One of the guards sat on a stool smoking in front of it.

Orange light reflected off the rifle that lay near the guard's feet. His cigarette hand dipped lower and lower, and his head nodded. He jerked up and looked around furtively, making sure nobody had seen him dozing. A few feet away a dark lump suspended in the night dark showed where the other guard slept in his hammock. One of the camp dogs scuffled its feet in its sleep at the awake guard's side. Zeitvogel wondered where the other dogs were.

They listened. Cicadas chirruped and buzzed in the background. A sleep cough came from the troop hootches. A few night birds called in their hunting flights. A dog barked twice somewhere distant. A lone truck rumbled in the main valley. Otherwise the night was silent.

Abruptly, Hempen slid into the kitchen and padded to the guard. He went so quietly, Zeitvogel didn't know he had moved until he saw the short Marine's shadow loom next to the guard. Zeitvogel saw that he carried his K-bar;

he didn't have his rifle with him. Hempen reached the un-suspecting guard and moved fast. His left hand went to the guard's mouth, clamping it closed; his right shoved the K-Bar up under his ribs, puncturing his heart. Hot blood spurted over Hempen's hand and belly. The dying guard spasmed, and his feet beat a brief tattoo on the ground until Hempen lifted him up so he pounded on air. Then the spasm ended and the guard went limp. The Marine care-fully lowered him to the floor of the kitchen and lay him on his right side so not all of his blood would flow out—it had stopped spurting by then. He didn't want a large pud-dle to flow and maybe catch someone's attention.

Hempen turned back to Zeitvogel and Huu and signaled them forward. The two men slithered over the top of the gully and through the bushes. In seconds they were in the kitchen. Strong cooking aromas surprised them; they hadn't smelled food from their earlier vantage point. A soft snore from nearby froze them, and they tensed for instant movement.

Hempen put his head near theirs. "The cooks," he whis-pered, and pointed out two forms lying on a straw mat in front of the kitchen. Where the women lay they were hid-den from view by the fireplace from where the three men had first watched. One of them was on her back. In the thin star- and moonlight that filtered through the trees the three saw that her form-fitting tunic was open from the bottom, exposing her belly to the air, and closed over her chest, concealing her breasts. Her head, pillowed on what might have been rolled-up clothing, lolled to one side. Her mouth was slightly open, and she snored lightly in her sleep. The other woman lay curled up, back to her. Her pants were twisted around her hips and legs. Her head was cradled on her arms; she didn't snore.

They waited longer, listening. There were no more un-

expected sounds. Zeitvogel looked at his watch; they still
had time. They waited a few more minutes, then the tall
man tapped Huu's shoulder. He nodded at him. Huu nodded back and rose to his feet. The chieu hoi stood still for a
moment, gathering himself for what he was about to do.
He patted his arm to make sure the red armband was in
place, checked that his knife was loose in his sleeve, and
slung his rifle muzzle down over his shoulder. Then he
stepped into the open and padded upright toward the headquarters hootch. Zeitvogel and Hempen watched him. Both
felt for their Vietnamese companion. They knew he had the
most dangerous parts of their operation. Neither of them
could do it for him; he was the only one who could walk up
to an enemy soldier without immediately being seen to be
an enemy.

The night was dark away from the lights, but Huu felt
totally naked walking through the clearing under the trees.
He felt as if he were completely exposed to hundreds of
eyes that were watching him, waiting to see how far he
would go before disintegrating from fear. Then the men to
whom those eyes belonged were going to kill him while he
lay huddled and helpless on the ground. They would shoot
so many bullets into him, his body would come apart into a
thousand times ten thousand parts that would be scattered
so far and wide that not enough of them could be recovered
for a burial. But in the darkness he was a shadow among
shadows in his black pajamas. Even if someone had been
looking, which nobody was, that person would have had to
be looking straight at him to see him. And even then he
might not have spotted his shadow movement. He almost
reached the veranda in front of the HQ before the guard at
its side saw him. Less than ten meters separated them.

The guard blinked, surprised. His surprise at seeing
someone approach him made him slow in challenging Huu.

The distance between the two men was down to five meters before he called out his soft "*Ai do*, who's there?"

"Messenger," Huu called back just as softly. He changed direction straight toward the guard, walking upright and openly, trying not to look like a threat.

"What are you doing here?" the guard demanded. He didn't have any idea he was about to be attacked. His orders were to keep the pharmacy from being being pilfered. No one had told him what to do if someone approached the command building—or that there was danger of enemy soldiers approaching him alone in the night.

"I have a message from Commander Couq for Commander Dong," Huu said, coming closer. Another step and he stopped at less than arm's length in front of the guard. "Is he in this building?"

The guard was suddenly suspicious. He didn't know who Commander Couq was, and his commander's name wasn't Dong. He started to raise his rifle, but it was too late. Huu saw the motion and stepped into the guard, slamming his shoulder into his chest. The knife flashed quickly in the dim light and slashed across the guard's throat. Huu wrapped his arms around him and grabbed his rifle to keep it from falling. He lifted his victim off his feet and held him away from the wall so his flailing feet wouldn't bang against the wall of the porch and make noise. Hot blood gushed from the VC's throat and poured over Huu's chest and shoulders. Some of it splattered onto his face, and he grimaced. It was a full minute before the VC's struggles stopped and his corpse went limp. Huu shifted his grip on the body to make it easier to carry. He hauled it around to the side of the building and lay it in the deepest shadows where the wall came down to meet the ground. He wiped his knife clean on the body's clothes and heaved a deep sigh of relief. He walked, seemingly calm but shaking almost violently, back to where Zeitvogel and Hempen waited for him in the kitchen.

The corporal clamped a hand on Huu's shoulder. No words were spoken, but Huu knew what Zeitvogel meant: You did well; it was a brave thing. The voiceless communication helped, and Huu's trembling eased. Now they had to deal with the guards at the cage. The PF took a deep breath: he had the hard part there, too. He put his hand on Zeitvogel's and squeezed. He was ready. The tall man signaled "let's do it" and handed Huu a piece of meat he had pulled from a large storage jar while the PF was killing the pharmacy guard.

They angled to the left leaving the kitchen, crouched over and moving fast to avoid detection from anyone who might be watching. When they were on a line from the HQ to the caged laborers, Zeitvogel and Hempen cut to their right on a route that would take them to the opposite side of the guards. Huu stood up there and walked openly toward the cage and its awake guard.

The guard on watch continued his struggle to stay awake, unaware of anyone approaching him. His head bobbed, jerked upright, gradually lowered until his chin almost rested on his chest, bobbed, and jerked up. He wasn't aware of Huu until the PF was nearly on top of him. He turned his droop-eyed face to see who his visitor was. It was too late for him to do anything about the only thing he saw—the knife slashing at his throat. The guard tried to jump back, but the knife was too close. The sharp blade sliced through his neck just below the larynx, opening his windpipe to the air; it severed his carotid artery, and blood spurted out. It slashed his jugular vein, and dark blood poured from it into his open throat. He tried to scream through his ruined throat, but the burbling he made only sounded like the noise a drowning man might make underwater. Huu grabbed him by the shoulders and lowered him to the ground. His heels tapped out a rapidly fading tattoo. The sleeping camp dog woke and woofed a soft question. Huu tossed him the piece of meat. The dog caught it and swallowed it in two bites, then lay lolling his tongue at his unexpected benefactor and wagging his tail.

The other guard shifted in his sleep; something told his unconscious to wake up. He never made it back to consciousness. Hempen slapped a hand over his mouth and plunged his K-bar up under his ribs into his heart and twisted hard. He bucked once, violently, convulsed, and went limp.

The three men squatted and looked around quickly, their eyes darting from place to place, never trying to focus anywhere. They saw no movement. Even the shadows cast by the soft glow of the fire were still. No warning sounds came from anywhere. Zeitvogel gave Hempen and Huu a curt nod. The short Marine scuttled to the fence around the laborers' cage and eased the gate open. Huu flitted shadowlike through the gate. He pressed tightly against the bamboo bars of the cage, trying to blend his silhouette with its to reduce the chance of anybody glancing his way being able to see him. He peered at the misshapen lumps crowded together on the cage's floor until he thought he knew which was the boy they had come for.

Cautiously, the PF reached a hand through the bars and shook the shoulder of the boy. The small form stirred and emitted a low moan. "Phao Kha Ai, is that you?" Huu whispered. In answer he got a louder moan, and the boy tried to flinch away from his hand, started trembling with fear. "I am a friend," Huu said. He made his grip firm without tightening it. "I have come to take you home." The trembling under his hand increased. "Your mother and sister are well; they did not die in the fire." The trembling abruptly ceased, and the shoulder he held went rigid.

"You lie," a tiny voice said.

"No, I do not lie." He fumbled in his pocket and withdrew the medallion. "Look at this and you will know." He pushed the medallion into the boy's hand.

Ai let the bronze disk rest loosely in his palm for a long moment, then closed his hands around it. He rubbed his thumb over the highly embossed surface, recognized the feel of it, and squeezed it tightly. A tear welled in the corner of his eye. He held the medallion close to his face and looked at it. Starlight glinted off the high points. He whimpered and went limp; he'd never thought to see it again. He rolled close to the bars and put his face against them. "How?" he whispered.

"Go to the door; do not wake anybody."

Ai gathered his feet and pushed up with his hands until he was crouching below the roof. Gingerly, he stepped over the bodies of his sleeping companions. One man cried out once in his sleep when the boy stepped on his outstretched hand and quieted immediately, his subconscious mind demanding silence so no guard would be attracted to him and beat him.

For the third time that night Huu put his knife to use, but this time it didn't draw blood; instead of fumbling in the dark with the leather fastener, he cut through it. He lifted up on the lattice door before pulling it open so its hinges wouldn't creak. He held his arms out, and the boy climbed into them.

"You are safe now, Ai," he whispered comfortingly. "Be quiet and we will get away from here. These are friends who have come to help me," he said when he felt the boy tense at sight of Zeitvogel and Hempen. "They are American Marines." He stepped through the gate and ran, still carrying the boy, after the two Marines.

Zeitvogel led them past the kitchen on the far side from where the two women still lay sleeping and into the gully. They followed the gully down a ways, then cut to their right and headed toward the trail leading from the valley floor to the POW camp. They kept going when they reached that trail. "Gotta go," Zeitvogel told them. "Time's getting short." The tall man took Ai from Huu; the PF assured the boy he was safe in the arms of the giant and ran with him.

The explosions started at midnight, just as planned.

CHAPTER TWENTY-ONE

Diversionary Tactics

At 2300 hours Zeitvogel led his team in one direction. At the same time Bell took Randall and Lewis the other way. They went slower than the three making the actual rescue, but it wasn't because they wanted to. Their packs were heavier, and they were going uphill. They also had farther to go to get to where they were going and more to do once they got there. That was okay with Bell since they'd be traveling lighter once they finished and didn't have as far to go afterward to the meeting place. In twenty-five minutes they were in the shadows of the brush under the trees behind the POW camp's watchtower.

The three Marines sat still for ten minutes observing the camp. Nothing moved in the lights, and the only guards they saw were two in the tower; one worked the searchlight, sweeping it from side to side, back and forth, and his fellow guard lounged against his machine gun watching where the light swept. They could see a straw mat spread on the openwork floor of the tower. Bell thought the other tower guard they'd seen earlier must be sleeping on it. The rope ladder that had climbed the side of the tower wasn't there anymore. No one else was visible anywhere except the prisoners in their cages. The prisoners were visible as the light moved over them, exposing them huddled in cramped fetal positions. No lights shined in any of the hootches. No noise came from anywhere in the camp; not even a snore broke the night silence. Somewhere in the distance a camp dog barked twice, then yipped at an object thrown to silence it. The guard operating the light said something; the other guard answered with a barking noise and laughed.

Bell looked at Randall and Lewis. Randall was watching the guards in the tower. Lewis wasn't; he was looking up at the tree they were under. Bell looked up also. The tree was spottily illuminated by the backwash from the searchlight. At first glance the bole seemed to go straight up to disappear in the darkness high above, but then projections became visible on it: the short stumps of branches that were cut off. The first branch that hadn't been removed was a few feet above the level of the tower floor, on the side away from the tower. Three feet higher was a branch that angled toward the tower and almost went over it. Bell felt a touch on his arm and looked.

Lewis tapped his own chest and pointed up. He made a swinging motion with his arm; he wanted to climb the tree and take out the guards with his Ninja throwing stars. Bell looked up again. The first branch stump was eight feet up. He held his head close to Lewis's. "Can you make it without noise?" he asked.

"No sweat," Lewis replied.

Bell looked up once more, his eyes tracing a route up the tree. He nodded and made a stirrup with his hands. The wiry Marine eased out of his pack and handed his rifle to Randall. He placed one hand high on the tree trunk and set one foot in Bell's hands. The two silently counted one, two, three—pressure down and then up. On three Bell stood erect and lifted his hands to chest height; Lewis pushed up and, straightening his bent leg, swung his free hand around and grasped the stub. Bell put a hand under each of Lewis's feet and pressed upward. Lewis shimmied his hands up the tree as high as he could reach, grabbed another projection, then pulled one foot up onto the first stub. The rest of the way he was on his own.

Bell crouched back down when Lewis's weight left his hands. Now all he had to do was wait—wait and hope Lewis was absolutely quiet and the guards didn't happen to look at the tree. This was the worst part of the operation. Randall looked at him; he felt the same way. If anything went wrong now, all they could hope to do was outrun their pursuit before it got itself organized. Then, if they were lucky, really lucky, they could all regroup somewhere else and make good their escape to the extraction point.

Lewis made sure his foot was planted firmly, then held tight with one hand and patted upward for the next handhold. When he found it, he gripped it tightly and raised his free foot, groping for the next foothold. It was a few inches too high. He grabbed the higher handhold with both hands and pulled himself up until he could step on the stub. At that point he could reach the lowest uncut branch. He chinned himself on it, then pushed off the tree trunk with one foot and swung the other leg out and up; his heel scraped on the branch going over it. He froze. On the ground Bell and Randall tensed when they heard the noise.

The guard leaning against the machine gun half turned toward the tree and said something about monkeys, then turned back to watch where the spotlight was shining.

Lewis hung there for a few more seconds, dangling under the branch by his arms and one leg. When he was sure the guard wasn't going to look at the tree again, he rolled onto the branch. He straddled it and rocked forward until he was close enough to the trunk to hold on to it and stand up. The light breeze shifting through the tree made enough noise rustling the leaves to cover the small noises he made moving along the branch. The next branch wasn't quite opposite him on the right. He leaned around the tree and snaked around it and onto the other branch. Part of his subconscious mind tried to imagine himself as a caterpillar inching silently along the branch; another part imagined him as a man-eating python. When he stopped, he was close enough to jump from the branch onto the tower floor. He sat up, straddling the branch with his feet hooked together underneath. He was ten feet from the guard working the searchlight, twelve from the machine gunner. There was a guard lying on the straw mat, sleeping. The rope ladder was piled in a corner of the tower.

He withdrew the plastic-wrapped package from inside his shirt and carefully opened it. He took two of the stars out of the oily cloth inner wrappings and very carefully held one of them between his teeth; he kept the other in his left hand while he deftly closed the package with his right and tucked it back inside his shirt. He held a star in each hand and jiggled to test his balance. Only twice before had he thrown the stars in combat; both times he had been kneeling with one knee on the ground, a very stable position. At this range he knew he couldn't miss his targets, but his balance was delicate enough that he was concerned he might overbalance and fall. He shifted his torso—right, left, right, left—to test his balance again, then nodded to himself, certain he could put enough force into his throws to do the job without knocking himself to the ground, more than twenty-five feet below.

He looked at the nearer guard, the light man, focusing all his attention on a small spot on the man's back, a spot just to the right of his spine, a few inches below the shoulder. He slowly coiled to the right and held his arm to the rear. Like a steel spring with the pressure suddenly released, he spun out of his coil and the pointed, circular blade flashed from his hand. On his follow-through the second blade was transferred from his left hand to his right and he twisted back; his eyes sought out and focused on his second target.

The light operator arched his back and sharply sucked air in through his teeth; an instant later the second blade was spinning through the air. The machine gunner started to look at his partner when the fiercest pain he'd ever known hit him in the back. He tried to bend away from the pain, but the human body doesn't bend in that direction, even if he could have gotten away from it. The searchlight clinked and spun wildly as its operator fell; he hit the floor with a dull thud. The machine gunner folded down and fell almost without making a sound.

Lewis scooted forward as soon as he threw the second blade and jumped into the tower. He drew his K-bar while he was in the air and plunged it into the throat of the sleeping guard as soon as he reached the floor. Then he turned to the two men who had been awake to retrieve his throwing stars. He had to roll the first body over to get at the back. Blood flowed copiously from the heart wound, and one point of the blade protruded. Lewis used his K-bar to lever the star out. He had to cut the wound in the other man's back big enough to reach in with his fingers to find the blade so he could pull it out. He wiped all three weapons dry on that body's shirt. It was then too wet and bloody to wipe his hands on; he had to clean them on the shirt of one of the other two bodies in the tower. Last, he turned his attention to the crazy-skewed searchlight and angled it over the cages, not directly shining on any of them but giving some illumination to most. If someone glanced at the scene and didn't look long enough to notice the light wasn't moving, it might look natural. He hoped.

On the ground, Bell and Randall craned their necks back, looking anxiously up. They saw the two rapid-fire flicks of the thrown stars and heard the first guard fall. Then they saw the briefly huge shadow of Lewis vaulting into the tower. Dripping blood plopped on the ground under the tower. They watched the searchlight stop shining into the trees and send its beam out over the cages, then become immobile. They knew what they thought was happening but didn't know for sure until Lewis popped his head over the railing and waved an all clear.

Lewis dropped the ladder and scrambled down it.

"Just like a wet net," he whispered to Bell when he got down, still holding on to the ladder.

Bell nodded. He had climbed rope ladders himself and knew they acted very much like the cargo nets Marines used to climb down the sides of troopships onto amphibious landing boats; the Marines called those cargo nets "wet nets." "Come with me, do the hootches," he said. "Tex, stay behind us, watch our asses."

Lewis took his rifle with one hand and picked up his pack with the other. Randall shrugged out of his pack and handed it to the sergeant. The two trotted low to the guard hootches. Randall waited for them to get fifteen meters away before he followed. He was going to be their eyes and ears while they were too busy setting the demolitions to watch out for themselves.

When they reached the guard hootches, Bell worked

deftly in the dark. He gratefully unslung the heavy coil of det-cord from around his neck and shoulders and lay it gently on the ground. From Randall's pack he withdrew a one-pound block of composition C. Fuses and trip wire came from his own pack. He placed the block of explosive on the ground flush against the hootch near its door and stuck one end of the det-cord into its side. He signaled Lewis to secure the cord in the block and picked up the coil. As rapidly as he could while keeping quiet, he walked around the hootch, reeling out cord as he went. When he got back to Lewis, he cut the cord and stuck its free end into the block of composition C. Then he inserted a fuse into the block, tied the end of a roll of fishing line to its cotter pin, stretched the line across the doorway a few inches above the ground, and tied it at that end. The next time someone walked through the doorway, the block of explosive would go off and so would the det-cord. The hootch would implode and go up in flames instantly.

Bell checked the block again to make sure everything was stable, then tapped Lewis. They picked up their gear and moved on to the next hootch. It got the same treatment with composition C and det-cord. They moved to the third hootch. After booby-trapping all four guard hootches, they went to the rear of the commander's wooden hootch. [Composition C is a plastic explosive; it is malleable and has a consistency similar to that of Plasticine, the oil-based clay young children use.] Bell molded a two-pound block to the corner of the command hootch two feet above floor level and inserted a fuse. He didn't attach the fishing line, not yet. There were two windows in the back of the building, and both had their sashes raised. He stuck a one-pound block alongside each of them, high, near the glass. Another two-pound block went on the other rear corner of the hootch. He stuck an end of the det-cord in that block and strung it back to the nearest window. He then looped the det-cord around the window, using small pieces of composition C to hold it to the frame. He pressed the det-cord into the block of explosive already in place. Then he strung it to the other window and did the same to it. Then back to the block with the fuse. He cut the cord and stuck its end into the block. When the detonator went, the entire back of the building would erupt and the glass from the windows would shatter and spray into it, as effective as any grenade. But the sergeant still didn't attach the fishing line. He put his pack back on and slung the remainder of the coil of det-cord around his shoulder. He and Lewis rejoined Randall.

He didn't say anything. They all knew what the next part of the operation was; Randall and Lewis were just waiting for the order. Bell pointed at the cages, and the three Marines trotted across the open ground to them. This was the dangerous part of what they were doing. They were exposed and could easily be spotted by anybody who happened to look in their direction. But the booby traps on the guard hootches would eliminate the most immediate part of that threat. If anyone sounded an alarm, the guards in the hootches would be killed or injured as soon as they tried to run out of them. The three Marines separated when they reached the cages. Rapidly, they ran from cage to cage. Each had a knife in his hand. They cut through the leather hinges on the cage doors, but they didn't open any of them. If some of the prisoners ran after the hootches were destroyed, the enemy was going to have just that much more to do; the chance of them getting organized enough to find Bell and his people would be reduced.

Some of the prisoners stirred in their sleep. One man opened his eyes and looked directly at Lewis when the wiry Marine was cutting. Lewis raised a finger to his lips and whispered in Vietnamese, "Wait. You will know when it is time to leave." The POW closed his eyes and didn't say anything.

Working as fast as they could while keeping quiet enough not to rouse the guards, it took just over five minutes for the three Marines to cut through the hinges on all the occupied cages. Then Bell led them back to the guard tower. They still had some det-cord and composition C to dispose of.

The sergeant stuck a one-pound block of explosive to each leg of the tower and strung det-cord from block to block; that took care of the remainder of the det-cord and all the explosives except a few pounds he kept in case they needed some to blow a landing zone for the helicopter when Reeves came to get them. He grimaced when he thought of how tight his timing was now; he had to be back in Camp Apache in a few hours to pack and be ready when the bird came to get him. He shook his head at the wonder of it—he was going home. Then he shook his head again to clear it of thoughts that had nothing to do with the mission and stuck a fuse into the block on the leg nearest the woods where they were going and tied a coil of wire to it. He handed the wire to Randall. "You two go into the woods as far as that wire will let you," he ordered. "Wait five minutes and give it a good yank, set this fucker off. I'm going back to arm the command hootch. When I hear the tower go, I'm going to set it off. Then I'm going to yell like hell to let you know where I'm at so we can regroup and get the hell out of here. Questions?"

"That's too dangerous for one man, Jay Cee," Lewis said. "Let me go with you for protection."

"Negative, Billy Boy. One man has a better chance of not getting spotted. Go."

"Let's di-di, Billy Boy," Randall said. He backed away,

feeding the line out. Bell didn't wait to see his order obeyed; he headed toward the command hootch.

Lewis hesitated a moment, then followed Randall, staying off to one side so he wouldn't accidentally hit the line and set off the explosives. The line was two hundred feet long. Randall checked the time when he reached the end of it and settled down to wait the five minutes Bell had told him to wait. He hoped that the line wasn't snagged on anything, that it would pull the pin out of the fuse when he yanked on it. Lewis lay down next to him.

Bell flitted from shadow to shadow, keeping as much out of sight as possible, to the command hootch. He attached the end of another spool of fishing line to the pin on the fuse and started to back away. Of course, nothing ever goes the way you plan it, not when you have to rely on people who you don't have any control over.

CHAPTER TWENTY-TWO

It Seemed Pretty Bad at the Time

He stood in his spider hole and looked through the concealing bushes to the northeast. He saw the same thing he would have seen if he had looked in any other direction: water. Water with isolated trees sprouting from it, and the scattered lines of wind-breaking trees seemed in the mist to drift above it. Water. The world was water. The fall rains had stopped two days earlier in the delta, and the dawn sun beat relentlessly down on the water that overlay the ground, making thick mists. Four months earlier, when he had first dug the waist-deep spider hole, it had stood on a low rise from which it commanded a fine view of the approaches from Saigon, the most likely routes the imperialist puppets would use if they came into this part of the delta. He had painstakingly constructed a strong, well-camouflaged cover for the spider hole. A man could stand on top of the hole when the cover was in place and not know it was there. Now the cover was useless. He stood in the waist-deep hole, and the water was up to his chest.

The depth of the water didn't matter; the only dry ground in nearly a kilometer radius was the roadway dike that angled across his front and came to within 150 meters of his position. The dike was a dimly seen line floating in the mist. If he was in any other position from which he could watch the dike, he would also be in water above his head. If he stood in a hole, as he did here. He held his Chinese Type 56 rocket-propelled grenade launcher balanced between his shoulder and the bipod he had constructed to hold its muzzle out of the water. An 80mm grenade was mounted on the front of the launcher; five more were in a waterproof bag that lay across his shoulders.

His job was to watch for enemy soldiers coming his way. If a small patrol or a single vehicle came along the dike roadway, he was to fire one grenade at them and wait to see what they did next. Probably the survivors would slink away; the puppet troops usually ran away when caught in an ambush. He didn't know himself. He'd never caught any of the puppet troops in an ambush; he had only his commander's words to go on. But the political officer told him the military commander only ever told the truth, so he believed him.

If more than a small patrol came along the roadway, he was to fire as many of his grenades as he needed to to kill them all or make them run away. If it took all of his grenades to kill them or make the survivors run away, he would wait until someone came to resupply him or relieve him. If the enemy came after him after he had fired all of his grenades, he would run away. But not run randomly and not run straight to the rise nearly a kilometer away. The rise that was barely above the water, where the rest of the company waited. Run in a direction that would lead the enemy past that rise. When the enemy was parallel to the rise, the rest of the company would open fire, ambush the enemy, destroy them.

He sometimes wondered about the last plan. There was no cover between there and the rise where the rest of the company was. Nothing to obstruct the enemy's view of him, nothing to stop the enemy's bullets from hitting him. Only the water, nearly a kilometer of water, water sometimes calf deep, sometimes deeper than his head was high. But the commander had assured him that the puppet soldiers were only good at oppressing unarmed people. They could not shoot; it was only by accident they ever hit what they shot at. He had no need for concern for his safety. So he sometimes wondered, but he never worried.

He had been there, standing chest deep in water in this waist-deep hole, since sundown. In another hour his relief would arrive and he could leave, climb into the flat-bottomed sampan and help pole it back to the rise, where he would eat and sleep until nearly sundown, when he would return to the hole for another twelve-hour shift as a sentry. After eleven hours listening and watching, his attention wasn't as sharp as it should have been. His mind wandered, lingered on his home in the central highlands and the girlfriend he hadn't seen in months, along with calculations of how many more days it would be until the water flowed off the plain, then how much longer until the water table lowered enough that the bottom of the hole wouldn't be filled with water. He might not be able to see much movement on the faint line of the dike, anyway, because of the mist, but he was sure to hear any vehicles long before they came into sight.

So he was very surprised to suddenly hear the thunder of many engines spread out along his front, the harsh clanking of armored vehicles rapidly closing on him. His eyes opened wide at the wall of steel rumbling toward him across the water. It was broad and nearly twice his height, and he could see many soldiers piled on top of whatever strange vehicle the wall was the front of. Reflexively, he looked through the sight of his RPG. It was centered on the wall. He squeezed the trigger. The rocket roared and flashed, and the launcher bucked on his shoulder. The grenade hit the wall and exploded with a great gout of smoke. The wall shuddered, and the entire vehicle slewed and stumbled to a halt. Mechanically, his shaking hands reached over his shoulder for another rocket-propelled grenade and fumbled it onto the front of the launcher. He looked for another target and found one immediately. He fired at it, reloaded, found another target, and fired at it. Angry voices shouted all around him, piercing the roar of the armored vehicles, the voices of soldiers now on foot heading for him.

Three amtracs—that's what they were, though he didn't know it at the time—sat still, killed by his first three shots. More were coming straight at him, and more and more angry voices shouted above the roar of the armored amphibians. He reloaded, fired, reloaded, fired, reloaded, fired, reloaded, fired, reloaded, fired, reloaded, fired, reloaded, fired. His sphincters let loose, and he urinated uncontrollably. Still the world around him filled with new amtracs, each one inexorably closing on him. Again he reloaded, fired, reloaded, fired, reloaded.

He stifled a scream and woke from the dream. His chest heaved, sucking in air through his clenched teeth. His wide eyes darted around, taking in the familiar bamboo walls, the dimly seen lumps of his fellows sleeping on their mats, weapons placed in comforting reach of each soldier's hand. Acrid sweat covered his body. Slowly his chest stopped heaving, the muscles of his jaw eased their tension, and his eyes lost their wild look and stopped darting about. Now he felt clearly the pressure of his bladder and sighed sadly. He wondered if this was to be his fate the rest of his life. Every time his sleeping bladder filled so he had to wake to empty it, he had this dream. Or was it every time he had this dream, his bladder lost its ability to wait until morning?

He told himself the dream was not the way it really had been last year. He had seen the infantry column on the road long before it and its two attendant amtracs were within range. He disabled the two amtracs and fired his other grenades at the foot soldiers before running away. He led the puppet soldiers on a chase as his commander had told him to. They didn't hit him despite all the bullets they fired at him, though many sang like angry hornets past his ears and many slapped the water close enough to splash him. And they were caught in an ambush as his commander had said they would be. But they had a radio and called for an air strike on the rise. He was one of very few men of the company to survive the battle.

Because of his shaken nerves he was next assigned as a guard at the prisoner of war camp. He had seen no action since that morning the year before. But still, every time his night-filled bladder needed relief, it used that dream to wake him. He rose to his feet, wondering how it was possible, with all the fluid he lost sweating from that dream, that he still had a large enough reservoir to need to urinate. He stepped the two steps to the doorway and through it. Something thin pulled briefly at his shin, then the entire world turned to flame and sound so bright and loud that it filled eternity.

Sergeant Bell was halfway from the rear of the command hootch to the trees when suddenly one of the booby-trapped guard hootches exploded. He dropped to the ground before the hootch broke into flames. The flash was on the other side of the hootch from him, and, as far from it as he was, the det-cord didn't give off enough light to show him. He froze for a couple of seconds, watching and listening. He heard shouts from men rudely awakened from sleep, dying screams of the men caught in the burning hootch. No one yet sounded like he was shouting orders. He jumped to his feet and ran into the trees. He didn't bother going all the way to the end of his fishing line; he couldn't afford the time it would take to feed it out carefully.

A second hootch exploded when one of its occupants tried to run out. The third went up almost immediately afterward. Bell decided he couldn't wait; he yanked hard on his fishing line. Nothing happened; the line was too loose. The final guard hootch exploded and went up in flames as he reeled the line in. He held the loose end in his hand and estimated that it broke when he dropped.

He thought quickly. The explosives he'd set on the command hootch weren't attached to any trip wires; they'd go only if someone deliberately detonated them. He heard shouting outside the wooden building. He guessed that the commander was up and out, that no one was left in it. On the other hand, there had to be important documents and records in the building, papers that would burn and prevent the VC from getting properly reorganized again immediately. Damn, he thought, I hate to go to all the trouble of setting that up and not having it go off. He dashed back to the clearing.

Many men were clearly visible in the flames, running about the area between the burning hootches and the prisoner cages, shouting in confusion. Bell dropped to all fours where he thought he'd gone to ground before and groped for the fishing line. He couldn't find it. He thought he had to give up. It was too dangerous to get closer; one of the Vietcong was sure to see him. He raised himself to a crouch and started to turn away, frustrated, when another explosion, louder than the earlier ones, went off. He grinned. "Good old Tex, right on time," he said softly to himself.

The shouting from the confused and disorganized VC renewed, and they all looked or ran in the direction of the downed watchtower. Bell changed direction and ran to the corner of the command hootch. He found the end of the line and tied it to the line he still held. He backed quickly away, feeding the line out. Under the trees he stopped, stepped behind a thick trunk, took the line in both hands, and pulled. This time his effort was greeted with a satisfying eruption punctuated by the shattering of glass as the entire back of the building was blown in. He looked around the tree trunk and saw flames start to lick at the wood. One last glance deeper into the clearing showed more movement hardly visible in the darkness at the edge of the fire glow; some of the POWs were taking advantage of their opened cages and the confusion to attempt an escape.

He ran deeper into the forest and started yelling for Randall and Lewis.

CHAPTER TWENTY-THREE

The Getaway

Randall beetled his brow and looked at the luminous hands of his watch when the first explosion rent the night. He looked at Lewis's night shadow; his unseen expression asked "What's that?" The five minutes until he was supposed to blow the guard tower hadn't passed yet. Something was wrong, very wrong. He heard voices shouting in the camp and asked, "What are they saying, Billy Boy?"

Lewis listened for a moment. "They're asking what the fuck's going on," he said.

Then there were two more explosions, and a fourth followed quickly. "Does it sound like they've got Jay Cee?" he asked.

"No."

Then it clicked on Randall what must have happened. "Somebody must have gotten up to take a piss," he said. "Jay Cee's probably waiting for us to do our thing." He took a firm grip on the fishing line and yanked hard. The blast from the guard tower was so loud, it sounded like they were next to it. The light the explosion flashed made shadows dance eerily around them, and the air pressure from the concussion pushed hard against them. Randall jumped to his feet. "Let's go," he said, completely ignoring noise discipline. They ran south, toward where they hoped Bell would be waiting. Another explosion, louder than the others, blasted through the night. "He did it," Randall said with a great feeling of relief. "Let's find him."

Seconds later they heard Bell shouting and angled toward him.

"Jay Cee," Randall shouted back, "here we come." He and Lewis crashed toward Bell's voice, mindless of the branches whacking at them and stinging their flesh, hoping they wouldn't trip over any roots.

They almost collided with the sergeant in the darkness.

"Damn, I'm glad you blew the tower when you did," Bell gasped. "My line broke when the first hootch went off, and I had to go back to reattach it. Your explosion distracted them enough to let me do it without being spotted."

"Shit, Jay Cee, it must be true what they say about Marine sergeants' balls," Randall said.

"You better believe it," Bell said, and chuckled. What they said was that Marine sergeants had balls big enough that they needed to carry them around in a wheelbarrow. "Billy Boy, think you can find where we're supposed to meet Stilts?"

"No shit," Lewis snorted. If he knew where his destination was relative to his starting point, he could always find it, even if he'd never been there before or through any of the terrain in between. "The question is, Can Stilts find where he's supposed to meet us?"

Commanding voices sounded from the POW camp.

Orders were being shouted; the enemy was getting organized.

"Sounds like they just realized some of the prisoners escaped," Lewis said. "They're starting to look for them."

"Sounds like a good time for us to be someplace else," Randall said.

"Let's di-di mau before they get organized enough to put a search party out looking for us," Bell said. "Or one looking for prisoners stumbles into us."

Lewis led them off as fast as he dared. He wasn't concerned about noise. He didn't go faster than he did because he didn't want to trip, get lost, or fall into a hole.

By the time Zeitvogel and his team reached the meeting place—the place where they'd waited that afternoon while Lewis had scouted ahead—the Vietcong in the POW camp were sending out parties to hunt down their missing prisoners. The Marines had no way of knowing it, but there was an undamaged radio in the camp and its commander was talking with other units in the valley. Most of the other units were preparing to defend themselves against the heavy assault they expected to hit any minute; they knew the strike against the POW camp could only have been the first blow in something big. Why else hit so small a target so hard? But some of the units were mobilizing to search for the escapees and for the raiding party that had hit the camp.

The two Marines, the PF, and the boy huddled, waiting for the rest of the team to join them. Whistles shrilled in the valley and on its fringes, voices boomed out through megaphones, and trucks and other motor vehicles rumbled from here to there. A deeper roar cut through the truck rumble.

"What the fuck's that?" Zeitvogel asked about the sound.

Hempen swallowed. "If I didn't know any better, I'd say tanks," he said.

The tall man looked at Hempen's shadow. "What makes you think you know any better?"

"Oh," the short Marine said in a voice that sounded far too small even for a man that short.

"Here they come," Zeitvogel said a moment later.

Hempen listened to the noises of a few men crashing through the brush toward them. "Someone, anyway," he murmured.

The running sounds stopped, and a hushed voice called out, "Stilts!"

"Over here, Jay Cee," the tall Marine said. He breathed a sigh of relief. He hadn't been positive the men they'd heard approaching were the rest of their team.

There was more crashing of underbrush, and the other three Marines emerged from the inkiness of the trees.

"They're sure as shit confused now," Bell said. "You got the boy?"

"You know it," Zeitvogel said, and hefted his small burden.

"Let's go, we've got a plane to catch," Bell said. To Lewis he asked, "Sure you can do it with dead reckoning?"

"No problem, Jay Cee. Just point me in the right direction."

They headed south at a rapid pace. Lewis was confident on the point.

The POW camp was still chaos, despite the commander's shouting incoherent orders at his men; most of the guards were dead or wounded from the explosions and resultant fires in their hootches. It was almost all the one medic

could do to sort the wounded into those who needed immediate treatment and those who could wait and those who
were too close to death to bother about. The commander
had a clerk, who slept in a corner of the command hootch
and therefore wasn't wounded, checking the prisoner cages
to see how many were missing. The clerk came back with
his report: Thirty-seven of eighty-five were gone, the
others were cowering in their cages, and the ties on every
occupied cage were cut. The commander swore and lashed
out in his anger at the bearer of bad news. There were five
guards left uninjured, and one of them was worthless from
the shock he had suffered—he'd miraculously escaped
from his hootch without injury because one of his hootch
mates had been directly between him and the explosion;
that man's flesh and blood were blown all over him. The
medic first thought the blood and gore covering him were
his own and put him with those too wounded to survive.
The commander put the other four guards to work rounding
up the remaining prisoners; he wasn't going to leave them
in unsecured cages.

An infantry sublieutenant leading a platoon reported to
the POW camp commander. The commander ordered him
to have his men search the surrounding area for escapees
who had gone to ground close by. The sublieutenant looked
dubiously at the darkness under the trees surrounding the
camp. He thought it was very unlikely his men would find
anyone even if someone was hiding close to the camp. But
he obeyed the commander anyway.

The explosions instantly woke everybody at the Vietcong
regimental headquarters, including the laborers huddled in
their cage. A few of the laborers sat up to listen to the
shouted questions and orders as the VC in the camp tried to
understand what was happening and what to do about it.

They watched, and their practiced eyes saw the order in the apparently chaotic running of the men of the two VC companies. They talked among themselves, wondering what that was going to mean to them, if anything.

One of the prisoners, the one with diarrhea, lay still and observed, with only the movement of his eyes to tell anybody he was awake. He ignored the fetid wetness of his affliction. He lay on the opposite side of the cage from the guards' fire. The first thing he noticed was that the two men assigned to guard them overnight weren't moving. He focused closer on them and understood they were both dead. His mind was in far better shape than was his body, and he thought quickly. The guards must have been killed by someone coming to rescue one of them. His eyes flickered as he examined the interior of the cage—the boy was missing. His eyes went to the door. It was closed, and he became angry that someone should come to get the boy and leave the rest of them captive. Then he noticed that the leather strap that held the door closed was hanging loose, its cut end showing ragged in the fire glow.

He looked beyond the cage at the soldiers still milling about, getting properly organized. Still no one had noticed the dead guards. He decided to take his chance and rolled onto his hands and knees.

"Be quiet, look like you are on an errand, and follow me," he said softly to the others.

They jerked around and looked at him, wondering what he meant. They didn't have to wonder long as he crawled to the door and pushed it open. The laborers gathered themselves into a line and followed him through the gate in the fence. They walked with their heads down, looking subservient. It wasn't subservience, though. It was fear that kept their heads down, their gaze averted. The ostrich principle: If I can't see you, you can't see me. They followed as much by smell as by sight as the sick man led them north to the nearest edge of the camp. Once under the trees he turned left and headed toward the mountains and Laos. When they were away from the valley, he reasoned, they could find a village whose people might give them assistance in making their way home. Or a village where the people would welcome them and accept them into its society. First, though, they had to put as much distance between themselves and the A Shau Valley as they could.

Gradually the small camps spotted around the valley stood down from their defensive alerts. The senior commanders had guessed correctly that there was not going to be a major assault. They added every possible unit to the search for the raiding party. It was very unlikely the raiders had come from the west, for that way was the Ho Chi Minh Trail and their own forces. They concentrated their search to the east and the south. That was where the raiders must have come from, where they had to be returning, not the north, because they had hit at the southern end of the valley. All small units located within twenty kilometers to the south and ten kilometers to the east of the valley were alerted to join in the search for the raiding party and the escaped prisoners. None of them realized they were looking for a group of only six men and a boy.

There were three platoons of local-force VC between the bottom of the A Shau Valley and the planned extraction point.

CHAPTER TWENTY-FOUR

March 15, 1967

There are events of cosmic significance. They don't happen all that often, and even when they do, they usually don't affect the entire cosmos. Usually their scale is so great that the only people who notice them are the scientists who study events of cosmic significance. That may not sound very cosmic, but they are certainly events of cosmic significance to those they do affect. One happened about dawn on 15 March. A spot on the surface of the sun facing the earth erupted, and a great gout of plasma flared away through the sun's atmosphere. It was big enough and had enough force that massive amounts of atomic particles were thrown free of the sun's gravity and radiated outward, some headed in Earth's direction. It took those particles seven or eight minutes to travel the ninety-three million miles from the sun to the Earth. When they got there, all hell broke loose in the ionosphere. It was night in Minnesota, and the northern lights were visible in the northern

part of that state. And the ionospheric turbulence broke up
radio transmissions on the dayside of the planet and clut-
tered them with static, making messages hard to hear. That
was for over-the-horizon ground communications. Aircraft
radio communications weren't much affected because their
altitude combined with the height of transmission towers
gave them a much farther horizon.

"Say again your last, over," Burrison said into the
handset.

"Zzzft problemzzzzoo-od buddy, over," the broken voice
said back.

"You are breaking up," Burrison repeated. "Say again
your last. And I don't need any damn problems. Over"

"Sorry about that zz-qth got them. Ovezzz."

"Ah, shit. Shit shit shit, I don't want to hear this," Burrison said without depressing the speak lever on the side of
the handset. He pressed down on the lever and said, "What
kind of problems? Over."

"Zzzay again your lazzz. Zzver."

"Shit shit, double shit," Burrison muttered, and repeated his question.

The turbulence cleared up momentarily, and Ensign
Lily's voice came through strongly for a few words before
getting garbled again. "My good buddy the driver can't
make it ozz zhtme. Zzpfz-zztot shot down. Over."

"What? What do you mean, he got shot down? Over,"
Burrison squawked. Then he remembered the speak lever
and had to repeat it. But the ionosphere was acting up
again worse than before.

"Zzzay agzzzn yozz lazzz. Zver," Lily's voice was barely
discernible through the static.

Burrison repeated his question about Reeves being shot
down.

"Zzzht zzhot dowzzq, he'll bzz zzo houzz zzatez." Lily

laughed. Burrison thought he had imagined it. To him it sounded like a cosmic laugh.

The Marine officer hung his head and propped his forehead on his free hand. "Let's try this again when the atmosphere clears up," he said into the handset. "Out." He put the handset down on the counter and rested his head in both hands, ignoring the few fragmentary words that still came at him through the buzzing of the static.

Swarnes sat a few feet away on his cot, staring wide-eyed at the lieutenant. Just from listening to one side of the conversation, he knew Burrison was having a lot of trouble getting through on the radio but not too much trouble to understand that there was a problem. Swarnes's lips moved, not forming words but inarticulately expressing confusion and concern. "Motherfuck a lucky duck," he finally muttered. "We're all up shit creek without a paddle. And no goddamn hip boots, neither."

Dawn broke over the wooded hilltop. Five men and a boy watched Sergeant Bell try to orient himself on the map and shoot an azimuth. He identified a spiky hill to the southwest and two high hills flanking a lower hill to the southeast. He shot azimuths at the spike and the two high hills and triangulated back on the map to pinpoint their position. He signaled Lewis to look over his shoulder and pointed out their position and the landmarks.

"Right here is where the photos show the clearing," Bell said, and tapped the map a grid square over from where they were and a little north of the three hills where the map showed another piece of high ground.

Lewis looked in the direction of the clearing. "Yeah?" he said. All he could see was treetops undulating toward the horizon, broken only by tree-covered hilltops and ridges rising above them. The high ground shown on the map was barely discernible, much less any sign of a clearing. He shrugged. "If it's there, I'll find it."

"Let's chow down quickly and then go. Tex, raise Camp Apache on the horn."

They broke out C-rations and started cutting the cans open. Except for Randall, who was busy with the radio, and Bell, who was watching them and the landscape around them. They all looked haggard, unshaven, with bags forming under their eyes. Except for the boy, none of them had slept in twenty-four hours. They moved slowly, as if their limbs were sheathed in lead. Zeitvogel opened extra C-rations for Ai; Lewis and Hempen opened rations for Bell and Randall.

Randall fiddled with the dials on the radio and spoke frequently into the mouthpiece. Bell watched expressionless as he turned the power off and on a couple of times. Finally the corporal flipped the power off and turned to Bell in disgust. "Too much static. I can't make out a damn thing," he said. "I don't even know if they could hear me." He accepted the C-rations Lewis handed him.

"Well," Bell said slowly, "the deal is, Reeves picks us up at that clearing unless we tell them different. So even if we can't talk to Camp Apache right now, we still go there and get picked up." He started eating. It bothered him, though, that they weren't able to confirm the extraction.

Lewis was the first one through eating. He started to cut open the bottoms of his cans to pack, but Bell stopped him.

"Leave it," Bell said. "We'll be back at Camp Apache two hours from now. If their search patterns come this far south, it'll be a long time yet before anybody from the A Shau gets here."

They finished their meal and left the trash, crammed into three boxes, under a bush. Lewis took the point again.

He figured an hour, hour and a half to the clearing. If it actually was there.

The man leading the VC squad hadn't been a squad leader very long, and he took his duties as a squad leader very seriously. Every now and then one of the five men in his squad complained about the waste of time and energy tramping around the hills looking for the raiding party that had hit the A Shau during the night. When one did voice his feelings, the squad leader cut him off. He reminded his men of the need for silence on patrol. It wouldn't do to make a noise that would alert the enemy to their presence, let the enemy get away or ambush them. And he told them that their leaders were very wise in the ways of the imperialist invaders and their Saigon puppets. The leaders would not have them searching that stretch of hills if it was not possible for their quarry to be there.

That was what he said out loud. Internally he cursed as much as any of his men did. He knew as well as they did that if the raiding party was as big as he'd been told, it would not be able to travel this far from the valley this fast; they were way ahead of it, if it even came this way. And if they did locate the raiding party, he didn't have a radio. The only way he had to report was by sending a runner. By the time a runner reached the company headquarters and more men reached where they had found the raiders, the raiders would be long gone from that location. It was a waste of time and energy, but he kept his grumbling to himself.

And it might have been a total waste of time and energy except that suddenly one of his men said, "Comrade leader," and knelt by the side of a bush on a hilltop.

"What is it?" he asked impatiently, and walked to his soldier's side. What he saw made him drop to his knees and peer closely. "Back off, it might be booby-trapped," he told his man. He waited until the man was what he hoped was a safe distance away, then weaved his hands through the air around the boxes hidden under the bush. He felt no trip wires. What if there is a pressure-release fuse under the boxes? he wondered. He watched the broad line of ants that had first attracted the attention of his man to the bush; the ants gave the appearance of a living rope the way they crawled over, under, and around each other on their way to and from the boxes, carrying small scraps of food on their way from it. The boxes rocked gently from the scampering of the mass of ants. He saw one ant struggling along, two legs holding high a piece of food nearly as big as it was itself, a piece bigger than any of the other ants carried. He held a small twig in this ant's path and lifted it away from the rope—no point in putting his hand where it would get many stings from the red insects. He plucked the piece of food from the ant's grasp and with a flick of his wrist tossed the ant back at its companions. Evidently unperturbed, the ant rejoined its colony of workers, staggered, and jerked its way back to the boxes for another load.

The small piece of tan-colored food was still moist to the touch. The squad leader held it to his nose and sniffed. It did not smell like it was turning, a good sign it had not been there long. He put it on the tip of his tongue and sucked. Its flavor was bland, like overcooked chicken, and it tasted fresh, though flat in flavor. He counted the three boxes and rocked back onto his heels, lost for a moment in thought. Those boxes could not have been there for long, probably less than half an hour. Otherwise the food would have started turning, if the ants hadn't completely cleaned it out by then. Three boxes. He had heard the Americans carried their meals in such boxes, though he'd never seen any himself, and that each box held one meal for one man.

That could not be the entire raiding party, he decided.
Maybe it was part of it—three men, not many more than
that. Maybe it was one of the Marine recon teams he had
heard about, though he didn't think the Recon Marines
would leave their trash behind to be so easily found. He
nodded decisively and stood up. This must be a few of the
raiders; they had broken into small teams to reduce their
chances of discovery in leaving the area. A very sound
tactic used by both the Vietcong and the North Vietnamese, but he hadn't known the Americans ever used it.

He told his men what he had concluded and finished,
"They are near. We will find them and kill them. Look at
the ground, look hard. The Americans are not good at forest movement; they will have left clear trace of their passage. We will find their track and follow until we catch
them."

The Marines' trail wasn't as easy to find as the squad
leader had said it would be, but they did find it and it was
easy enough to follow.

Lewis tried hard not to let the relief he felt show on his
face when he found the clearing. He'd almost gone past it a
little to the north, but some sign had told him to turn, and
he had turned and climbed the north face of the high
ground. The trees surrounding the clearing weren't particularly high; that meant their tops weren't much above the
tops of the trees on the low ground below, which was why
that high ground had been hard for Lewis to see when Bell
had pointed it out to him earlier. It was a good thing the
trees weren't high; the clearing was a rectangle little more
than sixty feet wide and a hundred feet long. A good pilot
could bring a UH-34 Sea Horse or a CH-46 Sea Knight
into it, but he'd have damn little room for error—and none
for maneuver. Lewis looked around and shivered. He was

getting the heebie-jeebies about the place; it was not an easy place to defend. He wanted to be somewhere else.

Bell looked at his watch. "Let's take cover," he said. "The flyboy will be here in less than an hour. Tex, try to raise Camp Apache, let them know we're here."

Randall attached the wire antenna and tossed it over a branch above his head. But the ionosphere was still in shambles, and Randall couldn't get anybody on the radio.

The insects and birds inhabiting the clearing and the forest around it stopped their cries and whispers when the Tango Niner patrol arrived, froze in place, and hid from those interlopers, those possible predators. Except for one hawk, a nesting female that screamed her anger and swooped close—though not too close—and told them to leave, poach on someone else's territory, go away from her nest. When they didn't go away or come closer to her nest, the hawk settled on a branch to warily watch them. After fifteen minutes of the strangers' not doing anything, the birds and insects forgot about them and returned to what they had been doing before they were so rudely interrupted, including the nesting female.

The VC squad leader knew that his squad was making better time than the Americans they were following and that it wouldn't be much longer until they caught up with them. He peered through the trees and brush ahead of them to their right and knew the ground was about to rise in that direction. He also knew there was a small clearing on that high ground, a clearing a helicopter might be able to land on. He decided to stop there for a few minutes to set a booby trap, just in case a helicopter ever used it. He signaled his pointman to angle toward the clearing. When they finished there, they would go back down and pick up the Americans' trail again.

They stopped just outside the clearing, close enough to see across it, deep enough in the trees that they couldn't be seen from it. A hawk screaming and diving at them was the only sound or motion in the clearing. The squad leader didn't think the Americans were there; they wouldn't know about the clearing and were probably headed farther to the southeast anyway. Besides, the hawk wouldn't be screeching and darting at him and his men if it were already pursuing another threat. Still, he decided to make sure. He motioned his point man to lead them in a circle around the clearing.

"Oh, shit, company," Bell said to himself when the hawk screamed and dove off her perch. The other four Marines and Huu had the same reaction. The high ground was silent except for the hawk. The bird of prey was trying to chase something—or someone—to their right, the direction they had come from. Then it darted to another spot farther away and farther away again. Someone was walking around the clearing in a counterclockwise direction. Bell held a hand out to Randall; he wanted the radio handset. He thought he heard a response, a few fragments of badly blurred, static-broken words but nothing he could understand. The hawk was halfway around the clearing.

"Let's di-di," he whispered to Randall.

Randall removed and recoiled the wire antenna. In less than a minute the short column was moving downslope away from the hawk zigzagging her circle around the clearing. Bell's map indicated a rocky spire a couple of hundred meters north. They could wait there until they managed to open communications with Camp Apache or until the helicopter came in range.

* * *

The Vietcong didn't exactly rush around the clearing. They took it at an easy pace; none saw any need to hurry even though they were trying to catch the Americans who were somewhere in the area. Neither did they go particularly slowly. The squad leader took less than three minutes to set his booby trap. He laid a dropped branch over a captured American grenade that was reset with a pressure fuse that would go off if anything added weight to the branch. They were sure the Americans weren't at the clearing. The trail the Americans had been following when they reached the clearing passed the hill on its north side. Then something changed the squad leader's mind.

The squad leader squatted and pondered the meaning of the crushed and bent leaves they had found on the north side of the clearing. Obviously someone had been there very recently as the ground leaves were still wet from the pressure of bodies sitting or lying on them. It looked like five or six men had been there on the north side of the clearing. Had the Americans they were following diverted from their route and come up there for some reason? Was this a different group of Americans? He knew it had to be Americans. His squad was the only friendly unit in the area, and the traces were too deep under the trees. Whoever had left them was hiding. If there were any hill people wandering through the area and they had paused there to rest, they would have settled on the edge of the clearing to rest in the sun. If these were the same Americans they'd been following, why had they come up here? Were they to be picked up here? Had that hawk alerted them? If it was a different group that had joined the others, the group was now too large for his squad to attack, and he should send his runner. He thought for several minutes before making his decision.

He stood. "See where these tracks go," he ordered his point man.

Fifty meters away they found the answers to many of his questions. The tracks showed the Americans had gone up the north side of the hill and then back down, headed farther north. A wrong turn, maybe? The squad leader thought about it more and decided they had gone to the clearing to be picked up by a helicopter and the hawk had warned them away. So what should he do now? Continue to follow them because they were headed toward an alternative extraction point? Go back to the clearing and wait to get the helicopter that might still come there? He raised his head and let his nose and ears absorb all the forest information they could. Nothing in the forest spoke to him of large numbers of strangers or the presence of an ambush. Here, they were beyond the range of American artillery, and if the Americans had fighter aircraft available to them, they would have used them the night before. His squad was six men who had grown up in those woods and knew how to move in them. There were five or six Americans. Everybody knew the Americans did not know their way around forests.

"Follow them," he ordered his point man.

CHAPTER TWENTY-FIVE

Closer and Closer

The jumble of rocks jutted more than fifty feet almost straight up into the air; its sides were jagged from the many generations of seeds that had tried and failed to germinate in its hostile environment. The few that had managed to take root and grow were stunted; they twisted and writhed in the agony of their harsh growth, clinging precariously.

"Go to the top," Bell ordered.

Lewis looked up the rock wall, picking out hand- and footholds along the way. He slung his rifle and started climbing. Several feet up he grabbed a treeling to pull himself up on. The dwarfed conifer's feeble root system tore loose from the thin dirt covering the rocks. Lewis slipped, let go of the falling tree and grasped at a protruding chunk of rock, caught it, and kept from falling. "Shit," he swore when he had his balance. He looked at his hand. Blood flowed from a ragged gash on his palm. He shook the injured hand and sucked at the cut, and a sliver of rock came out into his mouth. He spit it out, wiped his hand on his shirt, and continued climbing, taking hold of things more gingerly this time.

Randall followed closely, carefully watching each place Lewis picked for a hand- or foothold. Huu and Hempen came next, while Bell waited at the foot of the rise with Zeitvogel and the boy. They cinched a cartridge belt around him.

"We'll hand him up," Bell said. He waited until Hempen was ten feet up, then called for the climbers to stop. He climbed up himself until his head was level with Hempen's feet, then reached down to take the boy whom Zeitvogel handed up to him.

Zeitvogel's height and reach were so great that Bell was able to easily reach around and grasp the back of the cartridge belt and, in one continuous motion, hand him up to Hempen. Not everybody had it as easy as Bell did. Randall had to climb a couple of feet higher to hand Ai to Lewis. Lewis looked for a good place to deposit him; he found a rock just big enough for the boy to stand on two and a half feet below a stump that seemed rooted firmly enough to loop the belt over. It was more than halfway to the top. He said a few comforting words in Vietnamese. The boy looked at him sagely and gave no sign of concern about his position. In the past two years he had learned to trust nobody, but some ancient part of his soul told him to trust these men who must be the giants his teacher had told him about; if his teacher hated them, they must be good. Then Lewis continued. He clambered over the lip and quickly scouted the top.

The top was bigger than Lewis had expected from the map. It was rugged with holes but more flat than rounded, an oval about sixty feet by seventy feet. Vegetation grew more thickly on top of the spike than on its sides; scum-covered, malodorous water sat in some of the holes in the rocks. Animal droppings dotted the rocky ground. A few more minutes and everybody was up and hidden. Bell looked at Lewis's hand and wrapped a field dressing around the cut, then he positioned him to watch back the way they'd come from.

The sergeant looked at his watch—less than half an hour until the earliest time the helicopter was due. "Tex, try to get Camp Apache again," he said.

Randall already had the pack board off his back and was stringing the wire antenna. "Getting slow in your old age, Jay Cee," he said. When the antenna was ready, he checked to make sure the radio was set to the right frequency, then turned on the power and spoke into the handset. He listened for a moment, then spoke again. While listening he twisted the volume and gain dials. After three minutes of hearing nothing but bad static, he switched to the helicopter frequency; communications with the bird were going to be line of sight instead of bouncing off the ionosphere. It was probably too early to get the bird, but no harm trying. Nothing.

Lewis burrowed under a bush at the edge of the small plateau formed by the top of the spike. The trees growing on the ground fifty feet below him didn't start branching and leafing until they were half the height of the high ground. He had an almost unobstructed view of the ground and brush below the trees for a hundred feet beyond the foot of the scarp. His experienced grunt's eyes scanned the area quickly and memorized the foliage and breaks in it—if anything changed from someone well camouflaged, he'd see the difference. The fauna was silent, probably from their passage, he knew, possibly because someone else was coming along. He hitched forward slightly and looked down the route they'd climbed, or what he thought was their route up the cliff. It was impossible to tell on the rocks. Then he saw it and swore, a small splotch of red a few inches from a raw spot of dirt where the plant he'd grabbed lost its grip in the thin earth, a sure sign someone had come up that way. Then he examined the ground below. He couldn't spot any broken twigs or squashed leaves or boot prints from this distance, but that didn't mean they hadn't left any in their wake. Maybe whoever was moving around the clearing wasn't following them, hadn't gone all the way around to where they'd waited and found sign of their wait. Maybe, but he wasn't going to bet the farm on it. All he could do was watch and wait.

A movement seen in the corner of his eye caught his attention, and he turned his head to see Zeitvogel slipping into position under another bush; he saw Hempen beyond the tall man. He swept the visible area below once more before looking to his rear. He saw Huu lying along a fallen tree thirty feet away, looking around its end, covering their rear. Midway between Huu and his own position, Randall sat cross-legged, hunched over the radio. Bell knelt near Randall, head held high, looking in all directions. Lewis looked out again. He let all his senses do their own searching, didn't focus on anything, just absorbed. Time passed. His conscious mind noticed that the birds and insects didn't take up their calls again.

Bell checked the time again for what might have been the twentieth time since they had reached the top of the pile of rock. There was a one-hour window for the helicopter to arrive, and they were at the beginning of that window. "Try for the bird again," he told Randall.

Randall checked the frequency and spoke into the handset. No matter what he did with the dials, there was no response. He shook his head.

Bell looked south, into the treetops, and thought. He

looked around the high ground they were on and examined its trees. Maybe they could stay there, he thought, be picked up there. If the bird had a winch, they could. It was a Navy helicopter. It might have the gear for rescues from the sea, though that pulling up of one man at a time would be very time consuming. It would be no problem for the helicopter to land if—he scanned the hilltop again—they cleared out four midsized trees. But blowing the trees with the composition C he had kept for that purpose would make noise, and they were too close to the enemy in the area for him to be willing to make noise, especially with only six men. Maybe he'd be willing to do it if he had a whole platoon of Marines there—he thought a Marine platoon could hold the steep-sided crag long enough to blow down four trees and for the birds to come in and pick them up, if there was a gunship escort to cover the birds. No, he decided, their best bet was to go back to the prearranged LZ.

"Pack it up; we're going back to the clearing," he told Randall. He went to tell the three watching from the edge.

"No can do," Lewis said when told to get ready to climb back down. "We got company down below."

"Where?" Bell looked hard but couldn't see anything.

"I don't know. I haven't seen anybody, but I know they're there. No idea how many or where, but they're there. Probably spotted where I fucked up, pulled out that bush, and cut my hand."

"We'll go down a different side."

"Shit, for all I know there's enough of them that they've got us surrounded."

Bell didn't know what to think. He had absolute faith in Lewis's ability to know if someone was there, but they couldn't stay there. Especially if they were indeed surrounded, the helicopter wouldn't be able to hover long

enough to haul all of them away. He knew about a device
the Army used to extract its long-range reconnaissance patrols from situations like that. Lines that held many men;
hook them on and fly them away until they were someplace
the bird could set down long enough for the dangling men
to get off the line. If they were still in the boonies, the bird
would sit down and the men would climb in for the rest of
the trip to safety. He didn't think the Navy had any of
them.

"Let's go check the other side of the hill," Bell said.
"Maybe we aren't surrounded."

Lewis shrugged but slid back out from under his bush
and went with the sergeant.

The other side of the hill felt totally different, unsullied,
unthreatening. The most immediately noticeable difference
was the noise. Many birds sang and screeched, thousands
of insects buzzed, and two lizards *fukyoo*ed back and forth.

Lewis squatted and looked and listened and smelled.
After a moment he said, "You get everybody, Jay Cee. I'll
find a way down while you do that."

Bell grunted. He was supposed to give the orders
around here, not take them from a lance corporal, but he
trusted Lewis. He was back with the others in two minutes.
Lewis had a way down the back of the hill.

The point man stopped when he saw the wall rising to his
front and waited for the squad leader to come up. He examined the wall while he waited and was glad he had
stopped. When his leader joined him, he silently pointed to
a spot a third of the way up. Raw earth showed dark next
to a small blot that might have been red, but the color
wasn't completely visible in the light that filtered through
the treetops.

The squad leader dropped to a squat and studied the

wall. He was fully concealed from the hilltop by bushes he was behind and looked through without moving any leaves. His eyes shifted from side to side as his gaze traveled up the steep, rocky incline. It was apparent the Americans had gone up that cliff face, but why? He wished he had more experience as a squad leader; a more experienced leader might understand what was happening. It was only a small hill, and they could more easily have walked around it than climbed over it. Well, that was how one gained experience. He did what he knew how. At the top he visually probed every shadow in the brush at the edge. One shadow looked larger than the others, larger relative to the size of the bush that made it. He examined the other shadows to see how they were patterned, then focused on the larger shadow for a long moment. The others were black-dappled with white and yellow and pale green; the larger shadow wasn't; it was black and green instead. His patient watching was rewarded in a little while when the larger, odd shadow grew a twin, almost next to the bush instead of under it, another black and green shadow without any of the white and yellow dappling the other bush shadows had.

So, the Americans had gone to ground on top of the rock spire. They must have discovered they were being followed. It was probably the hawk that had screamed and darted at them when they had gone around the clearing that had given them away. How many Americans were there? Was it really the five or six he thought from seeing their waiting place near the clearing, or was it more? Had they met more Americans here? What were they doing on top of the spike? Were they waiting for his squad to walk into an ambush? They might wait a long time in their ambush for him and his men to appear. Or they might wait to see a tail, to learn how many were following them, then leave from

the other side. Whatever way it was, now that the enemy
held the high ground, his one squad was no longer enough
to deal with them.

He sent his runner to get help. Now, if only the Americans will stay there for another hour, he thought. In the
meantime he needed to post his remaining four men as
sentries in case the Americans decided to leave the top by
one of the other sides. He backed away from his vantage
point. Quickly, he gave his orders. He drew an oval repre-
senting the small hill on a bare patch of ground. He
showed his men where they were on his crude map and
where they were to go and watch. He finished with instructions on how to signal if they saw the Americans
coming down. Then he returned to his post, and his blood
raced at what he saw: The shadows that didn't belong were
gone.

It took longer to climb down the back face of the hill than
it had taken to climb up the front. It wasn't because the
back was more difficult or treacherous than the front; it
was simply the way those things normally went. Climbing
up, your face goes first, you get to see every hand- and
foothold before you need it. Going down, you have to
search for them; you do a lot of blind groping. Lewis was
first man down. He slipped into some bushes as a sentry.
Zeitvogel came second. Hempen handed the boy down to
Randall when he was the last one left on top, and the four
men on the cliff made a sort of ladder among themselves to
get him safely down in stages. Hempen was still on the
wall when something told Lewis they weren't alone anymore. He bunched his hands in front of his face and
twisted. When they came away, the left end of his mustache jutted aggressively up and forward and the right end
corkscrewed to the front.

The wiry lance corporal caught Bell's eye and flashed a signal at him. Then he disappeared deeper into the trees and circled around to his left. He carried his rifle ready in both hands as he moved, its muzzle pointed constantly where his eyes looked. He wished he could get his throwing stars out, but it took both hands to unwrap them, and he couldn't take the risk of slinging his rifle and being effectively unarmed long enough to do it. Silently, he slipped between slender breaks in the undergrowth and found spaces between leaves and branches where he could go without making noise. A bird trilled oddly, catching his attention. He took a step in its direction and almost stepped on it.

Except it wasn't a bird. Squatting in the brush in front of him was a Vietcong soldier making a birdcall. The man stopped to take a deep breath, and the Marine twisted his body around to the left, then uncoiled, directing the full force of his kinetic energy into his rifle and slamming its butt against the VC's head. The skull shattered with a wet crunch, and the body thudded to the ground. Lewis dropped to one knee and held his rifle ready to fire. He looked and listened in all directions but didn't see or hear anything.

He took a couple of seconds to wipe the butt plate of his rifle on the corpse's shirt, then, one-handed, he frisked the body. The shirt pocket gave up two documents. Lewis glanced at them. One was a diary entry that told of the man's local-force platoon searching for American raiders who had hit the A Shau; the other was a list of names with no explanation. There was no pack. The man had carried an SKS carbine. Working quickly, Lewis field-stripped it and pocketed the bolt. A bandolier carried five ten-round stripper clips for the rifle. Lewis draped it over his shoulder. He briefly shook his head. The VC was more heavily armed with those sixty rounds than most local-force VC were; he contrasted that with his own load of a 120 rounds. By American standards, he himself was very lightly armed. He left the body where it lay and rejoined the others.

"I found a sentry," he reported to Bell. "He was signaling the others with a birdcall."

"Shit. You didn't see any more?"

"That's a negative."

Bell thought for a split second. "Let's go around to the right," he said. Lewis nodded and led off.

The squad leader watched the cliff top for several tense minutes. He and his four men surrounded the spike at five points, like a pentagon. If the Americans were coming down, one of them would see them. If the Americans were too fast, they would be down and away before everyone was in position. If. It wracked his nerves. Then he heard it, a birdcall from his man on the far left corner. He sounded a call of his own as he started off in that direction. The near man on his right should follow him if his men understood the various calls he had told them, different calls that meant different things. He ran, not hard but fast, to the man nearest him on the left. At that point he wasn't much concerned about noise. He knew the sound of his running probably wouldn't carry around the hill in this forest. Once he joined that man, they would proceed more slowly, more concerned with quiet. He hoped the near man on the right would join them quickly. It was a good plan, even if he didn't have enough experience to fully trust himself.

The man on the left was ready and waiting for him. The young soldier looked jittery; his eyes were wide and didn't seem quite in focus, and his hands had a slight tremor. A crashing behind him told the squad leader his other man was on his way. He waited for a moment, then there were three of them there, ready to advance. Into what? He murmured a few words, and the three padded as fast as they could without making noise. They reached a place where they could see part of the back of the hill; the far left man had to be somewhere near. No one was visible, not the soldier, not the Americans. The squad leader gestured, and they went forward until they could see the entire back side of the hill. Still, they saw no one. The squad leader called out softly, telling the hidden watcher to show himself to them. Nothing. He got scared but tried to hide it. He looked around and picked out a place from which he thought he could see the entire quadrant of the hill and went to it. His two men followed him. His stomach twisted at what he found in that place. It was the first time he'd seen a man dead from a battle wound. An explosive gurgling and gastric odor behind him told of someone throwing up. He didn't bother to look. He knew which of his men it had to be. He knelt. The body had none of the documents the man had been keeping. The rifle was stripped; he found all the parts except the bolt. The ammunition was missing as well. The Americans were much better than he had been led to believe. He stood and looked around, memorizing the location so he could later lead others to the corpse so the man would receive proper burial.

He stiffened at the sound of another bird cry. He turned his head to localize it. It had come from the northeast corner of the hill.

"Let's go," he said, and headed toward the bird cry. None of the fear he felt of the Americans showed in his voice or movements.

CHAPTER TWENTY-SIX

Tighter and Tighter

Events of cosmic significance never last very long. The sun flare that kicked out the charged particles that played hob with the ionosphere and messed up the radio signals that had to bounce off it wasn't a terribly big one. The sun's surface settled down, and the particles flying off it got caught by its gravity and pulled back into it instead of escaping. The brilliant display of northern lights that was visible in northern Minnesota early that night dimmed and faded away by the time the farmers put their chickens to sleep and headed for their mountains of quilts and covers themselves. The ionosphere calmed and soothed itself, and radio waves started bouncing off it in a predictable and usable manner again.

When he heard the radios were working properly again, Lily got back on the horn to Burrison.

"What's this about your buddy got shot down?" Burrison almost screamed into the handset. "I've got people out there. What am I supposed to do for them? Over."

"Whoa, good buddy," Lily said. "He's not down, he's helping retrieve someone else who went down. He's just going to be a little bit late getting where he's going, that's all. Over."

"He's supposed to be there now. I've got people in a bad spot wondering where their bus is. How long is a little bit? Over."

"Couple of hours. This morning, anyway. Over."

"You're sure of that? Over."

"Positive. Over."

"You damn well better be. Out." Burrison turned to Swarnes. "Try to get Jay Cee. They should be at the extraction point by now. They'll have their radio on and be listening for word Reeves is on his way."

Swarnes took over his radios again. After a moment he started working his jaw and squinted at the dials. Yes, it was the right frequency. He sweet-talked to his radio as though that would bring in the team. He wondered why they weren't answering his call.

The rescue team wasn't answering his call because they were in the forest between the spike and the designated pickup landing zone and the radio was off. The radio was off not so much to preserve the batteries—they weren't going to be needed much longer—as because the radio waves might not be able to penetrate the dense foliage overhead, not using the whip antenna, anyway. Mostly the radio was off because if it were on, there would be some slight noise constantly coming out of the ear piece of the handset. They had to cut out all noise to make it harder for the bad guys in the area to locate them.

Lewis stopped halfway back to the LZ and turned to Bell. "You sure you want us to go back there?" he asked.

"I'm sure, Billy Boy," Bell answered. "If there are bad guys waiting there, they don't really expect us to come back. If Reeves is on his way, that's where he's going. We need to go there so we can try the radio again. If we don't find bad guys, everything's cool. If we do, we have to try to contact somebody, let them know we're going to the alternate."

Lewis looked at Bell for a short moment. He knew the sergeant was right; there were many compelling reasons to go back to the hill with the clearing. There was also one damn good reason not to. "You're the honcho," he said.

"You better believe it," Bell said. He was talking to Lewis's back since the point man had started off again without waiting for an answer.

They moved at a steady pace, following a game track so narrow that most men wouldn't have seen it. Lewis knew that if there were enough bad guys in the area, they might have an ambush on the game track. Maybe, if they found it, if they had enough people, if they thought there was a chance the men they were following might double back the way they had. That was enough ifs; he decided it was worth the risk. Especially since using the track allowed them to move more quickly and more quietly and left less trace of their passage. And he was confident his sixth sense would warn him in time if they were walking into an ambush. At least he hoped it would.

They were safer than they realized; the only nearby bad guys were four men trying to pick up their trail where they had come down from the spike. They reached the clearing without incident.

"Set up the radio, Tex," Bell ordered as soon as they saw the clearing.

Randall was already dropping the pack board to get to

the radio. He attached the antenna and strung it before turning on the power.

Bell took the handset and spoke into it. He heaved a sigh of relief when Swarnes answered immediately. Quickly, Bell described the situation. He had to do it again because Swarnes held down his speak lever and tried to talk at the same time. [That's the way military radios are; you can talk or listen but not both at the same time—depressing the speak lever turns it into a transmitter and disables it as a receiver until the lever is released, at which time it turns back into a receiver and won't function as a transmitter, just like a CB radio. That's why radio operators always say "over" when they're through talking. "Over" means it's your turn to talk while I listen.]

There was a pause after Bell told Swarnes the situation before Tango Niner's radioman came back on and told him to wait one while he got Burrison. The second pause didn't last as long as the first one. Bell didn't have to repeat his situation to Burrison, since Swarnes had already passed it on. Burrison told Bell about Reeves being delayed, and the sergeant sagged. "Roger," Bell answered at the end of it. "We are proceeding to the alternate and expect to get to it by—" He looked at his watch. "—Ten thirty hours. Over." He listened to Burrison sign off, then gave the handset back to Randall. He gathered his men around and told them:

"We've got a problem with transportation." Before anybody had time to get too upset about the news and think he was abandoned, he added, "It's being delayed until later this morning. Let's get our young asses to the alternate LZ." He didn't say out loud the rest of what he was thinking: It's too damn dangerous to stay here, and let's hope the bad guys don't manage to follow us there.

* * *

It took the VC several minutes to pick up the slight traces left by the Americans when they moved away. They lost it in far less time than it had taken to find in the first place, and they lost more time before the squad leader figured out the Americans must have followed the game track their path intercepted when it disappeared—part of that time was spent in finding the small track. At the foot of the hill with the clearing, the point man found traces that indicated someone had left the game track. A few growing leaves showed their pale undersides; closer inspection exposed a boot print in the moist earth underneath. The squad leader looked at the traces and where they led; he was puzzled. One thing the trainers emphasized was never to go back on the same route you went out on; another was never to go back to a place you had already rested in—unless absolutely necessary. Why would the Americans go back to the hill with the clearing? Then it dawned on him that this must be the place their helicopter was to come and pick them up. He became very excited. He had recognized the clearing earlier as a possible helicopter landing zone; now he knew he had been right. Never before had he seen a helicopter. Now he had a chance to shoot one down. He deployed his men on a line to advance up the hill. They went slowly, expecting to find the Americans.

Instead, they found where the Americans had stopped and then gone off in a different direction, east and a little to the north. The squad leader was puzzled again. That kind of back and forth movement by men who he was certain knew they were being followed didn't make any sense to him. He assigned one of his men to go back to the spike and wait for the others to come; that was where his runner would lead them. "Tell the commander what I think about the importance of this clearing. The Americans might come back here again. We will leave a clear trail for you to follow," he concluded his instructions.

The assigned man trotted back into the brush on the hillside, back to the rocky spike. He made no attempt to hide his trail or keep quiet. The squad leader looked at his remaining men. When they had first found sign of the Americans, they had been six and he thought they were strong enough to take on and kill the foreign devils. He had sent one man as a runner, one was dead, and now one more was staying behind as a guide. Only three men were left in his squad. He licked his suddenly dry lips and sucked on his suddenly dry mouth in an attempt to moisten it. Before he had thought he outnumbered the enemy; now he knew they outnumbered him.

"Let's go," he told his remaining two men. "Carefully." Had he been more experienced, he might have waited for reinforcements.

His men didn't say anything back. Their mouths were as dry as the squad leader's.

It was a difficult situation for the three. They had to follow quickly enough to catch up to the Americans, but they didn't know how far behind they were. And they had to avoid getting too close; they could not survive a fight with the superior numbers of the enemy. They followed, not as fast as they had earlier but faster than they had gone before they had found the first sign. It was more than half an hour after the squad leader had sent the runner.

"What do you think, Jay Cee?" Lewis asked. "Looks like it goes our way for a while."

Bell looked at the narrow, gurgling stream. It was clear and shallow, and the large pebbles and small rocks littering its bottom were easily visible. A few meters to the left, upstream, the stream bent to the north. It wandered off more than a hundred meters to their right, a little south of east, until it turned back to the left. He looked to the right and thought for a moment. "Good idea," he said at last. "We follow it as long as we can. That way there's nothing to show where we went unless they search far enough downstream to see where we leave it."

Randall joined them. He looked up- and downstream and at the opposite bank. "False trail," he said.

"What?"

"We leave a false trail," Randall explained. "Someone cross over it and go into the brush. There's got to be a game trail close to the water on the other side. Go to it, then walk backward to here. If they're still following us, they see where we left on the other side, follow the tracks to the game trail, then try to figure out what way we went from there. In the meantime, we're putting distance between us and them."

"They won't believe two sets of tracks left by one size boot. You and Billy Boy do it. That'll look better."

Randall shucked off the pack board with the heavy radio and handed it to Bell. "Be back in a skosh bit," he said. "Come on, Billy Boy, let's do this thing." He stepped into the water and slogged across with Lewis close behind. The stream was only midcalf deep in its middle.

They weren't too careful when they left the stream, since they wanted to leave some sign. When they broke through the brush on the opposite bank, they broke two or three large twigs, making their crossing even more visible to any followers. They crashed through the brush, making sure there were bent, broken, smashed bits of flora left in their path. Three meters deep they found what Randall had been sure would be there, a game trail. It was narrow, as though someone had taken a scalpel and sliced a thin line through the forest. Air showed through the foliage to both sides of them along the track and high above until the trees branched across it. The ground of the track was beaten hard and was more than two inches below the level of the ground on its sides. Tiny hoof and paw prints scarred the trail, showing recent and frequent use.

"Let's confuse the issue," Randall said. "Both of us walk a few feet in each direction, leave tracks. Then we'll bust into the other side." He chuckled. "The little fuckers will waste half an hour here trying to figure out what way we went."

Lewis laughed also. "And all the time we went someplace else."

They made tracks in both directions for ten meters and roughly stepped into the brush at each end of their false trails. On the left side, Lewis leaned farther into the brush and tied a short length of fishing line to the stem of a bush. He straightened the ring pin on a grenade, set the grenade behind a forked stem, loosened the pin, and tied the other end of the line to the ring. They walked backward to their starting point so all boot prints went away. Then they walked backward to the stream.

"That's going to fuck Charlie up something fierce," Lewis announced, grinning. He told Bell about his booby trap.

"Good," the sergeant said. "Now let's get the fuck out of here before someone comes along and doesn't need a trail to see where we are." He handed the radio pack back to Randall.

They were breathing a lot easier by the time they reached the alternate LZ.

* * *

The three VC reached the stream.

"Look, they crossed there," one of them said excitedly.

The squad leader grunted. He saw the place on the other bank where men had come out of the water. That was a problem; he saw it too clearly. He looked downstream and saw how the stream went for a distance tangential to the general direction the Americans had followed. Then he looked again at the other bank and wondered why the Americans had not tried to conceal where they'd crossed. He wanted to follow the stream, but he had to check out the marks on the other side. He nodded, and his two men splashed across. He followed more slowly, wondering if they were walking into an ambush.

A few meters away from the water he found his two men standing confused. He looked down at what they saw and felt a sinking in his stomach. It had to be some sort of trap. Had the Americans set an ambush to kill them while they stood there? But nothing happened and nothing seemed out of the ordinary. Except for the confusion of the boot prints. His men looked at him for instructions. The squad leader told them to go, one in each direction, to see where the tracks went. Each man went ten meters, stopped, and called back excited. The Americans were getting careless, the men said. They must have been frightened to leave such clear indication of where they had left the game trail.

The squad leader started to call his men back; the smell of a trap was too strong. But it was too late. The man on the left pushed through the brush to see if the Americans' trail stayed as clear as it was where it broke through. An explosion shattered the forest calm. And then there were two.

The squad leader trembled as he squatted over the torn

remains of his man, the same one who had thrown up when he saw his first battle fatality. One leg of the corpse was mangled and almost missing below the knee. The other was almost unharmed; it had been shielded by the hurt one. His lower body was pitted and pocked, and blood flowed sluggishly from the pocks and pits. A jagged piece of metal had torn into the dead man's throat and broken through the bottom of his skull to his brain. At least he had died instantly.

The squad leader stood and looked into the forest. All he saw out of place beyond the corpse was leaves ripped by the grenade, bark scarred by its shrapnel. He looked at the other place the Americans had broken through the brush on the side of the trail and saw it was also a blind marker designed to fool a follower.

Anger started to course through the squad leader. The Americans were nibbling at him, killing his men one at a time. Well, they had to be taught they couldn't do that. They must not be allowed to succeed—they must die, and he must kill them. Or die himself in the attempt.

"They went down the stream," he said to his last man. "We will follow them. They will not expect us now."

The last man quaked with fear of the Americans, but he followed his squad leader back to the stream and down it. He was more frightened of the look in his squad leader's eyes than he was of the Americans.

The men of Tango Niner were very careful to hide their trail when they got close to the alternate LZ. Bell didn't know how long they'd have to wait for the helicopter and didn't want to be followed in. They hid as well as all their accumulated and considerable skill allowed. Randall set up the radio and contacted Camp Apache. The situation was

as before; their transportation was delayed, nobody knew
for how long, stand tight.

They stood tight at this alternate, hidden in a bamboo
thicket that stood next to a hunk of granite that was barren,
swept clean by centuries of wind and storm. Insects sang
there, but there didn't seem to be any birds.

CHAPTER TWENTY-SEVEN

Real Close, Real Personal

The Vietcong reaction force stopped at the side of the stream. The commander looked back and forth between the clear markings the squad leader had left leading downstream and the equally clear marks of men leaving the stream on its other side. Then he sent his best tracker across to see what the other markings might mean. The tracker was back in two minutes. He reported the body in the brush, what the tracks looked like to him—half the boot prints between the water and the trees were walked backward; he could tell by the differing depth of toe and heel—the tire-tread footprints coming back to the stream. The commander barked an order, and his platoon set off downstream. They caught up with the squad leader and the last man he had with him where they had lost the Americans' trail. The two men were moving in widening circles trying to pick up the trail again.

The commander quickly analyzed the situation and returned the runner and the guide to the squad leader. He knew the squad leader was not at fault in losing his men. Those few untested soldiers were up against exceptional soldiers; it was a wonder the squad had tracked them as well as it had. He must remember to commend the new squad leader who had done so well. Who are the enemy soldiers? the commander wondered. Are they the U.S. Army's legendary Special Forces? Yes, the Special Forces were in the highlands, but they operated out of camps with their own irregular troops, whom they trained themselves. And the last SF camp in the area was the one in the A Shau Valley that a year earlier had taken an entire regiment to destroy, so it wasn't them. Were they U.S. Marine Recon, whom some people considered to be the best in the world? That didn't seem likely, either, not if they were some of the men who had participated in the previous night's raid. That was not the kind of operation Marine Recon made. It didn't matter. Whoever they were, they were good. Very good. He looked at his platoon. His men were good, too. And they greatly outnumbered the Americans, whoever they were.

The commander set all of his men to finding the trail of the Americans. Time was passing; surely, the Americans were on their way to an extraction point. He needed to find them and kill them. If one could be taken prisoner, so much the better. Then maybe they would learn why that raid had been made, what the Americans had hoped to accomplish. The Americans didn't think the way the Peoples Army did; to them simply to prove they could hit a sanctuary was not a good enough reason to do it.

It wasn't long before the commander realized the Americans were good enough at forest movement that his men couldn't pick up their trail when the Americans wanted to disguise it. Some of his men might have been good enough to find the signs, but too many others were tramping around looking. Any signs to be found by those good enough to find them were probably being obliterated by those who weren't. He thought about the area and consulted his map while his men continued their fruitless search—but let them keep it up anyway; it gave them something to do while he thought.

When he had decided, he called his platoon together and gave the men their new instructions: Break up into three-man teams, each with a different destination. Look for the Americans or for sign of them. If you do not find them or sign of them, return here immediately. If you do find them or their sign, two men stay to watch, the other returns immediately to report.

Eight three-man teams radiated from the place where the Americans' trail was lost. The squad leader and two of his men—the frightened one and the runner—were assigned a destination where there was a granite outcropping.

Randall curled, half-reclined against a thick bamboo tree. The radio handset was hooked onto the chin strap of his bush hat where he could hear anything coming over the airwaves while leaving both hands free. The volume was turned down as far as was possible to still let him hear transmissions, though he'd have to turn the volume back up to make out what was being said. Hempen lay prone near him, watching over the bare rock. The other three Marines lay pointing at the other compass directions. Huu was in the middle next to Randall. He sat cradling the boy in his arms. The four men watching lay with their legs forming a fence around Randall, Huu, and the boy.

"Oh, shit, company," Hempen suddenly whispered.

The tension that had melted during the forty-five minutes they'd lain there came back; the short hairs on the backs of their necks raised.

Hempen felt one of the others shift position and lie next to him. It was Sergeant Bell. "What'cha got, Short Round?"

Hempen pointed his rifle and lay his left fingers vertically against its stock. He squinted at the fingers and past them and shifted his rifle again. "See the tree that looks like it can't figure out what way's up?"

Bell looked in the direction Hempen's rifle was pointing. He picked out a pine tree that started off growing close to the ground, then climbed a couple of feet and turned back almost parallel to the ground, but in the opposite direction. "Got it," he said.

"Go about six fingers to the left; there's a break in the trees; just looks black because you're seeing into them."

Bell put his fingers up, sighted along them, shifted them to the left, and sighted again. "Right where you said it was."

"I saw somebody in there."

"You're sure?"

"Jay Cee, no fucking way I'd make that up."

Bell let his eyes go unfocused and put all his concentration into listening to the forest sounds. He didn't detect any difference in the buzz level of the insects. Probably, he thought, insects on this side won't stop because of strange movement on the other side, and maybe we can't hear the ones over there, anyway. "Billy Boy, watch my side," he said. "Everybody, look alive. Someone's in the area."

Lewis shifted his position so he could cover Bell's section of the perimeter as well as his own. Everybody watched and listened more intently.

The squad leader stepped back the instant he realized he had stepped into a natural tunnel through the brush from the outcropping. He knew that if someone was in a position on the other side where he could see into the tunnel, he could be seen in it. He squatted at the edge of the tunnel and looked deeper into it. It was only a few meters long. He looked at his men and led them around the bush at the end of the tunnel, then back closer to the bare rock. The path his route described was a rough circle five meters deep in the trees and bushes surrounding the open rock. He rationalized that if the Americans were there waiting for their helicopter, they would be close to the clearing, surely not more than five meters from the open. He hoped they were there. And not able to spot him before he discovered them. There were no birds around, no diving, screaming hawk to give him away.

They completed their circle of the granite slab without seeing anyone or any sign of people having passed through. The squad leader was frustrated; he desperately wanted to find the Americans, and the rock did seem a likely place—if they were indeed going to a place to be picked up. Had they gone back to the clearing where they had first waited? That didn't seem likely.

"We will go around again, ten meters deep this time," he told his men. Maybe the Americans weren't close enough to see the bare rock; maybe they were hidden deeper in the forest.

They weren't, of course. They were closer than five meters, and the VC's second circuit didn't find them, either. The squad leader wasn't ready to concede, though. He thought about the problem. He was certain they had seen into every place where a man could hide. Except that bamboo thicket. But it was too thick for men to enter and hide in, wasn't it?

The men of Tango Niner lay motionless, not even daring to breathe, the first time the three Vietcong came past. Randall turned the radio off to kill the small noise it made. The six of them could easily take the three VC, but by that point they thought that the jungle must be teeming with the enemy and that firing their rifles would bring too much down on them.

A few minutes after the VC disappeared Bell told Randall to try to contact the helicopter; maybe it was finally on its way.

"Earth Base Alpha, this is Flyboy," came the static-filled, faint voice in reply. "We will be at your number two in two zero. Do you copy? Over."

"Roger, Flyboy. You will be at our number two in two zero," Randall replied, louder than he intended to. He was too relieved at the word their pickup was finally on its way to be as quiet as he meant to be.

They all let out more air than they'd realized they'd been holding in their lungs when Randall passed the word. Then their hearts sank when the VC came by the second time. Until they realized the soldiers were deeper in the woods than they had been the first time. That meant the VC weren't searching the place they knew the Americans were in; they were simply methodically searching everywhere. As long as they kept going, everything was fine.

They weren't okay, though.

After they completed their second circuit of the granite outcropping, the squad leader led his men back to a place from which they could examine the bamboo thicket without getting too close to it, without, he hoped, being seen by anyone hiding inside it. They squatted behind the concealment of bushes and observed the thicket from one side for several minutes, then moved and looked at it from the side away from the granite, then moved again and examined it from the opposite side from where they had first looked at it. They saw the same thing from all directions: The segmented poles grew straight and close together; there seemed no place where a man could squeeze through. It was likely the thicket was that dense all the way through. Still, the squad leader thought that the thicket might be clear on its inside and that the Americans might have found a way into it. They had already proved themselves highly adept in the forest.

He thought about it. What he wanted to do was send a man as a runner to get the rest of the platoon, then attack that bamboo thicket—the more he thought about it, the more he became convinced that that was where the Americans were hidden. But he couldn't call for the rest of the platoon to come, not unless he knew for sure. He needed to get closer to the thicket to find out. He looked at his two men and decided he had to do it himself; he was the only one calm enough to have a chance to pull it off without giving himself away—and it was the kind of assignment he believed a good leader never gave to someone else unless he was willing to take the chance himself. He signaled his men and led them away from the thicket, then back toward it, more in the clear. He talked out loud as he walked.

"The Americans are not here," he said. "It is a waste of time to continue searching in this area. We will go and rejoin the rest of the platoon in its search half a kilometer north of here." He walked straight at the thicket while he talked and didn't look at it. His men gave each other glances. They didn't understand why their squad leader had suddenly decided there were no enemies in the area, especially since he'd been so suspicious of that thicket only moments earlier.

"Before we go I must relieve myself," the squad leader announced. "Wait for me here." If the Americans were in the thicket, maybe one of them understood Vietnamese and would know what he was saying. At any rate they could see what he was doing. Certainly they knew there were many Vietcong in the area searching for them and would not do anything unless he somehow showed he knew they were there. He hoped. He stopped in front of the thicket, opened the front of his trousers, and urinated into the bamboo trees. He tried to look totally unconcerned. He did not flare his nostrils as he tested the air with his nose. Finished emptying his bladder, he shook himself, tucked away, and turned from the thicket. He could hardly contain his excitement as he ambled back to his men and led them back into the trees.

As soon as they were out of sight of the thicket, the squad leader clapped his runner's shoulder. "Run to the commander," he whispered harshly. "Tell him the Americans are here." His nose had detected a faint odor coming from the thicket. It smelled like the inside of the cans they had found earlier.

They listened tensely to the VC walking toward them. Bell knew they could probably kill the three men easily with their knives, but there was too great a chance of one of them getting away, and they'd have to shoot him. That would alert the other VC who had to be nearby searching, a chance they couldn't take. So they watched and listened, though Huu and Lewis were the only two who could understand the man's dialect—and Lewis couldn't understand it fully. The VC stopped at the edge of the thicket, and Lewis cringed; he was facing him only a few feet away. He turned his face away so it wouldn't get spattered; he grimaced at the drops hitting the back of his head and his shoulder. Then the VC went away.

"You still take a shower once a week whether you need

it or not, right, Billy Boy?" Hempen asked when the VC were gone.

"I take a fucking shower every day, goddamn it," Lewis snarled.

"You didn't yesterday," Zeitvogel said. "I think you need one now."

"Better have Chief check you out," Randall said. "Gook might have hepatitis."

"Fuck you." Lewis tried unsuccessfully to pull away from the wet spots on his shirt.

"Shitcan the grab-assing, people," Bell said. "There's still bad guys around."

Huu gave Lewis a sympathetic smile but didn't say anything.

Randall turned the radio back on. In a few minutes a message came over it. He rogered the message and turned to the others. "Flyboy thinks he's got our position in sight, says he'll be here in a few minutes."

The commander squatted and looked at the thicket the squad leader had pointed out to him. He agreed it was a likely hiding place if it was open on its inside. The only question he had was how trustworthy the squad leader's sense of smell was. He had to believe him; it was the only lead they had. He prepared his men for an attack on the thicket. If the Americans were there, he was going to do what he could to speed the squad leader's next promotion.

CHAPTER TWENTY-EIGHT

Contact

"I can hear him," Zeitvogel said, excited. The helicopter's drone was dimly audible.

"I see him," Hempen said. "That big, bad beautiful bastard is coming straight at us." He pointed out the banana-shaped CH-46.

All six men fidgeted. The helicopter couldn't get there too soon to suit them. The boy, quiet until then, squirmed —he wasn't sure what was going on, and the nervousness of the adults made him anxious.

Randall listened to his handset and spoke into it. He turned to Bell. "He's got a visual on the LZ," he said, "and wants us to pop a smoke."

"Here goes," Bell said, pulling the pin on a smoke grenade and throwing it into the open.

Randall listened to the radio again and said, "He's got yellow smoke. That's us." When a helicopter coming in for an extraction called for smoke to mark the position, nobody said what color it was until it popped, then the pilot identified the color of the smoke he saw as a marker. That way, in case there were bad guys listening on the frequency who threw out a smoke grenade at the same time he asked for one, they wouldn't know what color to use. The smoke bellowing from Bell's canister-shaped grenade was yellow.

The helicopter changed its course to come into the wind and made its approach.

"Everybody saddled up?" Bell asked. He looked at his men. Each had all his equipment strapped on or in his hands; they were ready to go. "We break for it as soon as he clears the trees at the side of the clearing. Get ready, here he comes."

All six crouched at the granite side of the thicket, ready to sprint into the open. Zeitvogel held Ai, who was so frightened by the noise of the aircraft that he froze in the tall man's arms. It was all too much for the boy to comprehend.

Fifty meters away the VC commander swore at the sudden sound of the helicopter that burst across the forest overhead. The squad leader had been right about where the Americans were, but they might be too late to do anything about it. He stuck his whistle between his lips and blew as hard as he could. The twenty men he had with him dashed forward and opened up on the thicket.

The gunfire was a roar above the roar of the helicopter. Living bamboo splintered all around them. A four-inch spike of wood slashed open Randall's cheek. Another large splinter impaled Lewis's pack; the pack's thickness stopped it before it reached his body. Green tracers flashed around them, dazzling their eyes.

"Hit the deck!" Bell screamed.

They spun away from the clearing and escape and dove for the ground.

"Where the fuck are they?" Zeitvogel shouted above the din of the fire and the helicopter. When he went down, he was careful not to land on the boy held in his arms.

"Over this way," Hempen shouted, and started firing to his right, at the yellow-red flowers that appeared briefly, giving away the positions of some VC. "They're coming at us!" A bullet cracked past his ear.

"On the left," Lewis called, and let loose a ten-round burst at an automatic rifle blasting from that side.

"In front!" Huu cried, and fired at dimly seen shapes flitting through the trees to his front.

Bell looked all around and saw they were surrounded against the granite outcropping. Green tracers flew haphazardly through the air around them, clipping trees, kicking gouges out of them, breaking them, knocking them down. "Stay down," he shouted. "They're firing too high to hit us if we stay down." He flattened himself against the ground and flinched when a bullet hit the ground in front of him and kicked dirt in his face. But that round was almost the only one that wasn't too high.

Randall was on the radio. Behind them the roar of the helicopter changed to a higher pitch and dopplered away from them. "Flyboy says there's too much fire sweeping the clearing," he shouted to Bell. "He's going to orbit, wants to know where to have his gunner fire."

"Shit," Bell swore. "Tell him pick a place, any place outboard from us."

Randall spoke into the radio again. He hadn't yet noticed the blood flowing down his face. He turned back to Bell, who was putting out slow rounds at the muzzle flashes and running shapes he saw. "He wants to know how far out."

Bell glanced around. "Tell him they're thirty meters and closing." He resumed firing and had the gratification of seeing a body pitch forward, hit by one of his rounds.

The five Marines and the PF didn't fire wildly; they tried to pick targets. What had earlier been an almost solid wall of living bamboo had become an open latticework of broken poles. They were able to easily see the Vietcong charging their position, enemy soldiers ducking and dodging and zigzagging and dropping behind trees before leaping to their feet and darting forward again.

Ai whimpered at Zeitvogel's side. At first he had been elated to be rescued, but now he was terrified. If he'd been able to think clearly, he'd have wished they'd never come for him.

The sound of the helicopter had vanished from their consciousness for a long moment; now it washed over them again, hammering their senses like a fire-breathing dragon in full fury. It flew directly over the bamboo thicket. The crew chief leaned out of the door, swinging his mounted M-60 machine gun side to side, raining down a thousand rounds between the thicket and the oncoming Vietcong—a few, ahead of the others, crumpled or tumbled under the impact of the bullets.

The commander looked around, wide-eyed, and saw seven of his men down, and they hadn't yet reached the Americans' position. The helicopter was swinging around for a second pass, and he knew they couldn't reach the thicket before the great flying machine hit them again. Once they were in the thicket, he knew, the helicopter wouldn't risk firing at his men for fear of hitting the Americans. But there wasn't time to close with them. He thought fast and came up with another plan. He blew hard on his whistle, and his men withdrew. Except for the seven who lay broken on the ground between them and the thicket. He wished they had a SAM to shoot at the helicopter with, but no one had suspected they'd run into aircraft.

"They're breaking off," Randall shouted into the radio handset, then had to repeat himself because he had spoken too loudly and his voice was garbled.

The helicopter made another pass, anyway, and the crew chief let loose with another thousand rounds in twenty-round bursts, farther out than he had fired on the first go-round.

"They're coming in again," Randall told Bell. "Flyboy thinks that'll keep their heads down long enough for us to get out of here."

"You heard the word, everybody," Bell said to his men. He made a visual check of them. Randall's cheek seemed to be the only injury. Says a lot about keeping your fire low, he thought.

The droning roar of the helicopter changed pitch again and grew louder as it came in behind them.

"Everyone ready?" the sergeant shouted. He looked toward the trees the bird would come over on its approach and waited for it to appear. As soon as it did, he shouted, "Let's go!" and they were up and running hard.

The VC commander didn't use his whistle anymore. While the helicopter was making its second pass, chewing up the ground and trees where his men had been when it had made its first firing run, he used hand signals and softly spoken words to gather his remaining men together. Then he led them as fast as they could go in a circle around to the side of the thicket, where they could see both it and the clearing. He got everybody down and kept them quiet until the helicopter was settling down and the enemy were running through the open.

Zeitvogel, with the boy in his arms, was the first to the helicopter. He tossed Ai into it while it was still several feet above the ground, then jumped in himself. Lewis was the next to reach the bird; he had a hand on the door frame and a foot raised in the beginning of his leap when the VC opened fire again. He tumbled through the door and spun to the side, facing out to help the others. In seconds, they were all in. The crew chief bent over his gun, blazing away at the enemy fire. Bullets hit the skin of the chopper, and a few flashed through the cabin. The helicopter leaned and lifted away, followed by green tracers that fought through the air like manic bees swarming to kill the despoiler of their hive. The helicopter banked and climbed hard; its twin engines screamed in protest at being put through their paces at too fast a rate. No one in the cabin knew it, but the copilot was watching fearfully as half the gauges redlined and the other half continued their climb to red.

Bell looked out the open door and breathed a deep sigh of relief when the tracers stopped flying at them. They straightened out and flew along for a few seconds, then the helicopter shuddered with something more than the controlled turbulence of the opposing rotors and its wildly gyrating engines trying to tear it apart—if the parts of a helicopter weren't balanced as well as they should be, it would disintegrate long before it reached full power.

The crew chief listened to his headphone, and his eyes almost popped. He held his head next to Bell's ear and shouted. "Something got hit; we're losing pressure fast and have to get down before we crash."

Bell's eyes searched the crew chief's face while he frantically searched his memory of his map and the aerial photos he'd studied. Except for their original planned extraction point, he couldn't remember another clearing big enough to receive the helicopter within two kilometers.

"We're going back there?"

The crew chief nodded dumbly.

The helicopter banked and twisted in the air; then, through the door, Bell saw the granite outcropping getting closer.

The VC commander swore when he saw the Americans pile into the helicopter and fly away. His men's bullets seemed to be hitting the huge machine, but to no effect. The Americans had made their escape—he had lost seven men needlessly. He stood and ordered his survivors to cease fire, then led them to where the bodies lay so they could carry them home for proper burial. He snapped at one of his men, cursing him for wasting ammunition on that last, fruitless burst fired at the rapidly receding helicopter. He could hardly believe the good fortune that, a few minutes later, brought the helicopter back. He had his men respectfully lay the collected bodies down and headed back to the outcropping.

The wounded helicopter landed without opposition, and Reeves cut the power. He ducked through the hatch between the cockpit and the cabin; the Marines saw him for the first time on the extraction. "It's times like this I wish I was a fucking mechanic," he said. Then to the crew chief he said, "We lost oil pressure in the forward engine; check it out." He muttered to himself, "Now, how the fuck am I going to explain *this*? The only good thing is my bird's going down tomorrow anyway. Maybe nobody'll notice a few more holes in it."

The crew chief nodded dumbly and took off his radio

helmet. He climbed out and scrambled up the side of the bird to the forward engine cowling. Zeitvogel, Hempen, and Lewis followed him out, but they went to the ground instead of up. The Marines went into the edge of the trees and started prowling, looking for returning enemy. The crew chief popped the cowling open and peered at the oil-spattered engine. Fluid dripped slowly from a hole in a copper tube.

"I think I see the problem," he called down. "Hand up the patching kit." Helicopters carried kits that allowed the crew chief to make minor repairs on the machine gun and on the bird itself. Any crew chief worthy of the job had things in his kit that allowed him to make bigger repairs. The repairs might not be permanent, but they could usually last long enough to get the bird home in one piece. Reeves handed the kit up, and the crew chief started working to repair the leak. The skin on the back of his neck crawled, and the muscles between his shoulder blades bunched from expectation of the quiet VC opening up on them now that they were down and helpless, but he didn't look, instead concentrating on the work at hand.

Inside the helicopter Randall took hold of the gun and checked to be positive a round was chambered and the ammo belt was free of kinks. If the VC came back, he was going to use the gun on them.

"Oh, shit, they're close," Lewis said as quietly as he could but still loud enough for Zeitvogel and Hempen to hear.

"Where?" the tall black corporal asked.

"Right the fuck in front of us."

The three Marines spread out a little more and crouched deeper. They kept going, but not very far.

Hempen, on the left side of the short line, was the first to see them. He didn't waste time or energy shouting a warning. He leveled his rifle at the man he saw getting into position to fire on the sitting bird and squeezed the trigger —his AK-47 was already set on automatic, and a four-round burst battered into the crawling VC's back, killing him instantly.

Zeitvogel and Lewis didn't look for targets. They saw where Hempen's rounds hit, saw the crawling man, and guessed the other VC were on line from him. They let loose with long bursts of their own on a line with the first man. Their fire was answered by the screams of wounded men. One shot came back at them, then another, then a burst, then half the VC opened at them. The enemy soldiers scrambled to get on line so they could shoot back without hitting their own men.

"Who is that?" Randall shouted when Hempen's burst went off. "Is that us or the bad guys?" He wanted to fire in support of the Marines in the bush but didn't know where to aim.

"Wait," Bell said, and put a hand on his forearm. There were two more bursts, then sporadic fire started to the left of the first bursts and slowly built up to a crescendo. "Bad guys are on the left," he said. "Hit them."

Randall pointed the machine gun toward the Vietcong and pulled the trigger. Huu stood to one side of him and fired his rifle at the same place.

"Ah, shit," Reeves said. "I'm a goddamn Navy helicopter driver, not a fucking mud Marine. I'm not supposed to be doing this kind of shit." And he drew his .45, stuck it out the door, and added its banging to the steel wall of fire flying at the enemy.

On top of the helicopter the crew chief worked frantically. His mind was ablaze with the expectation of bullets slamming into his body at any second, but he still managed to maintain his concentration on his work and didn't make any mistakes. Finally he was finished. He shouted down to the cockpit, "Crank it up." He watched the engine closely as fresh oil pumped into it from the reservoir and it started working. His patch held. He popped the cowling closed and climbed back down. Randall had to stop firing for a few seconds to let him back in. He took over the gun without words.

"They're trying to flank us," Lewis shouted, and fired at a shadow flitting through the trees on his right. The shadow shuddered in its forward motion and toppled backward.

"Short Round, keep them pinned down in front," Zeitvogel ordered, and turned to help Lewis fight off the flankers. He saw two drop but couldn't tell if they had hit the deck or were knocked down by his fire. One thing he did know—they weren't taking as much return fire as they had a couple of minutes earlier. Suddenly what he could only characterize as a screeching maniac rose in front of him and ran straight at him, screaming and waving a handgun that he fired without bothering to aim or even point. The apparition jammed a whistle between his lips and blew. Zeitvogel cut the whistle call off in midtrill with a burst into the running man's chest.

There were sudden cries of consternation, and the return fire stopped. "Cease fire," Zeitvogel shouted. Abruptly, the only sounds in the forest were the crashing of a few men running through the trees and bushes, away from them, and the droning of the helicopter's engines. Then there was another sound, Bell's voice.

"Stilts, get over here, we can go now."

Zeitvogel ignored the order for a few seconds, listening to the forest. The crashing sounds were more distant. He jumped up. "Cover me," he said to Hempen and Lewis. He ran the few paces to the man with the whistle; he was wearing lieutenant's insignia on his collar. Quickly, the tall man stripped him of his insignia, whistle, and pistol. "I gotta have these to show my grandkids," he muttered. Then he rose and made a rapid circuit through the woods, looking for more bodies. He rejoined the other two in two minutes. "Let's di-di," he said, and sprinted to the impatiently waiting bird. Five SKS carbines and two AK-47s hung from his wide shoulders, along with two tube packs and half a dozen web ammo belts. His hands were filled with smaller objects he'd taken from the bodies of the dead.

The flight back to Camp Apache was uneventful.

CHAPTER TWENTY-NINE

Fare Thee Well, Old Friends

"Talk to me, Lieutenant," Captain Hasford said. He was wearing his Marine captain's stone face. "I told you yesterday a bird was coming out here today to take Sergeant Bell on the first leg of his trip back to The World. The bird's here. Where is Sergeant Bell?"

Burrison swallowed. He noticed all too clearly that Hasford called him by rank and didn't use Jay Cee's nickname; it was about to become official. If it wasn't already. "I got him on the radio last night," he said in a tight voice. "He knows about it, and he's on his way. At least earlier this morning he was. I had Big Louie—" He paused a beat, then decided to stick to formality. "—Corporal Slover pack his seabag yesterday afternoon so he'll be ready as soon as he gets here. Sir." He added the last almost as an afterthought.

Hasford used his Marine captain stone face to stare down the young lieutenant; Burrison didn't wilt under the hard look. "Raise him on the radio; get his exact location. I'll have this bird go out and pick him up." He waved at the helicopter he had come in on, the one that was to take Bell away.

Burrison was backed into a corner. How could he tell Hasford that Bell was on his way back, flying in a Navy helicopter that had just gotten shot up getting him? He hemmed for time to think of something to say. Before he hawed he was saved by Swarnes, who ran up at that moment.

"Scrappy," the radioman said, then saw the expression on Hasford's face and drew himself into an approximation of attention. "Uh, sir?" he started over again, uncertainty evident in the way he pronounced the unfamiliar word "sir." "Just got a call. Jay Cee's zero five out."

Hasford took a few long strides to where he could see over the open ground to the west of Camp Apache's hill and looked at it. "What's he doing, flying? Unless he's in an aircraft, I don't believe he can get here in five minutes."

Swarnes looked at Burrison. He didn't know what to say. Neither did Burrison.

A distant thrumming made Hasford raise his eyes toward the western ridge. "I don't want to believe this," he said slowly, looking at the approaching helicopter. Then to Swarnes he said, "Is that Jay Cee's ride?"

"You better fucking believe it," Swarnes said, then paled and stammered when he remembered he was talking to an officer who showed all the signs of being angry. "I mean, sir, yessir, I do believe Sergeant Bell's on that bird. Sir."

Hasford looked away and shook his head. "I *do* not want to believe this," he repeated.

Slover ran to his squad tent before he went to the helipad, despite the fact that he already had his Ping-Pong paddles in his hip pocket.

Hasford looked at the bullet holes in the body of the helicopter when it landed and shook his head again. He watched wondering while the five Marines and the PF, all armed with AK-47s, dismounted from it. He raised his eyebrows at the boy Zeitvogel handed to Houng and his wife, both happily crying. Then he watched very interestedly as Bell handed his Communist rifle to Slover, who handed him his own M-14—along with something else, it appeared. The two NCOs exchanged a few words, and Bell clapped his old friend on the shoulder with a word of thanks and marched to the officers.

"Captain Hasford," he said, nodding in greeting. "I hear I had to cut my fishing trip short because I'm going home." He held up the fly rod tube Slove had handed him, trying to look as though he had carried it off the helicopter with him. "Fishing wasn't very good. We only caught enough to eat ourselves while we were out there.

"Too bad about the fishing," Hasford said slowly, nodding back, suspiciously eyeing the fly rod tube. "But that's right about you going home. Now tell me, Jay Cee, is that something I shouldn't know about?" He pointed at the gray helicopter.

"What's that, sir?" Bell asked. He didn't turn to look where the captain was pointing.

"Turn around. That."

Bell waited until he heard the pitch of the rotors on Reeves's bird change before he turned his head and looked at the bare ground where it had been a few seconds earlier. "What, sir? I don't see anything." He turned back, wondering what Hasford's reaction was going to be to his actions, actions that could very easily convince a court-martial board he was insubordinate.

"That's what I thought," Hasford said dryly, shaking his head. "Scrappy tells me Big Louie packed your gear. Get it and get aboard." As long as Bell was back, he didn't see any point in continuing his hard act. They were all better off if he didn't know what the shot-up helicopter was about—or who the young boy with Houng and his wife was.

"Can I have a few minutes to say good-bye, sir?"

The pilot and copilot of the helicopter there to pick Bell up were the same two who had flown in the daily hot meal two days earlier and wondered about the Navy helicopter passing them on its way to Camp Apache. The copilot had to look across the pilot to see the Navy bird and didn't notice the bullet holes in it.

"Son of a bitch," the copilot said. "Not only do they get the Navy to fly roundeyes out to them, they get the Navy as their own personal taxi service when they go on fishing trips." He thought for a moment about the two hot combat assaults and the hot recon extraction he'd been on during the past week. "Fuck this shit, soon as we get back to Da Nang I'm putting in for a transfer to one of those CAGs."

The pilot looked at him and cocked an eyebrow. What's the matter with this boy? he wondered. He got a heavy-duty death wish or something? The pilot had seen the bullet holes and realized what the weapons the Marines were carrying when they got off the Navy bird meant. "You're dinky dau, you know that?" he said.

"You still gonna come visit me in Maryland when we get back to The World and out of the Crotch, Stilts?" Bell asked. He and several of the others were standing near the helipad.

Zeitvogel cocked an eye at the sergeant. "And double date?" he asked.

"You mean like me, my girlfriend, my sister, and you?"

Zeitvogel chewed on his lower lip and slowly nodded.

"Well." Bell shrugged elaborately. "I think that's up to my sister." He stood to his full height, chest expanded, and continued. "If she says no because you're a basketball player and she can't stand roundball, you're shit out of luck, man. But," he said in a slower, more measured voice, "if she says no because she's white and you're black, well—" His voice dropped. "—then I'm just going to have to take her out behind the woodshed and teach her something about the value of people."

Simultaneously, the two Marines reached their hands out to each other.

"You two don't think you're leaving me out of this, do you?" Randall grunted. He reached for the two clasping hands. "You both *will* report to Texas when we all get back to The World." His right hand slapped down on top of the other two.

"And if you don't come up to north Jersey, all of Paramus is coming after your young asses," Slover said, clamping his hand on top of the others.

"I'm in on this, too," McEntire said, wide-eyed, slapping his hand onto the others. "Any of you guys really got a sister?" He shook his head. "Shit, I ain't been laid in so long, I forgot what end to stick it in. So—" He grinned. "—your sisters are safe with me."

"Shit, man, lemme in here," Hempen said, and added his hand.

"Jay Cee, for a sergeant, you ain't half bad," Lewis said, shouldering his way into the circle.

Bell's eyes blurred with tears he couldn't shed as he looked at the other six Marines whom he was about to maybe never see again. They intertwined their fingers and held tighter.

"Aren't you forgetting someone?" Burrison asked. He came up on them quietly. They turned toward him. Houng and his son and Huu flanked the young lieutenant.

Bell's face churned its way to a wry smile. "Shit, no, we just thought you officers thought you was too good for us."

"Make way," Burrison said, shouldering his way into the circle of Marines.

They shifted about without letting go of each other's hands. Burrison, Houng, and Huu stuck their hands into the grips of the others. Houng's son hung back until Randall grabbed him with his free hand and drew him in and stuck the boy's hand into the middle of the others.

"Brothers," they all said, six white Americans, two black Americans, and three Vietnamese. "Brothers forever." Even Houng's young son piped his thin tenor into the chorus.

Then Bell boarded the helicopter. A few days later the rest of the Americans of Tango Niner left Bun Hou.

Eventually all the Americans in the country went home; the Vietnamese were already there.

ABOUT THE AUTHOR

David Sherman served as a Marine in Vietnam in 1966, stationed, among other places, in a CAP unit on Ky Hoa Island. He holds the Combat Action Ribbon, Presidential Unit Citation, Navy Unit Commendation, Vietnamese Cross of Gallantry, and Vietnamese Civic Action Unit Citation. He left the Marines a corporal, and after his return to The World worked as a library clerk, antiquarian bookstore retail manager, deputy director of a federally funded community crime prevention program, manager of the University of Pennsylvania's Mail Service Department, and sculptor.